Jacking In to the *Matrix* Franchise

Peter Bondanella:
Italian Cinema, 3rd Edition

Will Brooker:
Batman Unmasked: Analyzing a Cultural Icon

Will Brooker:
Using the Force: Creativity, Community, and Star Wars Fans

Donald Bogle:
Toms, Coons, Mulattoes, Mammies, and Bucks:
An Interpretive History of Blacks in American Films, 4th Edition

Danny Fingeroth:
Superman on the Couch

Geoff Klock:
How to Read Superhero Comics and Why

Rémi Fournier Lanzoni:
French Cinema: From Its Beginnings to the Present

Alison McMahan:
Alice Guy Blaché: Lost Visionary of the Cinema

Philip Nel:
Dr. Seuss: American Icon

Jonathan Rayner:
The Films of Peter Weir, 2nd Edition

Maurice Yacowar:
The Sopranos on the Couch

JACKING IN TO THE
MATRIX FRANCHISE

Cultural Reception and Interpretation

Edited by
Matthew Kapell and William G. Doty

continuum
NEW YORK • LONDON

2004

The Continuum International Publishing Group Inc
15 E 26 Street, New York, NY 10010

The Continuum International Publishing Group Ltd
The Tower Building, 11 York Road, London SE1 7NX

www.continuumbooks.com

Printed in the United States of America

Library of Congress Cataloging-in-Publication Data

   Jacking in to the Matrix franchise : cultural reception and interpretation / edited by Matthew Kapell and William G. Doty.
      p. cm.
   Includes bibliographical references and index.
   ISBN 0-8264-1587-3 (hardcover : alk. paper)—ISBN 0-8264-1588-1 (pbk. : alk. paper)
   1. Matrix (Motion picture) I. Kapell, Matthew. II. Doty, William G., 1939-
   PN1997.M395J33 2004
   791.43'72—dc22
                                                                          2004001971

Dedicated to:

My own personal Trinity and Oracle, respectively:
Stephanie (*semper toujours!*)
and
Zoe Blythe (all the inspiration needed)
—M. K.

Contents

CONTENTS

Acknowledgments

T his book would not be possible without the help of a host of different people, and we wish to thank them all. Our editor at The Continuum International Publishing Group, David Barker, provided both encouragement and support; he has our thanks. Gabriella Page-Fort did a wonderful job organizing the copy-editing of the manuscript, which would be quite inferior without her input. We thank her. John Shelton Lawrence, a contributor, acted as a de facto third editor of this volume, and his insight and wisdom have helped to make it a much better book. Stephanie Wilhelm also read a large percentage of the chapters as they came in, and her reaction to them guided our editorial process. Peter Wilhelm provided very useful insight into the *Enter The Matrix* game, and we thank him as well. Our colleague Mary Fran Lebamoff of Loyola University in Chicago also provided encouragement to the senior editor and read a number of essays—her influence was tremendous and she has our thanks. A number of students at the University of Michigan-Dearborn also read many of the essays and provided critical responses to the readability of the volume. Among those to thank are, most importantly, Kristen Chapman, whose continual input on a number of chapters made them all better.

It goes without saying that any errors remain our own, but much of what makes this book worthwhile belongs to the above-mentioned individuals.

About the Contributors

ELIZABETH BAKER lives and writes in Durham, North Carolina. She graduated from the University of North Carolina.

RUSSELL BLACKFORD is a writer, critic, and student of philosophy, based in Melbourne, Australia, where he is Honorary Research Associate in the School of Literary, Visual and Performing Arts, Monash University. His formal qualifications include a PhD from the University of Newcastle, and a Master of Bioethics degree from Monash. He is co-author of *Strange Constellations: A History of Australian Science Fiction* (1999), and a contributor to many magazines, journals, reference works, and anthologies. His recent publications include a science fiction trilogy, *Terminator 2: The New John Connor Chronicles;* the novels in the series are *Dark Futures* (2002), *An Evil Hour* (2003), and *Times of Trouble* (2003). Russell is currently thinking up new ways to destroy humanity as we know it.

WILLIAM G. DOTY retired from the College of Arts and Sciences at the University of Alabama–Tuscaloosa in 2001, but continues to teach in premier student programs at the university. His books have included *Myth: A Handbook* (Greenwood Folklore Handbooks, 2004); *Mythography: The Study of Myths and Rituals* (2nd ed. 2000); *The TIMES World Mythology* (2002), *Myths of Masculinity* (1993), and several edited and co-edited volumes such as *Picturing Cultural Values in Postmodern America* (1995); *Interdisciplinary Studies Today* (1994), and *Mythical Trickster Figures: Contours, Contexts, and Criticisms* (1993). He edited the two published volumes of *Mythosphere: A Journal for Image, Myth, and Symbol.*

FRANCES FLANNERY-DAILEY, PhD, is an assistant professor of Religion at Hendrix College, in Conway, Arkansas. In addition to teaching courses in Biblical Studies, she also teaches classes on Religion and Culture, including "Religion and Film," "Apocalyptic Thought and Movements," and "Religion and Monsters." She has written several articles on film and most recently a book entitled *Dreamers, Scribes, and Priests: Jewish Dreams in the Hellenistic and Roman Eras* (Brill, 2004). Her secret writing partner is twenty-month-old Samuel, who, alas, does not type well. Her spouse Mike and the dogs (Maggie, Casey, and Bucky) also lend a hand from time to time.

BRUCE ISAACS is a final year PhD student at the University of Sydney, Australia. His research interests include theories of postmodernism, as well as the films of Quentin Tarantino and David Lynch. His is currently completing a chapter on postmodern narrative theory for *Post-Punk Cinema* (ed. Nicholas Rombes) to be published by the University of Edinburgh Press.

RICHARD JONES is Assistant Professor of Anthropology at Lee University in eastern Tennessee and an ordained minister. He, his wife Sheila, and their daughter, Rebecca, have a Lab-Bassett hybrid named Daisy who tends to occupy a lot of their time. Richard also likes reading science fiction, playing softball, and fishing.

MATTHEW KAPELL is a doctoral student in history at Wayne State University in Detroit who holds a Master's degree in anthropology. From 1998-2003 he was Visiting Lecturer in anthropology at the University of Michigan–Dearborn where he also taught courses in women's studies, sociology, and linguistics. He has published widely on topics as diverse as the genetics of human growth and *Star Trek: Deep Space Nine*. When his daughter Zoe grows up, she either wants to be just like Trinity or have a horse and cat farm. *Jacking In to the* Matrix *Trilogy* is his first book.

C. RICHARD KING is Associate Professor of Comparative Ethnic Studies, Washington State University in Pullman, Washington. His work has appeared in a variety of journals, such as *American Indian Culture and Research Journal, Journal of Sport and Social Issues, Public Historian,* and *Qualitative Inquiry.* He is also the author/editor of several books, including *Team Spirits: The Native American Mascot Controversy* (a *CHOICE* 2001 Outstanding Academic Title), *Postcolonial America,* and most recently *Telling Achievements: Native American Athletes in Modern Sport.* He is completing work on a book on race and racism in American popular culture.

GRAY KOCHHAR-LINDGREN is Associate Professor of English, Central Michigan University, and the author of *Narcissus Transformed, Starting Time,* and *TechnoLogics.* He lives near Useless Bay among the deer, fox, and banana slugs.

JOHN SHELTON LAWRENCE is Professor Emeritus, Morningside College at Sioux City, Iowa. He taught philosophy and interdisciplinary courses in American culture before retiring in Berkeley, California. He is a Senior Fellow in Conservation at the Sierra Club in San Francisco, doing research on corporate environmental policies and behavior. He writes frequently on American popular culture and politics, most recently in books co-authored with Robert Jewett: *The Myth of the American Superhero* (2002)—winner of the John Cawelti Award of the American Culture Association for the Best Book of 2002, and *Captain America and the Crusade Against Evil: The Dilemma of Zealous Nationalism* (2003). He has mortal envy for the success of the Wachowski brothers in popularizing philosophical ideas for the college age group—and isn't expected to survive a sequel to the *Matrix* trilogy.

DAVID J. LEONARD is Assistant Professor of Comparative Ethnic Studies, Washington State University, Pullman, Washington. His articles have appeared in *American Jewish History, PopMatters, Colorlines,* and at conferences sponsored by the Popular Culture Association and the Organization of American Historians. He is working on a manuscript on race, gender, and national identity within video games, and another examining race and Kobe Bryant.

MARTINA LIPP is currently a Fulbright Scholar and German Language Teaching Assistant at Hollins University in Virginia. She is doing research in feminist film studies and cultural studies, and is working on her PhD on "Alternative Spaces: The Postmodern Female Hero in Contemporary U.S. Fiction and Film" at the University of Graz, Austria. She graduated from the University of Graz with a Master's Thesis on "The (M)Other: Femininity, Sexuality, and Maternity in *The Matrix.*" Lipp has also studied at the University of La Laguna in La Laguna, Spain, and at the University of New Mexico in Albuquerque, New Mexico. She really wants to be a hero, but does not know how to fit into the latex outfit.

TIMOTHY MIZELLE teaches in the First Year Writing Program at Duke University. His prose and poetry have appeared in *The Paris Review; Mythosphere: A Journal for Image, Myth, and Symbol; The Carolina Quarterly;* and other journals. He was a Morehead Scholar at the University of North Carolina. He is currently working on a novel, *The Left Hand Path;* a collection of stories, *Red Feather;* and a project on films by Lang, Godard, Fellini, and Lynch called "Silencio: The Weight of Silence," with Elizabeth Baker. When he is not losing himself in his own imaginings or those of the directors named, he lets himself be dazzled by the pretend adventures that he encounters with his daughters, Celia and Madeleine.

MICHAEL SEXSON has lived for the past three decades in an alternate reality where he has posed not always successfully as a professor of English at Montana State University in Bozeman. He teaches and writes primarily on topics related to religion, literature, and mythology. He is the author of a book on the insurance salesman Wallace Stevens who, thinking himself an artist, poetically pondered the shifting currents between reality and imagination.

THEODORE LOUIS TROST is Assistant Professor of Religious Studies and New College at the University of Alabama. He is the author of *Douglas Horton and the Ecumenical Impulse in American Religion* (2002) and, with Carolyn Medine Jones, the co-editor of *Teaching African American Religions* (2004). He is currently writing a book on religion, popular music, and film.

RACHEL L. WAGNER, PhD, is a visiting assistant professor of Religion at Southwestern University in Georgetown, Texas. Wagner teaches a variety of courses on monotheistic religions and Religion and Culture, including "Religion and Film," "Islam and Media," and "Spiritual Journeys," and also has a particular interest in the cultural significance of Harry Potter. Her dissertation, now being revised and submitted for publication, is an intertextual analysis of biblical structures in William Blake's epic poem *Jerusalem*. When not writing or teaching, Wagner plays soccer on three recreational teams and tries to keep up with her brilliant nine-year-old son Isaac, Yu-Gi-Oh master and computer programmer extraordinaire.

STEPHANIE J. WILHELM is a graduate, with distinction, of the University of Michigan–Dearborn with degrees in English and history. At the time of publication, she will be a graduate student in English literature at Wayne State University in Detroit. Her relationship with her cats, Sasha, Boris, and Nikita, it has been pointed out by friends, borders on the pathological.

The Deeper We Go, the More Complex and Sophisticated the Franchise Seems, and the Dizzier We Feel

WILLIAM G. DOTY

The Matrix changed the way we see things.

—Joel Silver (Salisbury 46)

Welcome to a series of discussions of one of the most widely viewed entertainment-culture productions of our decade: the *Matrix* franchise. The year 1999 saw the first episode, then 2003 brought both a second and a third film. This book provides enrichments to the first—and the second and the third, and all the franchise elements in between and beyond. They include a computer/video game, *Enter* (see abbreviations list in the Appendix), and the DVD, *Animatrix*—consisting of nine short animé films serving to whet appetites for *Reloaded* and *Revolutions*—and I haven't even mentioned the series, *Comics,* introduced on the Warner Brothers Website (whatisthematrix.warnerbros.com) before the print publication (which is identified in advertising as Volume 1 Fall 2003), or other materials.

Announced as we were going to press, the "Massively Multiplayer Online Role-Playing Game," *The Matrix Online* (abbreviated in releases as MxO; 2004+), supposedly takes the *Matrix* story beyond where the film trilogy left off and provides "deep insight into the world of the Matrix" (http:// thematrixonline.ubi.com/US/gamedata.php). I will suggest below that to stage so extensive and complex an artistic and commercial production can be compared to what Richard Wagner attempted in his German opera house: he sought to produce *ein Gesamtkunstwerk,* a total, all-encompassing, and synthesizing work of art that would provide nationalistic ideals.

This book has been written by academic contributors, most of them college or university faculty. But these folks make their living speaking to

1

"ordinary people"—students!—and have been under our editorial mandate to "make it clear, eliminate technical scholarly debates, and express your-selves the way 'ordinary people' talk."

On the other hand, we don't intend a sort of *The Matrix for Dummies* crib sheet, either. This introduction clarifies some of the concepts and terms used by critics in analyzing these works, and the Appendix supplies expla-nations of terms, names, and concepts found in this book—note especially that it identifies cast names of actors, so that our contributors need not refer to them at each reference, e.g., "Neo (Keanu Reeves)."

This volume appears to be the first to encompass the entire *Matrix* fran-chise, and in contrast to other volumes on *The Matrix,* this one does not pro-mote a narrowly rationalist branch of academic philosophy, or various the-ological claims, or specialized studies by science-fiction writers and critics (see Irwin; LaVelle or Seay and Garrett; and Haber or Yeffeth). Instead, we provide a wide range of approaches to the whole franchise that is engag-ing thinkers and analysts all the way from conservative Christians to post-modernist critics (a *Christian Science Monitor* feature on "The Gospel accord-ing to Neo" surveys several of the recent books—see Burek).

Not surprisingly, serious philosophical issues are often addressed here in terms of images, characters, and plots of the *Matrix* materials (Kochhar-Lindgren, Sexson, Wilhelm and Kapell, Blackford: epistemology—how knowledge comes about; ontology—the nature of reality; ethics; and posthu-manism—thought reaching beyond traditional Western philosophy). A num-ber of philosophical essays are posted on whatisthematrix.com and salon.com; Hollywood.com Staff provide "*The Matrix* and Philosophy: An A to Z Guide."

Such discussions jostle those of popular culture analysis, with analyses of the role of computers in the films and in everyday life, as well as repre-sentations of gender and race (King and Leonard, Lipp, Kochhar-Lindgren). Contributors explore issues in the social sciences (Blackford, Mizelle and Baker: the role/s of the individual and the collective in society today, the presentation of "self" in hypertechnology and ideology), as well as the fields of mythological or religious studies discussed by Isaacs and Trost, Flannery-Dailey and Wagner, and Jones: Neo as—or *not as*—a Christ figure, "salva-tion eschatology" (Bartlett and Byers 39). There are treatments of how East-ern and other religious teachings are represented—and perhaps misrepresented, and reference to the significance of Trinity as a contempo-rary goddess-incarnation of Isis/Inanna or the much later Christian aspects of female deity.

Here the movie trilogy and all its action toys (!) are placed in the contexts of the history of thought (from romanticism to analogous contemporary sci-fi films and novels that highlight the search for "the real," or explore the status of the posthuman cyborg—King and Leonard, Sexson, and Kochhar-Lindgren) and cinema (several contributors make comparisons with other films, Hong Kong kung fu movies, and genres such as paranoia-thriller films).

Feminist issues meet cyberpunk, cosmological perspectives meet mythological and literary analysis; violence in contemporary society and various ethical issues are explored, as well as other psychological and communal factors of contemporary life; and American values, politics, and heroic models return to view frequently (Lipp, Lawrence, King and Leonard, Jones).

Although the Wachowski brothers state that the "whole idea [of the *Matrix*] sort of exploded over a period of about three days" (Wachowski interview), the trilogy itself—planned as a large enterprise from the beginning and then efficiently executed by the Wachowski brothers with assistance from a huge number of media specialists, and incorporating many different influences—provides an enormous arena for many of the conceptual and practical issues just named. Its reiteration of details allows for multiple perspectives in analysis and interpretation, and we have tried to shape contributions so that they can be read by themselves apart from the book. Authors here indicate just how deeply our culture has been touched by the franchise, how its films and other components speak to issues explored by conservative Christians no less than presumably secular postmodernist analysts.

Teaching the *Matrix* franchise seems relevant to many contexts in the social sciences and humanities—and even, as seen in these essays, neurobiology and ecological studies. The extent of interest across educational institutions has been stunning, although readers may be surprised to realize that hundreds of courses worldwide focus upon elements of the *Matrix* universe. When initially we used a couple of electronic mailing lists to invite professional scholars to propose chapters for this book, we were forced to close submissions after only three days, because of the huge number of responses that flooded in. Within ten days after our initial deadline, we had received more than 150 proposals.

Much of the distinctiveness of this volume derives from its *multidisciplinary* scope. Its editors selected contributions that spanned many of the intellectual areas presently engaged across contemporary world discussion of the present status of our culture and our prospects. Contributors examine mythological models and issues (Jones, Isaacs and Trost, Lawrence, Lipp).

They range from practical matters (feminism, racialism—Lipp, King and Leonard) to abstract theorizing and religious practice (cosmology, theology—Isaacs and Trost, Flannery-Dailey and Wagner, Mizelle and Baker), and comments on contemporary social issues and prospects (Blackford, Kochhar-Lindgren, Wilhelm and Kapell). The world of science fiction and cyberspace is engaged (Blackford, Sexson, Lawrence), as well as the characteristics of our postmodernist times (Wilhelm and Kapell, Kochhar-Lindgren, Isaacs and Trost), and how we deal with ironic interpretations of "the real" (Sexson's fictional classroom discussion).

Such a broad scope is precisely what characterizes two academic areas that have gained recent prominence: Cultural Studies (originated as a leftist perspective in England, it became closely allied with American Studies in the United States) and Popular Culture Studies. Both are indicative of present-day reaching across traditional disciplinary divides that have long ruled university life modeled upon nineteenth-century German distinctions between the humanities, social, and "natural" sciences. For much of the twentieth century, turf wars among academic disciplines led mostly to rigid classifications and restrictions, seldom to interdisciplinary cooperation—precisely what the great majority of "real world" applications of complex knowledge require. Graduate law and medical schools are now impressed by undergraduate majors in music and literature, not just in the sciences.

Both cultural studies and pop culture studies are interdisciplines that are seldom institutionalized in professorial chairs, yet are well known, even if people on the street would not recognize them as huge barns in which a large variety of theoretical and analytical animals have been given stalls. These are quite sociable animals, and most contemporary cultural studies work (as compared to in the earlier British-influenced writings that followed primarily socialist or Marxian orientations) takes place not in the closed stalls, but in the open center of the barn—a sort of "come who may" pub scene where for one to operate on the basis of more than one highly specialized theory or technique is rather suspect (a wide-ranging reader by Grossberg, Nelson, and Treichler is useful for an overview).

An apparent danger is that the variety of disciplinary perspectives may become too extended, too multiple in approaches, so that there are few authentic criteria by which "to credential" any particular practitioner (primarily a concern of academic administrators who have minimal connection to the processes by which new knowledge is produced and verified). On the other hand, some of us tend to see such openness to non-institutional venues as a healthy response to restriction of scholarship to only a small list of "approved" academic approaches within higher education. To our way of thinking, it is in areas of *interdisciplinary overlap* that important intellectual breakthroughs occur.

This arena is what anthropologist Victor Turner explored as the *liminal,* that place/period between the beginning and end, initiation and gradua- tion, of a ritual or social process. And Thomas Kuhn refers to the situations where traditional scientific paradigms are shattered when new and multi- disciplinary perspectives are coming into their own—a "paradigm shift" may be marked by the introduction of a new scientific journal of physics and biology, say, or medicine and philosophy.

The *Matrix* franchise materials have occasioned extensive explorations of social and individual values, even of the mythological and scientific nature of "reality" and its artificial simulation in communications media, financial markets, and advertising (see Taylor). When a body of work expands to include the influence of the animated Japanese adult comic books and films— animé (see Napier, and TheAnimatrix.com)—as well as video gaming, the power of its marketing in seizing and holding contemporary interest is extraordinary. There has been a spoof piece, Mark Lowton's "Matrix 4 in the Pipeline," in which President George Bush commissions the first AI machines, as well as a humorous take entitled "Matrix Jedi" (http://home. netcom.com/~jskipper/mj/mj.html) in which the post-*Revolutions* rebels develop a Jedi Virus and Light Sabers (guess where they come from?) that are very effective against the Agents—and even pornographic Internet sites that capture only *the name,* in order to lure clients.

The "Jacking In" of our title refers to the way audiences are often enchanted, fascinated, when the movie screen is first illuminated: I feel this in my own living room when DVDs bring to my home stereo system the feeling of being in a cathedral or IMAX theater. But of course another ref- erence is to the cyberworld of novelist William Gibson, who initiated the idea of direct physical connection of the human body and electronic resources through a sort of physiological phone jack (see especially "Johnny Mnemonic," and the cyberpunk classic, *Neuromancer*). At the same time, in the *Matrix* franchise itself, there is clearly another darker overtone: that of the rape of human beings by the evil Über-Machine, the subjugation of the human to the program, and the threat of apocalyptic end to civilization.

Hundreds of analytical and critical responses to the work lead us to see it as a sort of pop culture Rorschach test: as illustrated in this book, practically any possible interpretation of its components has been attempted. This is the case because the *Matrix* franchise was never from the beginning a simple jack-in-the-box, but has remained stubbornly *polysemic,* that is, it opens itself to a fantastically wide range of possible interpretations and applications. Bruce Sterling provides a handy list (although speaking just about the first film):

> *The Matrix* is a postmodern philosophical movie in which fragments of *philosophy* do this *Casablanca* cliché dance. There's Christian exegesis, a Redeemer myth, a death and rebirth, a hero in self-discovery, the *Odyssey,* Jean Baudrillard (lots of Baudrillard, the best parts of the film), science-fiction ontological riffs of the Philip K. Dick school, *Nebuchadnezzar,* the Buddha, Taoism, martial-arts mysticism, oracular prophecy, spoon-bending telekinesis, Houdini stage-show magic, Joseph Campbell, and Gödelian mathematical metaphysics. (23-24)

Beyond the initial movie, *The Animatrix* provides back-story as well as thrusting forward into the second and third episodes. A fold-out poster at the back of Doug Walsh's *Enter the Matrix Official Strategy Guide* provides a chart from "In the Beginning [...] when 'man' makes the machine in his own likeness" down to the point where *Enter* begins. The *Comics* volume provides extra details about the Matrix world that were not covered in *The Matrix.* And chat rooms and now the online multi-user video game (*Online*) need to be taken into account as well. For many of these we could also list several potential modes of interpretation, and others will doubtless be proposed, since fascination with the franchise remains high.

Such rich polysemy might reflect a series that wandered around aimlessly, but I think part of the charm of these works is their intensely focused cinematography—both in the films and in *Enter,* since the Brothers shot much of the action scenes while filming the movie trilogy. And of course one can admire the spectacular special effects, the success of which already in *The Matrix* led to an almost unimaginable intensification in the subsequent episodes and associated materials, even if the plot seemed to drag a bit. The actor Keanu Reeves (Neo) catches this perfectly: "There's no extraneous movement, gesture, behavior [....] It's very pure. What [the directors] do in their films is like a samurai strike with a sword—one perfect gesture all concentrated in that one moment" (Salisbury 46).

The filming (and the months of physical training of the actors for the wired action scenes) is just as cyberpunk as one might imagine: it opens the way to imagining incredible human/cyborg beings that redefine the limits of physical reality as we have known it. It graphs worlds almost unimaginable—and yet a paranoid part of each of us wonders whether or not just such *Matrix* worlds might not be just around the corners of our postmodernist lives (or, perhaps, we're already there?).

Meanwhile, *Reloaded* and *Revolutions* move progressively away from the fetus-bank batteries of *The Matrix* and "Second Renaissance II," toward the possible "real world" futures presented primarily through virtual reality. And if we take the glorious golden streaming light on the horizon at the end of *Revolutions* as prophetic, the denizens of the matrix can anticipate a very pleasant new era indeed.

The fantastically imagined contexts of the franchise are already pretty "believable" to us. The concept of simulations have become natural and real—think of the way many national leaders have physically identical doubles who stand in for them in dangerous situations (as is portrayed in *Star Wars* with respect to Queen/Legislator Amidalla)—that we forget their constructedness, their arbitrary fabrication (Baudrillard 1994; the postmodernist concept of simulation is discussed by several of our contributors).

Exposé after exposé has left us pretty shell-shocked: we know that what the public sees is never more than a tiny fragment of the actual political or economic realities, a tiny part of the back-story of the simulation. Finally, the whole nature of "the real" certainly suffers when reduced to a clearly phony "reality TV" presentation of an obviously highly orchestrated and staged spring break in Cancun, Mexico (a sleazy film released in April 2003).

The key issue involves the nature of knowledge, the "epistemology" of the philosophy classroom; or the shape of interpretation, as explored in biblical and film studies (here, especially by Isaacs and Trost); or the relative role of the morally-good or -evil. *The Sopranos,* a recent television series that constantly makes us aware of how it is posing such moral issues (and hence is especially postmodern), also portrays an existential time of gender confusion, corporate financial mayhem, questioning of "family" (and ethnic and gender) values, and recognition that traditional orientations to the environment or to society have now to be radically rethought (see Barreca). The title of another volume highlights just how aware we have become about how a whole artist's self/persona can be self-orchestrated: George-Claude

Guilbert, *Madonna as Postmodern Myth: How One Star's Self-Construction Rewrites Sex, Gender, Hollywood, and the American Dream.*

Our lives are staged amidst an interpretive shift away from a singular Cartesian "objective" normality (what's real is what we can see displayed before us) to some of the many postmodernist perspectives, in which the whole system of a culture's thought is considered at most an arbitrary selection of choices *socially constructed* by those with the greatest wealth and power. We have learned from feminism how completely female voices can be excluded from decision-making (including about how a woman controls her reproductive function), and from post-colonialist studies how whole ethnicities and "races" have been subjugated to the capitalist projects of the supposedly enlightened Western powers. The works of the French historian of ideas Michel Foucault teach us to recognize how many noble truths and practices (in law, medicine, sexual moralities) were religiously or ideologically driven constructs of a particular politics of one or another historical period.

The *Matrix* materials, somewhat like *Star Wars,* encourage reliance not upon the brain, but upon the bodily intuitive ("Trust the Force, Luke!" and "Neo, I believe!"; see Slack). In many ways they are the identity materials of the adolescent male, learning how to balance impulses with education and life experiences. But they are also curiously neo-utopian (Wilhelm and Kapell) in holding out the hope of evolutionary development of conscious species toward a new society of decency and fairness available to all.

Obviously the *Matrix* franchise has been big-time since 1999, and widespread interest is still being cultivated by the Wachowskis—witness the multi-user online game, *Online,* that debuted in 2004. The film trilogy (and associated licensed spin-offs) represents one of the most affective productions of recent time—psychologically and economically: the first two *Matrix* episodes generated $1.9 billion here and abroad from box-office sales, the video game, soundtracks and music CDs for each film, and other merchandise: "the entire franchise will [...] near $3 billion in sales" (Pulley; Holson; many of these are available at The Matrix Shop, www.whatisthematrix. warnerbros.com).

By November 2003, *Enter* had sold 3.25 million copies for a total of $162 million in revenue; *Animatrix* sold 2.7 million for $68 million; the soundtrack for the first film, 1.85 million copies for $37 million; and assorted merchandise brought in $3.5 million. *Reloaded* is the top-selling R-rated movie of all time, $200 million ahead of #2, *Terminator 2* (Pulley).

Some inkling of the vast international fascination with the franchise can be intimated by the fact that a simple search for "Matrix" on the search engine Google in January 2004 brought forth pages of links to 22,400,000 sites—it would take months to read through them all! That its appeal is so tremendous indicates that these movies touch down upon a wide range of social issues faced by late-twentieth- and early-twenty-first-century populations around the world.

That a work based primarily in cinema (albeit a very complex conception of theater: see Mizelle and Baker, Isaacs and Trost, and Doty in this volume) expanded under the Brothers' direction to so many other related media is certainly impressive. I find it typical, however, of a new openness to the technological complexities of contemporary communications media: a colleague in Germany, for instance, stages terrifically involved dramatic works contributed to by participants around the world in real Internet time, electronically. Each multimedia theater production involves a live performer at a computer before an audience (who view projections and taped visual segments projected on screens) and live actors/authors around the world contributing in sequence to an agreed-upon sketched-out dramatic/musical/artistic scenario (see Marlena Corcoran's projects: http://www.marlenacorcoran.com).

A number of classic sci-fi films are familiarly referred to as "space operas," and that is warrant enough to discuss the *Matrix* materials as comprising all together a contemporary form of Wagner's *Gesamtkunstwerk,* as indicated at the outset of this introductory chapter. Beyond what has already been mentioned, there are the storyboard constructions that led to underwriting of the initial parts of the franchise by Warner Brothers Pictures—to be viewed along with various conceptual designs and sketches for camera work in *The Art of the Matrix* (Lamm).

And of course any discussion of the *Matrix* franchise has to take into account the quite revolutionary cinematic technology (such as Bullet Time and the wire-work kung fu scenes) that the storyboards and eventual scripts made mandatory—the extra tracks on the movie DVDs or *The Matrix Revisited* VHS/DVD are also full of information. Of course music is also merchandized (now including music CDs "inspired by *The Matrix*"), as well as extremely carefully orchestrated advertising such as the coordinated worldwide debuts of *Reloaded* and *Revolutions,* various documentaries about various segments of production, and spectacular clothing effects (see The Matrix Shop, or The MATRIX 101 "Get Stuff!" segment). Let me sketch some of the background of the Wagnerian concept and see if it doesn't add to appreciation of the franchise.

Beyond writing extremely long and complex operas and having an enormous impact on orchestral music, Richard Wagner was one of the most creative theatrical geniuses of the last quarter of the nineteenth century, and at his *Festspielhaus* (festival theater) in Bayreuth, in southern Germany, produced in 1876 the nearest experience to virtual reality before the invention of sound movies (Krukowski). He was the first to design a theater in which daylight was excluded in order to control very carefully the lighting effects on the stage. His music was so strikingly original that it led to the invention of special musical instruments (notably the Wagner tuba).

And clearly his concept of *Festspiel* leaped ahead of any previous conception of theater (one might argue that he went back to ancient Greek dramatic models) in its synthesis and integration of art (design, costumes, sets), architecture, statuary (on the grounds and in the interiors), and obviously, music, poetry, drama, and dance: the first multimedia spectacle, if you will.

It was all ideologically driven, to be sure: Wagner's intent was like that of ancient Greece, namely to develop in his dramatic presentations the true values of the democratic community, under—and here his closeness to fascism enters, which would eventually repel his early champion, Friedrich Nietzsche—one single director. He was responsible in his productions for every aspect such as the texts (libretti) of the operatic works to the details of the sets and costumes—and for those many-hour performances broken up with time for meals, he even tried to orchestrate the local cuisine.

Perhaps the Wachowski brothers didn't go quite that far, but their orchestration of the worldwide simultaneous launch of the second two films of their trilogy was pretty impressive. Their command of Internet resources certainly went beyond Wagner's capabilities, of course, but I suspect that Wagner would have gotten right on board.

One aspect of the concept of the *Gesamtkunstwerk* that I find most interesting is the fact that it has not been frozen in nineteenth-century limits, but—as witnessed by a collaboration in 2002 between the Musée du Louvre and the Solomon R. Guggenheim Museum in which many contemporary aspects of the "total work of art" were explored (see http:///www.guggenheim.org/press_releases/total_art_pr.html, accessed 29 October 2003). Topics included the relationships between avant-garde arts and popular culture during the twentieth century, the vast eco-works of ecological artists Christo and Jeanne-Claude, and discussions of artworks that do not become materialized works of art to be hung in museums.

A 2002 performance at St. Mark's Church in New York, entitled "Maria Del Bosco (Sex and Racing Cars: A Sound Opera)," by Richard Foreman, explicitly correlates Wagnerian (and Nietzschean) attempts to break down distinctions between artistic genres. Reviewing the production, Joseph Nechvatal suggests that "What Wagner prognosticated for us, here Foreman/Nietsche deliver: the idea of an artwork made up of a synthesis of all the arts: a fused combination of music, poetry, dance, architecture, sculpture, and painting into a multimedia-spectacle" (http://216.239.41. 104/search?q=cache:P22yJsGUIPIJ [...], or at nyartsmagazine.com; accessed 29 October 2003). Here three "ravishingly beautiful, sex-starved fashion models [...] fall in love with a racing car that turns out to be human consciousness in disguise" (Nechvatal, par. 2). Such incongruence reflects something of the "pastiche" of postmodernist art, where particular images from elsewhere or the past may be brought in apparently by arbitrary importation, not because they are significant in the plot by themselves (Easthope 22; see also Isaacs and Trost in this volume).

In Foreman's production, Nechvatel suggests, "our culture is presented to us as a dramatic conflict between Dionysian and Apollonian energies— chock full of American excesses and their corrections." I would just annotate: "and in the *Matrix* franchise in its most stretched-out elements." "Space Opera" takes on new connotations as the matrix or matrices which we all inhabit become through this Wachowskian *Gesamtkunstwerk* more and more visible as we look around our cities, homes, and bedrooms. It will be a long time before another such encompassing artwork is conceived, even by the extraordinary Brothers and their co-conspirators. Perhaps contributors to this volume add to that conspiracy to dis-close, re-veal, what may happen when one dares to take the red pill, indeed when a society as a whole challenges the artificial virtual realities a government substitutes for democratic growth of real—not just virtual—communal values.

Works Cited

Barreca, Regina, ed. *A Sitdown with the Sopranos*. New York: Palgrave-Macmillan, 2002.

Bartlett, Laura, and Thomas B. Byers. "Back to the Future: The Humanist *Matrix*." *Cultural Critique* 53 (Winter 2003): 28-46.

Baudrillard, Jean. *Simulacra and Simulation*. Trans. Sheila Faria Glaser. The Body, in Theory: Histories of Cultural Materialism. Ann Arbor: University of Michigan Press, 1994.

Burek, Josh. "The Gospel according to Neo." *The Christian Science Monitor* (9 May 2003), <http:www.csmonitor.com/2003/0509/p16s01-almo.htm>. Accessed 11 November 2003.

Easthope, Anthony. "Postmodernism and Critical and Cultural Theory." *The Routledge Critical Dictionary of Postmodern Thought*. Ed. Stuart Sim. New York: Routledge, 1999. 15-27.

Gibson, William. *Neuromancer*. New York: Ace, 1984.

———. "Johnny Mnemonic." *Burning Chrome*. New York: Ace, 1986 [1981]. 1-22.

Grossberg, Lawrence, Cary Nelson, and Paula Treichler, eds. *Cultural Studies*. New York: Routledge, 1992.

Guilbert, George-Claude. *Madonna as Postmodern Myth: How One Star's Self-Construction Rewrites Sex, Gender, Hollywood, and the American Dream*. Jefferson NC: McFarland, 2002.

Hollywood.com Staff. "'The Matrix' and Philosophy: An A to Z Guide." http://www.hollywood.com/sites/matrix/feature/type/red/id/1716447. Accessed 11 November 2003.

Holson, Laura M. "An Elf and a Bear Trip UP the Final 'Matrix.'" The *New York Times* 10 November 2003. Accessed online on that date.

Irwin, William. Ed. *The Matrix and Philosophy: Welcome to the Desert of the Real*. Popular Culture and Philosophy. LaSalle: Open Court, 2002.

Krukowski, Damon. "Jean-Luc Godard on CD." *Pulse Magazine* April 2001. Accessed online on 29 October 2003, <http://216.239.41.104/search?q=cache:iXj9mz2w4-AJ:pulse [...]>.

Kuhn, Thomas S. *The Structure of Scientific Revolutions*. 2nd ed. Chicago: University of Chicago Press, 1970 [1962].

Lamm, Spencer, ed. *The Art of the Matrix*. New York: Newmarket and WB Worldwide Publishing, 2000. [With the script of *The Matrix* by Larry Wachowski and Andy Wachowski, also published separately, and rich background for many aspects of the production of the film.]

LaVelle, Kristenea M. *The Reality Within the Matrix*. Wisconsin Dells: Saxco, 2002.

Napier, Susan J. *Animé from Akira to Princess Mononoke: Experiencing Contemporary Japanese Animation*. New York: Palgrave—St. Martins, 2001.

Pulley, Brett. "Cliff-Hanger." *Forbes*. 10 November 2003. Accessed at <http://www.forbes.com/forbes/2003/1110/100_print.html>.

Salisbury, Mark. "Rage Against the Machines." *Premiere: The Movie Magazine* Special Collector's Issue (May 2003): 44-53, 97-99.

Seay, Chris, and Greg Garrett. *The Gospel Reloaded: Exploring Spirituality and Faith in the Matrix*. Colorado Springs: Pinion, 2003.

Slack, Jennifer Daryl. "Everyday Matrix: Becoming Adolescence." *Animations (of Deleuze and Guattari)*. Ed. Slack. New York: Peter Lang, 2003: 9-29.

Sterling, Bruce. "Every Other Movie Is the Blue Pill." *Exploring the Matrix: Visions of the Cyber Present*. Ed. Karen Haber. New York: St. Martin's, 2003: 17-28.

Taylor, Mark C. *Confidence Games: Money and Markets in a World without Redemption*. Chicago: University of Chicago Press, 2004.

Turner, Victor. "Frame, Flow, and Reflection: Ritual and Drama as Public Liminality." *Performance and Communication*. Ed. Michel Benamou and Charles Caramello. Theories of Contemporary Culture, 1. Milwaukee: Center for Twentieth-Century Studies, and Madison: Coda: 33-55.

Walsh, Doug. *Enter the Matrix Official Strategy Guide*. Signature Series. Indianapolis: BradyGames-Pearson Education, 2003.

Yeffeth, Glenn, ed. *Taking the Red Pill: Science, Philosophy, and Religion in* The Matrix. Dallas: Benbella, 2003.

Wachowski, Andy, and Larry Wachowski. Interview: "Matrix Virtual Theatre." 6 November 1999. <http://www.warnervideo.com/matrixevents/wachowski.html>.

Welcome to the Sexual Spectacle:
The Female Heroes of the Franchise

MARTINA LIPP

In *The Myth of the American Superhero,* a contributor to this volume, John Shelton Lawrence, along with co-author Robert Jewett, comment on the dominance of white males in American popular culture. Looking at the mythological aspects of what they call "the American monomyth," they ask: "Why do women and people of color, who have made significant strides in civil rights, continue to remain almost wholly subordinate in a mythscape where communities must almost always be rescued by physically powerful white men?" (8). The question leads to reflections on how character roles are still being played out in movies today.

Did you ever imagine being a casting director? Sometimes when I watch a film I particularly like, I do. I try to imagine whether a film with one actor would have been similarly successful with another. And on my badass feminist days, I go even further and rewrite the whole script: I try to imagine whether it might have been possible to substitute a female actor with a male, and vice versa.

Exchanging the two leading actors, Trinity and Neo in the *Matrix* franchise would not present much of a mental challenge: They look so similar that one could even mistake them for brother and sister, and both have fighting skills that are far beyond ordinary human physical possibility. However, the one major difference is that he is the chosen one and destined to save the world, and well, she is not and dies at the end.

With Luke Skywalker in the *StarWars* series or Paul Atreides / Usul Muad'Dib in *Dune* (David Lynch 1984) to name two examples, there are already plenty of films out there featuring a white male hero/savior figure. These films reflect what bell hooks frequently refers to as a white supremacist capitalist patriarchal worldview: the story repeats itself, only the settings change.

In their book *The Female Hero in American and British Literature,* Carol Pearson and Katherine Pope comment on this orientation as follows:

Our understanding of the basic spiritual and psychological archetype of human life has been limited, however, by the assumption
that the hero and central character of the myth is male. The hero is
almost always assumed to be white and upper class as well. The journey of the upper-class white male—a socially, politically, and
economically powerful subgroup of the human race—is identified
as the generic type for the normal human condition; and other
members of society—racial minorities, the poor, and women—
are seen as secondary characters, important only as obstacles, aids,
or rewards in his journey. (4)

One would assume that it might be time for a retelling of the hero myth
with a female and/or non-white hero. But would the world be ready for a
female messiah portrayed by Trinity? And a more practical question: would
the whole *Matrix* franchise still have been as successful as it is with a heroic-
female messiah figure?

Science fiction has been notorious for its stereotypical and frequently
even sexist representations of women. At the same time, science fiction has
given us some of the strongest—both physically and mentally—female characters in film history. I am thinking of the *Alien* series' Lt. Ellen Ripley, as
well as Sarah Connor in *The Terminator* (1984) and in *Terminator 2: Judgment
Day* (1991), or the Terminatrix in *Terminator 3: Rise of the Machines* (2003).

And, of course, there is Trinity. In this chapter I will focus on the role
she plays as the story of humanity's war against the machines unfolds from
The Matrix through *Reloaded* to *Revolutions*. In fact, the *Matrix* trilogy offers
a wide range of interesting female characters worth analyzing, particularly
in the second and third installments (the first film is rather short on significant female characters): The Oracle, played in the first two films by the
late Gloria Foster and replaced by Mary Alice in *Revolutions*, Niobe, Persephone, or Zee just to name a few. An in-depth analysis of every individual
female character is impossible here, but I will refer to significant scenes featuring other relevant female characters.

Annette Kuhn, in her book *Women's Pictures: Feminism and Cinema*, poses
some useful questions essential for the textual analysis of a film from a feminist perspective:

What function does a woman character perform within the film's
narrative?

How are women represented visually?

Are certain fixed images of women being appealed to, and if so
    how are they constructed through the film's image/narrative?

How do women not function, how are they not represented in
    the film? (79).

Representations (especially of gender) can be a tricky terrain. Very often
they are not consistent in their approach, which is why one has to be prepared to look at these representations from various perspectives.

Like film in general, the *Matrix* trilogy never offers just one possibility
of a way of reading it. Frequently a film works on various levels combining
various degrees of dominant, mainstream ideas and revolutionary approaches.
As bell hooks argues in her book *Reel to Real:*

> Even though many traditional academic film critics are convinced
> that popular art can never be subversive and revolutionary, the intro-
> duction of contemporary discourses of race, sex, and class into films
> has created a space for critical intervention. Often multiple stand-
> points are expressed in an existing film. A film may have incredibly
> revolutionary standpoints merged with conservative ones. This min-
> gling of standpoints is often what makes it hard for audiences to
> critically "read" the overall filmic narrative. (3)

Coming to terms with the various standpoints presented is a problem
to be faced in the analysis of the *Matrix* franchise: in comparison with other
(science fiction) films, we have a huge cast of very strong and powerful
female characters. However, their empowerment is frequently toned down
by the use of a range of different narrative methods.

In my analysis, I focus upon the heroic, empowered, and what I consider positive qualities of the women portrayed in the trilogy. But what actually makes a woman heroic? The next section is devoted to this question.

We Could Be Heroes Just for One Film— The Female Heroes in the Franchise

Studying heroines portrayed in the mass media can give historians
a clue not only about the values of women of that era but about dis-
crepancies in social demands for heroic symbols. (Hume 26)

Is a heroine just a female version of a hero? Not necessarily. In fact, the term "heroine" is very gender specific and has rather negative and diminutive connotations attached to it: "The heroine is most often praised for her dedication to traditional feminine qualities. She is pure, gentle, generous, quiet, stoic in the face of adversity and responsive to her roles as mother and wife. She epitomizes the feminine" (Dilley 141). For the purpose of this chapter, I use the more neutral term "female hero" instead of heroine.

In her essay, "Changing Characteristics of Heroic Women in Midcentury Mainstream Media," Janice Hume tries to come to a definition about what is considered heroic in a woman. She cites Ralph Waldo Emerson, who states that heroes "mirror the ideal morals of the community" (9), and this definition definitely can be applied to our analysis.

However, given the fact that "ideal morals" are not the same for men and women, we can conclude that a heroine is not just a female version of the male hero, especially because, for a long time in American history, "the very actions that would distinguish a woman as 'hero' if she were living by male standards of morality, might just label her as unladylike and thus make her an unfit symbol of 'heroine' for women of her day" (Hume 10). Mass media in general—and here I would also include film and fiction—has always played an important role in the creation and perpetuation of the dominant culture's heroic role models.

So, how and to what extent have these heroic role models been transferred to science-fiction film in general? In many cases, as I have mentioned already, women in Hollywood cinema are frequently represented as passive narrative figures: "they tend to be fought over rather than fight, avenged rather than avenge" (Tasker 17).

In the *Matrix* franchise, women often appear as the incarnation of one of the basic definitions for heroes—they are brave warriors or warrior queens. The history of the brave women warriors goes back to the figure of the Amazon in Greek mythology, a tradition sustained in recent sword-and-sorcery fantasy tales (*Xena–The Warrior Princess,* or *Red Sonja* [Richard Fleischer, 1985]), in feminist utopias, and in science fiction of today. The Amazons were unwilling to submit to male rule, escaped from patriarchal societies, and created independent separatist communities, which they significantly "defended with *force of arms*" (Rohrlich xvi, emphasis mine).

In science-fiction films today, the female partner, although far more empowered than the passive women in the films of the 1950s and 1960s, often serves to confirm the heterosexuality of the male hero or acts as a secondary sidekick:

> Whilst the woman in the action narrative may operate as some kind of symbolic guarantee, a place for the fixing of difference and heterosexual desire, she is simultaneously rendered increasingly marginal. [The male figure] controls the action at the same time as he is offered up to the audience as a sexual spectacle. (Tasker 16)

This is definitely true for *The Matrix,* where women, no matter how empowered they are, always have someone above them on the social ladder.

Trinity might be important for the plot, but she will never be the chosen one: She is there to support, love, and nurture Neo, but he is the one who saves humankind from extinction. The same is true for Persephone: she is powerful, especially through her strong sexuality, but she is never shown to act out of her own initiative. The only meaningful and heroic act in *Reloaded* and *Revolutions* (where she only has one line) is when she betrays the Merovingian after he has betrayed her with the blonde babe—"Cause and Effect" as he first calls it—and Persephone later mocks him. This is one of the methods we frequently find in fiction and film: strong and heroic women are often portrayed as villains and traitors, using their power to destroy rather than to create. However, here Persephone's treason of the Merovingian actually becomes a heroic act to help humankind.

When examining all three films of the trilogy, it is one of the secondary characters, Niobe (who only appears in the second and third parts), who is the most empowered among the women in the film (she is one of the main action fighters in *Enter*). Her strength and independence could also be attributed to the fact that she is not caught in any intense relationship with one of the male characters. Her relationship with Commander Lock obviously does not prevent her from helping her former lover Morpheus.

The only character who, at least in the beginning, seems to operate in a complete self-determined manner, if one can say that about a computer program, is in fact The Oracle. She becomes a heroic figure through her wisdom and through her "commitment to a truth beyond that recognized by social convention" (Pearson and Pope 9). Pearson and Pope also comment that "often, the female hero is in tune with spiritual or natural values that the society advocates but does not practice" (9). These values often make it possible for the female hero to survive, as does The

Oracle in the end. However, her spiritual heroism stands on shaky ground, since she relies on men like Seraph to protect her, and in the end she patiently awaits Agent Smith and Agent Smith and Agent Smith to become another Agent Smith. While most of the other women in the franchise are constructed as warriors, relying very much on their physical abilities, The Oracle is the only female character who is not established as a sexual or physical spectacle.

As we can see, names obviously play an important role in the Wachowski brothers' universe. The main characters in their first movie, the thriller *Bound* (Wachowski Brothers, 1996), have rather evocative, not to say descriptive, names such as "Corky (buoyant), Violet (clinging), and Caesar (dictatorial)" (Strick 260). And in the *Matrix* franchise this tradition is ambitiously continued: all of the characters have highly significant (or signifying?) names. Trinity, whose "unifying presence links—and exchanges—the powers of Morpheus the dream-master with those of the long-sought savior Neo (note the anagram) who is at once the New Man (as in, by useful coincidence, Neo-Tokyo subsumed by *Akira*) and the neophyte disciple" (Strick 260).

The word "trinity" is generally used to refer to a unity of three parts, following the Wachowskis' obvious and intentional Christian symbolism (http://awesomehouse.com/matrix/parallels.htn). Taking her name literally would then mean that we can conclude that Trinity represents the essence of things, of life, of humanity. Or is she, as proposed by Philip Strick, just the spiritual and physical link between Morpheus and Neo? Because then we would have to assume that, since Morpheus is God(father)-like (or is he the God of Sleep?), and Neo is associated with Christ, Trinity represents the transcendental condition of Christianity in the figure of the Holy Ghost.

The significance and importance of names as a descriptive reference to the person is a tradition well known in various parts of the world. Especially in many Native American cultures, names and the act of naming play an important role: In many groups, for example, children are named when they reach adulthood and become full members of the community (Beck, Waters, and Francisco 194-95). Other tribes name the young child when an ancestral spirit is reincarnated (Hultkrantz 81-83, 137). In all instances, the act of naming or a change of name marks a transition from one stage in life to another.

In the *Matrix* franchise naming is a process connected to the widespread and common—and not so spiritual—practice of adopting an alter ego when entering cyberspace. While Keanu Reeves is Thomas Anderson in the real (or rather not so real) world, when joining Morpheus and his group, his hacker identity as "Neo" becomes his new real identity. The change of name thus marks his transition and an act of initiation.

As one usually chooses one's cyberspace name oneself, instead of being named by parents or other authorities, this act precludes an aspect of intentional self-reference involved in the process. In cyberspace one can choose what and who one wants to be, one enters a parallel world and creates one's own "residual self image," as it is called, in the matrix, thus leaving one's restricting real physical self behind. In the *Matrix* franchise, the cyberpunks Trinity, Neo, and Morpheus have to assimilate their chosen alternative identities in order to meet their real selves. Hence the process is reversed: the characters leave what they think is the "real world," in order to find the "truth" and their actual physical identity.

The Wachowski brothers draw on various kinds of mythological sources to name the other female characters: in Greek mythology, Persephone is the goddess of spring, married to the king of the underground Hades, and—surprise, surprise—this also parallels her position as the girlfriend of the Merovingian in the narrative of the *Matrix* franchise.

Niobe's name also draws on Greek mythology: She is a woman who repeatedly boasts to the goddess Leto about her capacity to have given birth to twelve children while Leto has only two children. As we frequently see in Greek mythology, characters such as Icarus, who question divine authority and superiority, have to be put in their places by divine intervention. Hence, Leto sends her two children Artemis and Apollo to kill all of Niobe's children and thus reminds Niobe "not to mess with the goddess," i.e., not to devalue divine femininity and motherhood.

Out of grief over her children's death Niobe later turns into stone. Fortunately, the *Matrix* films express a far more empowering message to self-confident women, who transgress not divine but patriarchal role models: in an act of spaceship navigation that extends the imagination and capabilities of her male counterparts, Niobe safely returns her ship to Zion to witness the final peace between the machines and humanity in *Revolutions*.

The Delphic oracle is also an important and very powerful figure in Greek mythology, who interprets presumably divine symbols to predict the future for those who seek her advice. Her answers are, however, never straightforward messages, but are enigmatic and delivered in verse form. The inquirer then has to make sense of the message on his or her own.

The Wachowski brothers obviously learned their Greek mythology lesson well, and in the films they give The Oracle a very similar position: She tells the individual characters enigmatically what they need to hear to fulfil their role in the future. However, in contrast to the historical oracle, who only advised male inquirers, the Oracle in the *Matrix* franchise also helps women in need for advice. While Greek mythology is shaped by stereotypical role models not only in relation to gender, but also in relation to human-divine interaction, the Wachowskis use these myths and rewrite them by eliminating, at least to some extent, the sexist and/or supremacist messages the original myths perpetrated.

Welcome to the Sexual Spectacle!

(Lieutenant) I think we can handle one little girl.
(Agent Smith) No, Lieutenant, your men are already dead.

In the script of *The Matrix,* Trinity is described first as a "woman in black leather," then as a "leather-clad ghost," moving "so smooth and fast, inhumanly fast" (Wachowski 275-274). This is certainly not your ordinary next-door neighbor, this is an almost superhuman creature, able to fight and bear pain unimaginable to the average human being. At the same time she wears clothes that are usually associated with the glitzy glamour involved in sado-masochism circles, with Trinity as "the leather-clad dominatrix," thus "emphasizing her sexuality, her availability within traditional feminine terms" (Tasker 19).

The Wachowski brothers' attraction to the kinkier/outlaw side of sexuality is apparent in *Revolutions,* when Trinity, Morpheus, and Seraph have to make it through a BDSM club on their way to talk to the Merovingian. Trinity's hypersexualization could be also considered as a masquerade in the sense of Joan Riviere: she has to hide her possession of power behind an exaggerated femininity, thus reaffirming her status as a woman by constructing her sexuality as a spectacle: "Womanliness therefore could be assumed and worn as a mask, both to hide the possession of masculinity and to avert the reprisals expected if she was found to posses it—much as a thief will turn out his pockets and ask to be searched to prove that he has not the stolen goods" (as cited by Doane 138; see also Judith Butler, "Prohibition, Psychoanalysis and the Heterosexual Matrix").

21

Interesting in this respect is the fact that Larry and Andy Wachowski both worked as writers for comics, and the genre of comic/cartoon art is strongly shaped by exaggerated visual role models (Tasker 26). Keeping in mind that the storyboards for all three films are conceptualized in comic-book images, based on drawings by Steve Skroce (responsible, for example, for *Spider-Man* and *Wolverine* of the *X-Men*) and Geof Darrow (*Hard Boiled*), exaggerated representations of gender do not come surprising (Morrisson).

A similar phenomenon can be found in the computer-game world, where exaggerated femininity—and masculinity as well—play an important role. When talking about exaggerated sexuality, it is inevitable to think of Lara Croft, the first entirely digital star. Mary Flanagan compares her with Theda Bara, the first cinematic sex symbol, whose star persona was similarly constructed around masculine expectations (Flanagan 81).

Croft is a simulacrum of femininity, a copy without an original (her claimed measurements 88-24-84 are obviously far from realistic), onto which the viewer can project his or her desire. This hypersexualization of the female body can also be seen a response to the fact that the majority of the computer-game audience, as well as the creators of the games, are in fact male. They seem to project their ideal of a woman, which I argue is more a result of pornographic fantasy rather than based on real-life images, into the game world.

Hence the computer-game universe is one of the strongholds where sexist gender categories are still highly emphasized. Thus the potential of cyberspace has so far very often been used to reinforce and express a misogynist worldview: "The current narratives offered on the gaming market, work against these possibilities [to present authentic or alternative representations of femininity] by offering hyper-sexual or victim characters" (Flanagan 91). Despite their hypersexualization, it has to be noted, however, that many fight games always had female fighters one could choose from, even at a time where "sexy fight chicks" were not as much in vogue in Hollywood as they are now. One could also argue, by using Judith Butler's concept of gender as a performance, that by choosing a game character from the opposite sex the player is able to transgress traditional and limiting gender boundaries.

The Matrix film iconography is heavily influenced by the video-game aesthetic, thus it comes as no surprise that the Wachowskis also produced the video game *Enter,* based on the films' narratives. Interestingly, as I have mentioned before, one of the strongest female characters in the movie, Niobe, together with Ghost, becomes one of the two main characters the player can choose in the video game. In contrast to Lara Croft, Jada Pinkett Smith's body is not sexually exaggerated in *Enter,* however, it is clear that the programmers were working with Lara Croft as a model for the game.

But let us come back to the *Matrix* film trilogy: it has to be noted that the construction of Trinity, Niobe, and Persephone in terms of sexual spectacles inside the matrix is a process not limited to the female characters, but extended to the male characters in the film as well. In the real world, be it on board the *Nebuchadnezzar* or in Zion, the characters wear clothes in different states of decay. This scarcity is placed in opposition to the excessively sexual, hyper-stylized fetish clothes they wear when they are operating inside the matrix.

While it can be assumed that the larger majority of the action/science fiction audience is still male, the popularity of *The Matrix* among many women can be attributed to the attractiveness of Keanu Reeves as a sexy action hero (in contrast to more beefy colleagues such as Arnold Schwarzenegger in the *Terminator* trilogy). But I would argue that another important reason for the film's success among female viewers is the overall message that the film sends out to women by having many strong women in the cast that act as powerful role models. Especially in the beginning of the trilogy, we frequently watch from Trinity's point of view: The initial scene in *The Matrix* features a voice-over conversation between Trinity and Cypher that illustrates this argument:

> TRINITY: I said, is everything in place?
> CYPHER: You weren't supposed to relieve me.
> TRINITY: I know, but I felt like taking a shift.
> CYPHER: You like him, don't you. *You like watching him?* [My emphasis]

Trinity is established as the (female) subject who watches over Neo, the unaware male object of her desire, and the audience shares her point of view. Her position as the active observer also serves as a reversal of the stereotypical phallocentric subject-object relationship often discussed and criticized in feminist psychoanalytic film theory. The woman here has the active part—she is the one who looks—while the man becomes the one who holds the look, who becomes a source of visual pleasure. In this scene Trinity becomes the screen figure of identification for the desiring gaze of the female spectator (Mulvey, "Visual Pleasure and Narrative Cinema"). This scene is also an indication of the fact that the pleasure we conceive from watching film is not necessarily linked to fixed gender identities. I think Yvonne Tasker is right when she argues that the pleasures we derive from watching film, "are not dictated by any rules of same-sex identification or by heterosexual understandings of desire" (136).

Postmodern spectatorship is a product of constant negotiations and renegotiations of gender identity. By classifying certain forms of behavior or entertainment as essentially female or male, psychoanalytical film theory often ignores and oversimplifies the dynamics and the potential of the whole identification process (hooks 2; see also Butler, *Gender Trouble*).

Women and Technology or: A Manifesto for Cyborgs

(Neo) Who are you?
(Trinity) My name is Trinity.
N: Trinity? The Trinity? The Trinity that cracked the IRS D-Base?
T: That was a long time ago.
N: Gee-zus.
T: What?
N: I just thought … you were a guy.
T: Most guys do.

This conversation from the first encounter between Trinity and Neo in *The Matrix,* challenges the widespread characterization of the hacker culture as "almost exclusively white, masculine, and middle class" (Ross 116), and, in addition, profoundly chauvinistic.

"A Detective Story," a short *Animatrix* film, gives the audience some background information on Trinity's hacker identity. It also illustrates the above assumption: until the detective actually finds her, he automatically assumes that Trinity must be a man. When in fact, Trinity and the other Zion women in the trilogy, actually serve as contradictions to the stereotype that women are not as competent with technology as men are: they are shown as professional in the use of all kinds of technical equipment including computers, spaceships, mobile phones, motorbikes, helicopters, cars, or weapons. The issue of femininity and technology leads us to another important issue:

Up to this point, we have considered Trinity and other protagonists as purely human creatures, while if we follow Donna Haraway's definition, they are actually cyborgs: "hybrid creature[s] composed of organism and machine" (1). Cyborgs incorporate two essential characteristics: an organic/human creature and "machines in their guise as [...] communication systems, texts, and self-acting, ergonomically designed apparatuses" (1). Their ability to enter and exit the matrix as they please is only possible through a socket in the back of their necks where they can "jack in."

The same socket also serves as a data path for direct downloads to their brains. This concept of "plugging in" or "jacking in" actually goes back to William Gibson. However, while "jacking into" the matrix for Gibson's character Case in *Neuromancer* is a highly sexualized, erotic act, for the crew of the *Nebuchadnezzar* it is in fact the complete contrary. The matrix is established as the site for the manifestation of sexual difference through clothes/appearance, but it is in fact a place where the sexual act itself is completely insignificant and obsolete. On the other hand, the matrix is a feminine not to say maternal site. Critic Fred Botting comments: "machinic processes, networks and connectivities promise new relationships and present something entirely Other, an otherness, however, presented as provocatively and ungraspably feminine" (147).

In the process of cyborgification, gender differences become obsolete (or should become obsolete), they should be, as Haraway calls it, "techno-digested" (177). While the *Matrix* franchise takes advantage of the potential of female cyborgs—especially in the fight and action scenes—when it comes to the representation of general human interaction, the Wachowskis, as we have already mentioned, still draw heavily on established gender role models.

Kung Fu, Guns, and "Dodge This!"

As is obvious in the many fight scenes, Asian martial-arts movies were an important point of reference and inspiration for the *Matrix* franchise. The presence of the many female fighters is one of the characteristics that make martial-arts films like the Oscar-winner *Crouching Tiger, Hidden Dragon* (Ang Lee, 2001) so interesting and visually attractive. In fact, Asian martial-arts cinema "may be the only place in the world where men and women fight as equals" (Giukin 56). In this respect it is important to note that Hong Kong action movies differ from traditional Hollywood action flicks in their emphasis on technique and speed, rather than upon the muscular body and physical strength. This brings with it a

> [s]trong masculinization of the heroine [which] often creates a break with the classical representation of feminine passivity in cinema, a transformation that affects her body representation to a degree that questions the received notion of gender. In order to control the more and more fluid boundaries of gender, the hero or heroine's more and more ambiguous body is frequently marked as feminine or masculine through costumes and/or other techniques, such as masquerade. (Giukin 55)

Giukin also draws on Joan Riviere's theory of femininity as a masquerade to hide the transgression of gender boundaries, later taken up by Mary Ann Doane in the article I have already mentioned. Masquerades and costumes are important characteristics of traditional Chinese culture, especially in the incarnation of the Cantonese/Chinese opera. This old tradition also influences the representations of gender in the Hong Kong action movies, where clothes play an important role as manifestations of gender.

As I have already mentioned, the *Matrix* franchise also takes advantage of costumes to convey gender difference. The female and male heroes are constructed according to the rules of the Hong Kong martial-arts film. The focus is on the "spectacle offered by fighters' bodies in interaction and the ballet of movements within the shot" (Giukin 57). *The Matrix* has adopted traditional characteristics from the Asian martial-arts movies and introduced them to the broader Hollywood audience.

The use of weapons is another issue I have already touched on. In the hands of men, guns and weapons have been traditional symbols of dominance and oppression, even when being used in the maintenance of the law. However, in the hands of women, guns and other technical gadgets become symbols for empowerment. While the combination of men and guns seems almost natural, especially because guns often act as signifiers for masculinity and phallic power, women using guns are still a contradiction to their traditionally presumed passiveness and weakness. In many action films women's use of guns is turned into a fetishistic spectacle—the narrative of *Blue Steel* (Kathryn Bigelow, 1990) is even outspokenly structured around the fetish/phallic image of a woman with a gun (Tasker 158-162).

In her discussion of *Thelma and Louise* (Ridley Scott, 1991), Tasker proposes that "[t]he possession of guns and the possession of self are inextricably linked through the dilemmas that the film poses about freedom and self-respect" (139). The film thus makes a strong connection between empowerment and the possession and use of guns: the professional use of a gun marks the heroine's independence and strength. However, again this empowerment has to be reduced by emphasizing the heroines' femininity through clothes or stereotypical feminine behavior, or, as in the case of *Thelma and Louise* and the *Matrix* trilogy, the main female characters have to die in the end so that patriarchal order can be reestablished.

The union of guns and women is strongly embedded within outer space and/or post-apocalyptic science-fiction film. Only rarely are the female protagonists unfamiliar with the handling of guns: "In the often barbaric and excessive world of the post-apocalyptic narrative, women are freer to act tough and be independent, because it is evident that the world has been turned topsy-turvy. In such a universe, girls are sometimes free to act like boys" (Inness 123).

This scenario has often been criticized by feminist critics, who note that by taking up arms, these women, like the mythic Amazons, are portrayed as female versions of men, continuing patriarchal law and behavior instead of developing alternative models of living. However, and here I agree with Tasker, there is a certain amount of masochism involved in this criticism. The use of technology and weapons can certainly have a liberating and empowering effect especially for women, who have been oppressed for a long time by all kinds of institutional and physical violence. For some critics there seem to be an irresolvable dichotomy between women as life givers and life takers.

Hollywood Love Affairs?

In this section I discuss another narrative device frequently used to reestablish a patriarchal world order within the plot. While on the one hand, Trinity and the other female characters are presented as—physically and mentally—strong female heroes, on the other hand they follow the stereotypical mainstream Hollywood female role model: "If a woman is in a nonnormative role in economic control and production, she will cede that control to a man by the end of the film. Romantic love seems to be the normative role which most strongly influences the decision" (Haralovich as cited by Kuhn 35; Dowling).

Laura Mulvey discusses the importance of marriage in the Western, and the function of woman as signifier in this process. Her observations can easily be transferred to the science-fiction film, since space is often characterized as the new "final frontier." In reference to Vladimir Propp's analysis of folk tales, she proposes that "an important aspect of narrative closure is 'marriage'" (Mulvey, "Afterthoughts" 33). Frequently, the act of marriage is the "main rationale for any female presence" (Mulvey, "Afterthoughts" 34), in a narrative dominated by men.

Although obviously nobody in the movies is married, we find that in the *Matrix* trilogy, all the main female characters, with the exception of The Oracle, are paired off in traditional, and very importantly, same-race, heterosexual relationships. However, and here I take Mulvey's argument a bit further, one could argue that these relationships are also necessary to confirm the heterosexuality of the female characters.

To come back to the initial quotation by bell hooks, one of the striking characteristics in the narrative of *The Matrix* is that it is motivated by a continuous shift between revolutionary and stereotypical positions. This becomes particularly evident in the relationship between Trinity and Neo from film to film, often even from one scene to the next. When one looks at all three parts of the trilogy, one notices a certain pattern within the narrative development: Trinity is always initially positioned in a very powerful position, but during the run of the film(s), her position of power is gradually taken away. This becomes particularly evident in the final (kiss) scenes between Neo and Trinity in all three films, *The Matrix, Reloaded,* and *Revolutions.*

While these scenes are not exactly marriage ceremonies, they are highly meaningful symbolic acts, which offer insight into the construction of gender in the narrative. Trinity's decline of power while in *The Matrix* is only marginal; in *Reloaded* it is she who has to be saved by Neo in a truly Superman act, followed by a reanimation scene reminiscent of underground voodoo practitioners. She comments on her rescue in her own true "Dodge this!" style: "I guess this makes us even," which is not something you would expect to hear from an ordinary damsel in distress.

In the beginning of *Revolutions* we find the couple in a similar situation as in the beginning of *The Matrix,* Neo has to be freed and it is Trinity who undertakes saving him. However in the end, she herself cannot be saved anymore and dies a heroic death. On the one hand this could be interpreted as a traditional way of closure for a female sidekick character, who has, similar to the main characters in *Thelma and Louise,* become too powerful and so has to step out the way for the male hero. However, I would like to offer a possible alternative reading as well, since Trinity's death could also be interpreted as the glorious end on the battlefield traditionally associated with male heroic warriors.

Conclusion

The Wachowski brothers certainly present a very empowered and thus positive image of women in the *Matrix* franchise, especially in comparison with other, more traditional, science-fiction films. At the same time, as in real life, female empowerment always ends where the glass ceiling begins. No matter how strong the female characters are, there is always some man placed above them in importance. Furthermore, the Wachowskis draw on some of the traditional narrative or visual devices, like hypersexualization, death, or heterosexual romance, to tone down the significance of the female characters. This of course sends out a mixed, not to say negative, message to the female audience: You can be powerful, but only to the extent those in power let you.

I think it is time for a female hero, who actually is the chosen one and not just the one who helps another male messiah figure to fulfill his heroic path. I would like to conclude my chapter with the following quotation from Pearson and Pope:

> Freeing the heroic journey from the limiting assumptions about appropriate female and male behavior, then, is an important step in defining a truly human—and truly humane—pattern of heroic action. [...] Until the heroic experience of all people—racial minorities and the poor as well as women—has been thoroughly explored, the myth of the hero will always be incomplete and inaccurate. (5)

Works Cited

Beck, Peggy V., A. L. Waters, and Nia Francisco. *The Sacred: Ways of Knowledge, Sources of Life.* Tsaile, AZ: Navajo Community College Press, 1992 (orig. 1977).
Botting, Fred. *Sex, Machines, and Navels.* Manchester: Manchester University Press, 1999.

Butler, Judith. *Gender Trouble: Feminism and the Subversion of Identity.* New York: Routledge, 1990.

———."Prohibition, Psychoanalysis and the Heterosexual Matrix." *The Visual Culture Reader.* Ed. Nicholas Mirzoeff. London: Routledge, 1998: 422-427.

Dilley, Kimberly J. *Busybodies, Meddlers, and Snoops: The Female Hero in Contemporary Women's Mysteries.* Westport: Greenwood, 1998.

Doane, Mary Ann. "Film and the Masquerade: Theorizing the Female Spectator." *Screen* 23.3 (September 1982): 74-87. Repr. *Feminist Film Theory. A Reader.* Ed. Sue Thornham. Edinburgh: Edinburgh University Press, 1999: 131-145.

Dowling, Colette. *The Cinderella Complex: Women's Hidden Fear of Independence.* New York: Summit, 1981.

Flanagan, Mary. "Mobile Identities, Digital Stars, and Post Cinematic Selves." *Wide Angle* 21.1 (1999): 77-93.

Gibson, William. *Neuromancer.* New York: Ace, 1984.

Giukin, Lenuta. "Boy-Girls: Gender, Body, and Popular Culture in Hong Kong Action Movies." *Ladies and Gentlemen, Boys and Girls.* Ed. Murray Pomerance. New York: SUNY Press, 2001: 55-70.

Haraway, Donna J. *Simians, Cyborgs, and Women: The Reinvention of Nature.* New York: Routledge, 1991.

hooks, bell. *Reel to Real: Race, Sex, and Class at the Movies.* New York: Routledge, 1996.

Hultkrantz, Åke. *The Religions of the American Indians.* Trans. Monica Setterwall. Hermeneutics: Studies in the History of Religions. Berkeley: University of California Press, 1979.

Hume, Janice. "Changing Characteristics of Heroic Women in Midcentury Mainstream Media." *Journal of Popular Culture* 34.2 (Summer 2000): 9-29.

Inness, Sherrie A. *Tough Girls: Women Warriors and Wonder Women in Popular Culture.* Philadelphia: University of Pennsylvania Press, 1999.

Kuhn, Annette. *Women's Pictures: Feminism and Cinema.* London: Verso, 1994.

Lawrence, John Shelton, and Robert Jewett. *The Myth of the American Superhero.* Grand Rapids: Eerdmans, 2002.

Mulvey, Laura. "Visual Pleasure and Narrative Cinema." *Screen* 16.3 (Autumn 1975): 6-18. Repr. *Feminist Film Theory. A Reader.* Ed. Sue Thornham. Edinburgh: Edinburgh University Press, 1999: 58-69.

Mulvey, Laura. "Afterthoughts on 'Visual Pleasure and Narrative Cinema' inspired by King Vidor's *Duel in the Sun.*" *Visual and Other Pleasures.* Bloomington: Indiana University Press, 1989: 29-38.

Morrisson, Grant. *The Invisibles: Say You Want a Revolution.* New York: DC Comics, 1996.

Pearson, Carol, and Katherine Pope. *The Female Hero in American and British Literature.* New York: Bowker, 1981.

Rohrlich, Ruby, and Elaine Hoffmann Baruch, eds. *Women in Search of Utopia: Mavericks and Mythmakers.* New York: Schocken, 1984.

Ross, Andrew. "Hacking Away at the Counterculture." *Technoculture.* Ed. Constance Penley and Andrew Ross. Minneapolis: University of Minnesota Press, 1991: 107-134.

Strick, Philip. "The Matrix." *Action / Spectacle Cinema. A Sight and Sound Reader.* Ed. José Arroyo. London: British Film Institute, 2000: 259-261.

Tasker, Yvonne. *Spectacular Bodies: Gender, Genre and the Action Cinema.* London: Routledge, 1993.

Wachowski, Larry and Andy Wachowski, ed. *The Art of the Matrix.* New York: Newmarket, 2000.

Wachowski, Larry and Andy. Online chat. http://awesomehouse.com/matrix/parallels.htn. 26 March 26, 2001.

Films

Alien. Dir. Ridley Scott. Perf. Sigourney Weaver. 20th Century Fox, 1979.

Aliens. Dir. James Cameron. Perf. Sigourney Weaver. 20th Century Fox, 1986.

Alien 3. Dir. David Fincher. Perf. Sigourney Weaver. 20th Century Fox, 1992.

Alien: Resurrection. Dir. Jean-Pierre Jeunet. Perf. Sigourney Weaver. 20th Century Fox, 1997.

Blue Steel. Dir. Kathryn Bigelow. Perf. Jamie Lee Curtis, Ron Silver, Clancy Brown. Lightning Pictures, 1990.

Bound. Dir. Andy Wachowski and Larry Wachowski. Perf. Jennifer Tilly, Gina Gershon, Joe Pantoliano. Republic, 1996.

Crouching Tiger, Hidden Dragon. Dir. Ang Lee. Perf. Yun-Fat Chow, Michelle Yeoh. Sony Pictures Classic, 2001.

Dune. Dir. David Lynch. Perf. Kyle MacLachlan, Francesca Annis. Universal Pictures, 1984.

The Matrix. Dir. Andy Wachowski and Larry Wachowski. Perf. Keanu Reeves, Carrie-Anne Moss, Laurence Fishburne. Warner Brothers, 1998.

The Matrix Reloaded. Dir. Andy Wachowski and Larry Wachowski. Perf. Keanu Reeves, Carrie-Anne Moss, Laurence Fishburne. Warner Brothers, 2003.

The Matrix Revolutions. Dir. Andy Wachowski and Larry Wachowski. Perf. Keanu Reeves, Carrie-Anne Moss, Laurence Fishburne. Warner Brothers, 2003.

Red Sonja. Dir. Richard Fleischer. Perf. Brigitte Nielsen, Arnold Schwarzenegger. Dino de Laurentiis Productions, 1985.

Star Wars. Dir. George Lucas. Perf. Mark Hamill, Carrie Fisher, Harrison Ford. Lucasfilm Ltd., 1977.

The Terminator. Dir. James Cameron. Perf. Arnold Schwarzenegger, Linda Hamilton, Michael Biehn. Cinema 84, 1984.

Terminator 2: Judgement Day. Dir. James Cameron. Perf. Arnold Schwarzenegger, Linda Hamilton, Edward Furlong. Carolco Pictures Inc., 1991.

Terminator 3: The Rise of the Machines. Dir. Jonathan Mostow. Perf. Arnold Schwarzenegger, Kristianna Loken, Nick Stahl. C-2 Pictures, 2003.

Thelma and Louise. Dir. Ridley Scott. Perf. Susan Sarandon, Geena Davis. MGM, 1991.

"Xena: Warrior Princess." (TV-Series) Created by John Schulian and Robert Tapert. Perf. Lucy Lawless. MCA Television Entertainment, 1995-2001.

2

Is Neo White?
Reading Race, Watching the Trilogy

C. RICHARD KING AND
DAVID J. LEONARD

African American philosopher, Tommy Lott, author of *The Invention of Race,* has recently termed the *Matrix* trilogy the greatest contribution to contemporary Black cinema. Lott's comments strike us as odd, if not misplaced. Although the films feature a multiracial cast, noteworthy for the prominence of African American actors, they were written, directed, and produced by three Euro-Americans, Larry and Andy Wachowski and Joel Silver. Moreover, we argue that the *Matrix* franchise is a racial project that despite its pretension as a radical undertaking offers conservative, if not reactionary, interpretations of race.

On the one hand, it not only tries to say something about race, but also reinforces commonsense understandings of race. On the other hand, it reiterates racist stereotypes about African Americans and Asian Americans. Taken together, we assert that these elements reveal the *Matrix* franchise to be nothing new, but an heir to a longer history of bringing racial ideologies to life through the media.

To begin, we trace the location of race in science fiction. Against this background, we connect the trilogy to some of the more important mainstream interpretations of race and diversity in the contemporary United States, color blindness and multiculturalism. Next, we examine the racial stereotypes central to the *Matrix* franchise, linking these images to those found in other recent cinematic genres. Then we discuss the centrality and significance of whiteness. In conclusion, we argue that despite the ample celebration of the *Matrix* trilogy—for its challenges to racism, its multiple inclusion of characters of color, for the "humanity displayed" within these characters, and, most importantly, because of its radical departure from past efforts from Hollywood, the *Matrix* franchise reflects at most a continuation of Hollywood's (and America's) long-standing ideas, images, and ideologies of race (Corliss, "'Matrix Diversity'"; Smith).

Odd Absences

The *Matrix* trilogy has invited serious reflection about the philosophies inform-ing it, the messages imparted through its characters, settings, props, and narra-tives, and the importance of its ruminations on the human condition. More specifically, intellectual reviews and accounts of the film series have displayed intense interest in cyberpunk and postmodernism (Barnett, Haber); the liter-ary influences and philosophical foundations of the film (Haber, Irwin, Yeffeth, Žižek); the nature of the real (Haber, Irwin, Yeffeth); the religious subtexts of the series (Horsely, Lavelle, Seay and Garnett); and the import of violence, style, and technology (Haber, Irwin). As intriguing as these analyses and arguments may be, critical discussions of the trilogy to date have totally omitted race.

Discussions of the movies have ignored race, literally erasing it from the cinematic texts and the interpretive contexts in which it has circulated. Rather than take up the implicit and explicit racial meanings of the trilogy, scholars and critics have opted instead to address a "matrix" of questions (supposedly) unburdened by race (whether construed as ideology, utopia, identity, or hierarchy).

Nowhere is this silence more audible than in three recent anthologies (Haber, Irwin, Yeffeth) that pose questions about freedom, the real and its rep-resentation, agency, spirituality, and violence, but do not interrogate the ways that race is taken up in the films or in turn how racialized histories, communi-ties, and identities shape the sorts of answers the films or its critics offer. Hold-ing race under erasure results in partial, if not faulty, understandings: How can one begin to make sense of free-will, the "real," violence, subjectivity, and the like, without race, racism, and/or racial stratification? Simply put, one cannot. Importantly, unlike the intellectuals we have cited, both the filmmakers and their audiences have not only used the trilogy to pose challenging questions about reality, humanity, technology, cosmology, and the like, but have also seized upon the *Matrix* franchise as representing important occasions to reiterate, reproduce, resist, rework, and otherwise engage common sense understand-ings of race, racism, and race relations in the contemporary world.

Racing the Future

To get at the racial meanings of *The Matrix,* it is necessary first to under-stand the place of race in recent science-fiction novels and cinema. Science fiction has long offered authors and audiences spaces in which to engage meanings of race. In many respects, the genre has confronted racialized fears and fantasies, the nature of racial hierarchies, and the future of race relations (see Bernardi, Greene, Guerrero, and Roberts).

Science-fiction cinema has built upon and reaffirmed widely accepted cultural values and ideologies. It has tended to place the white and the male at the center of its narratives, marking both as the norm in contrast to abnormal others—supplemental non-white/non-human helpers and sidekicks and threatening aliens. Although seemingly focused on future possibilities or distant universes, science-fiction films render the present, frequently fashioning the here and now through the flat binaries of Manichean logic seen in films like *Enemy Mine* or through nostalgic reiterations of the order and sensibility of racial hierarchies as in *Star Wars.* This underlying conservatism, moreover, has encouraged the use of science fiction to formulate reactionary responses to contemporary cultural crises.

As a case in point, the imaginary worlds of science fiction easily translated the panics about urban (read black, Latino, and poor) America in the 1980s: *Blade Runner* encapsulates white fear and loathing of the city and its multicultural, chaotic, dismal futures. *Aliens* displaces concerns about unwed black mothers, welfare queens, and the urban underclass onto the hyperfecund, threatening body of the grotesque black alien that the white, nurturing heroine literally exterminates. And *Predator* uses a dreadlocked, savage, extraterrestrial warrior-hunter who kills for sport in the war-torn rain forests of Latin America to work through a growing uneasiness about the black gangsters and pushers of a mythic urban jungle during the escalation of the war on drugs (see Bernardi; Roberts 119).

Science-fiction films also have taken up immigration, offering diverse (if almost invariably anti-immigrant) narratives, ranging from *E. T.*'s story of the ideal immigrant who "arrived alone, cannot reproduce, and has no intention of seeking citizenship" (Guerrero 1993a: 58) to *Men in Black* which trades upon the cultural capital of blackness to render a hip, even irreverent retelling of efforts to police, absorb, and exterminate aliens (Roberts).

While science-fiction cinema allows for more than the dispersal and intensification of racial panics in reactionary terms and hegemonic forms of power, it also affords a means to envision the future shape of race relations. In some cases, as in *Logan's Run,* the future is starkly white; however, increasingly over the past three decades, several projects have endeavored to present more diverse prospects, and multicultural futures. *Star Trek,* in all of its various renditions, exemplifies the desire for a more colorful future in which peoples from an array of racial and ethnic communities will work together toward a common end (Bernardi).

The specter of white supremacy has always haunted this utopian vision. For in the worlds of *Star Trek,* white males have remained the gatekeepers, power brokers, and central agents; people of color and the other-worldly allegories for them remain supplemental, marginal, and supportive. Importantly, science fiction does not merely reinforce hegemonic ideals, but often clears a space to question and challenge existing categories and relations. For instance, as Greene and Guerrero reminds us, films like *The Planet of the Apes* series and *Brother from Another Planet* foster critical reflections on slavery and its legacies in the United States.

Although science fiction is a largely white domain, we wish to stress that (particularly off the screen) black characters have been common, and several African American authors, such as Samuel Delany and Octavia Butler, have had a profound impact upon the genre. Indeed, while presence or absence says much about prevailing understandings of race at any given socio-historical conjuncture, more telling is what authors and audience make of and do with "diverse" casts and characters: Who centers the action? Who is secondary or supplemental? What characteristics adhere to racialized characters? What are the social relations? Who does what? How do they contribute to our racial common sense? And in our own immediate context, in what ways does the *Matrix* enterprise, as well as its connected projects, "create, inhabit, transform and destroy" racial categories, our understanding of socially constructed ideologies? (Omi and Winant 55). Regardless of the setting and the specifics, the genre of science fiction has centered on race, often times legitimizing and reaffirming widely accepted ideologies, while at other moments resisting and reworking "common sense" understanding of race, racism, and race relations.

Stop the Celebration!
Or, the *Matrix* Franchise as a Racial Project

Although the *Matrix* franchise is not about race, racism, or the particular experience of a community of color, race is central to its plot, message, and narrative structures. It is, in short, a rather fully realized racial project. As with all forms of popular culture, it employs racialized ideas and lenses, at the same time, as we elaborate below, it denies the existence and importance of race through a discourse of color blindness. It utilizes and contributes to commonsense understandings of race inside and outside of Hollywood. The *Matrix* franchise enters into widespread discussions about the meaning (and desirability of such meaning) of race in the future.

Ideas of race are at once constantly on display and held under erasure: race is visible and tangible to contemporary audiences who live in racially saturated and stratified societies, yet in the film it is little more than surface color, detached from racialized communities and histories, so that race no longer matters—a message that is central to the trilogy. Thus, the *Matrix* franchise represents a space in which ideas about race are cultivated, challenged, and reinforced, one that unfolds as an endeavor that centers on and further develops our understanding of race in the twenty-first century.

For many, the *Matrix* franchise is a cause for celebration. For example, African American philosopher Cornel West, who stars in *Reloaded* and *Revolutions* as a member of the Zion Council, remarks upon the casting and vision of the trilogy: "It's not just the representation or numbers but the humanity displayed ... The acknowledgement of the full fledged and complex humanity of black people is a new idea in Hollywood, given all the stereotypes and distortions" (Smith). This reaction, we would argue, reflects the long-standing privileging of inclusion and presentation over antiracist or ideologically progressive images.

Critics of Hollywood have long emphasized the importance of actors and actresses of color securing job opportunities and the positivity of said images before engaging in sophisticated analysis of the trilogy's inherent racial projects. A more cynical reading might suggest that the overabundance of racial referents in the trilogy reveals the tendency of filmmakers increasingly to employ race as a commodity and fetish, as a means to attract minority consumers (blacks represent 30% of moviegoers), while simultaneously validating the progressive orientation of the film.

Worse, the inclusion of people of color in the trilogy more often than not flattens out the role of racial representations, merely extending Hollywood's historical use of characters of color as scenery or background characters in novel directions. Here, in short, race has no depth; it is all surface. People of color possess particular physical characteristics through which viewers read their race; they do not, however, possess *racial identities,* grounded in history or community. In contrast with those who celebrate these films, we assert that the inscription of race in the characters and narratives relies upon commonsense cues and classifications, and consequently, only recycle accepted stereotypes. Race, especially in the *Matrix* films, then, offers a spectrum of meaning ideally crafted for consumption in a society that increasingly thinks of itself as colorblind.

Color Blindness and Multiraciality

Although great fun, the various media products composing the *Matrix* franchise do important ideological work, advancing rather than countering prevailing understandings of race. "Ideologies," Eduardo Bonilla-Silva argues, "are about meaning in the service of power" (25-26). In other words, on the symbolic level, ideologies legitimize and explain the realities of our material conditions: Why does inequality exist? Why are white men paid more than anyone else? Why do people of color disproportionately inhabit prisons?

Ideologies anchor privilege and enable oppression. "Whereas rulers receive solace by believing they are not involved in the terrible ordeal of creating and maintaining inequality, the ruled are charmed by the almost magic qualities of a hegemonic ideology" (Bonilla-Silva 26). In this context it is clear that the presence of master frames is central to the deployment of racial ideologies, which "set paths for interpreting information" (26). The predominant master frame and racial discourse of the post-civil rights era in the United States has been that of color blindness—that race no longer matters.

Within this context, *multiraciality* has equally gained prominence—it has come to represent racial progress and progressivism. Relationships, particularly sexual relationships, across racial boundaries, as well as "mixed" communities, workplaces, and children, signify personal, if not social, enlightenment, sophistication, and improvement. Multiraciality, long a source of contempt, fear, desire, and violence within American history, has more recently crystallized as an *antiracist signifier*.

The *Matrix* franchise is emblematic of this pattern: the ubiquity of multiracial people (Keanu Reeves, Marcus "Tank" Chong, Jada Pinkett-Smith, and Nona Gaye) conveys equality, progress, and diversity, in short a colorful world where race does not matter. In fact, through all three films, the majority of the freed humans living on Zion and even those on Earth (in *Reloaded* and *Revolutions*) are black or Asian. For example, the rave party in *Reloaded* (a visually powerful scene) consists of mostly blacks and Asians dancing to tribal drumming and chants.

The scene takes the viewer into a world of sexual energy, as bodies of color exist as a backdrop for the love and passion of Neo and Trinity. Numerous quick shots of dark-skinned breasts are juxtaposed with the faces of Neo and Trinity engaged in lovemaking. While some journalists and intellectuals like Cornel West and Tommy Lott celebrate numeric visibility as a source of progress, the sexualized peripheral presence of people of color, compared to that of Neo-Trinity, reflects the long-standing history of Hollywood using the "other" as a source of "spice, seasoning that livens up the dull dish that is mainstream white culture" (hooks 1992: 21).

Embracing color blindness leaves audiences blind. On the one hand, for all of the prominence of diversity and hybridity, the *Matrix* films and video game in particular, seem to work against their superficial presence. In fact, *Matrix, Reloaded,* and *Revolutions* actively reinforce the notion that races should not mix and that miscegenation is problematic. For instance, all of the romantic relationships (Neo/Trinity; Niobi/Locke; Link/Zee; Morpheus/Niobe) are between individuals of the same race.

On the other hand, the visibility of mixed-raced or lighter-skinned characters of color, especially black women, reflects historically based ideas of "lighter being brighter," white supremacy, and the sexualization of the mixed-race other. Virtually all of the black women who appear in *Reloaded* and *Revolutions* are light-skinned, playing to white supremacist ideologies that "put a premium on lightness and softness mythically associated with" whiteness (West 90). Niobe, Zee, Cass, and a slew of extras are played by light-skinned, oftentimes mulatta women.

The hyper-visibility of the exotified light-skinned other demarcates a space of sexual desire. As evident in the rave scene in *Reloaded,* the exotic presence of Asian women within the *Animatrix,* and the visual appeal of Niobe in *Enter the Matrix,* the sexual appeal (even in the absence of sexual relations) of women of color is clear. A review of *Enter* within *Time Magazine* makes this clear when Chris Taylor writes, "It's Jada's body, but you can use it" (74). Color blindness opens a space for "eating the other" and the reproduction of stereotypes in the absence of critique (hooks 1992: 21-22).

Traditional Stereotypes

The entire *Matrix* franchise accepts and disseminates traditional ideas about race through its representations, racial deployment, narrative structure, and larger themes. Repeatedly, it reiterates well-worn stereotypes of the black other as being a more natural, libidinal, and animal-like creature. To offer only three illustrations: the majority of natural humans, residing in Zion and participating in the resistance—literally outside the system— are black and mixed race. In *Reloaded,* Neo and Trinity make beautiful romantic love in a room bathed in soft light, while anonymous people of color undulate en masse at a public celebration resembling a rave in a darkened cavern; whereas, Link arrives home not to bestow his love to his wife, but greets her with "where's my pussy?" In *Animatrix* "Second Renaissance," a gang of Latinos and blacks attack, strip, and kill a white female robot, subtly recycling troubling notions about the improper, uncontrolled, sexualized, and violent proclivities of black and Latino men. More troubling than these brief examples is the manner in which the characters and stories reproduce racial stereotypes.

In *The Matrix,* both Tank and Dozer, the only African Americans and ("home-grown") humans on the Nebuchadnezzar, are servants. Dozer spends all of his time cleaning and fixing the ship, while Tank, a computer expert (a near cliché that has become common in recent films, beginning perhaps with *Die Hard*) serves the predominantly white crew by jacking them in and out of the matrix.

Throughout the history of black images within Hollywood, the Uncle Tom represents one of the most long-lasting characters. The Uncle Tom, visible in Hollywood's first films and still present today, reflects a white imagination of a loyal black servant. Donald Bogle describes the Tom characters in the following way: "Always as toms are chased, harassed, hounded, flogged, enslaves, and insulted, they keep the faith n'er [sic] turn against their white massas, and remain hearty, submissive, stoic, generous, selfless and oh-so-very kind" (6).

While always subjected to harassment in the form of physical abuse and insults, the Uncle Tom does not waver in his allegiance to his white master. The Tom reveals black satisfaction with subordination as well as an innate black stupidity, as who else would be happy with such subjugation? While Morpheus does not necessarily embody the Tom character in its classical form, he does represent its modern incarnation. In fact, he reflects the longstanding tradition of loyal black servants—a sidekick whose subjectivity is limited to association with the essential white character, in this case "the One," Neo. While certainly a modern incarnation in that Morpheus possesses power as a leader of the ship and all those who live in Zion, he still represents a flat character. Like many African American characters in these films, he lacks a family or any sense of sexuality, reminding the viewer of Sidney Poitier in *Guess Who's Coming to Dinner?*

The Oracle, a stereotypical servant in her own right, embodies the Mammy. Similar to the Tom, the mammy functions as a servant for whites. She is often fat, angry, cantankerous, and bossy; she is dark, dowdy, and asexual; her existence is defined by her ability to take care of white children. When we first meet The Oracle, she is not surprisingly making cookies inside a house that very much looks like a nursery (white children are everywhere). Despite her extensive wisdom and powers, her purpose is to care for and serve whites. She presumably takes care of those children, and throughout *The Matrix, Reloaded,* and *Revolutions,* she mothers Neo.

bell hooks argues that "mass media consistently depict blacks folks either as servants or in subordinate roles, a placement which still suggests that we exist to bolster and caretaker the needs of whites" (hooks 1996: 114). Notwithstanding the praise for their depiction of "black humanity" in these films, common in the media (Smith, "*Matrix* Diversity,") and among intellectuals like Tommy Lott, the Wachowski brothers offer a very traditional racial project in terms of the deployment of racialized and gendered stereotypes across the *Matrix* franchise.

Ultimately the films reinscribe black characters as powerless as contrasted to white figures. One might wonder why Thomas Anderson is the ONE: when he initially arrives at the ship, he is awkward, confused, unable to fight and not extremely bright. Nevertheless, Morpheus and The Oracle recognize him as their savior, while the diverse citizens—predominantly non-white residents—of Zion worship him. The audience never learns why he is the ONE, or what makes him so special.

Without any other cues, one must assume that Neo is destined to save, and lead the battle against the machines, *because of his whiteness.* Neo, unlike a majority on the *Nebuchadnezzar,* and within multiracial Zion, possesses the powers associated with masculinity and whiteness. Without the help of Neo, played by a Hapa (Hawaiian for half-Asian/half-white) actor (Reeves) passing for white, the world may not survive.

Morpheus, who despite his knowledge and skills, is unable to combat cyborgs, and even The Oracle, who can tell prophecies, needs Neo! The films thus reinforce widely held racist ideas about white intelligence, leadership, and centrality, precisely what bell hooks suggests: "While superficially appearing to present a portrait of racial social equality, mass media actually work to reinforce assumptions that black folks should always be cast in support roles in relation to white characters" (hooks 1996: 114). While the films offer increased job opportunities and increased positivity in the images of black folks, they remain entrenched in white supremacist ideologies that repress non-whites as inferior and peripheral.

Buddy Picture

While many critics have celebrated the *Matrix* trilogy for its sophisticated plot line, its philosophical messages, and its amazing cinematography (Barnett, Haber, Irwin), these films embrace a classical or traditional narrative formula: the biracial buddy formula. This narrative strategy is nothing new to Hollywood productions, having graced the screens for more than four decades. Amid racial tensions of the 1960s, with increasing calls for nationalist revolution, a number of films, such as *In the Heat of the Night* and *The Defiant Ones,* elucidated the nonviolent potential of intergroup cooperation. Such films gave way to the all-white buddy pictures of the 1970s (*Butch Cassidy, Easy Rider,* and *Midnight Cowboy*), each of which repositioned masculinity and maleness at its rightful center just as the Women's Liberation Movement challenged American patriarchy.

The 1980s saw the reemergence of the biracial buddy picture within a series of comedies. As evidenced in *48 Hours, Trading Places, Lethal Weapon, The Toy,* and several others, the 1980s biracial buddy picture "presented the audience with escapist fantasy narratives and resolutions, which in some instances articulate allegorical or metaphorical dimensions that mediate America's very real and intractable racial problems" (Guerrero 1993b: 240). Not surprisingly, during the Reagan presidency, these films engaged discourse surrounding immigration, criminality, welfare, and urban plight through racially coded cinematic language.

Such a formula did not die at the end of the Reagan era or the Cold War, and has only changed slightly with Hollywood's return to blockbusters and sequels. In an environment of police brutality, urban uprisings, the prison industrial complex, and a worsening economy, "Hollywood has put what is left of the Black presence on the screen in the protective custody, so to speak, of a white lead or co-star, and therefore in conformity with dominant, White sensibilities and expectations of what Blacks should be like" (Guerrero 1993b: 240).

The last ten years have brought about a wave of popular films featuring the buddy formula. The trilogy, while being part of the science-fiction genre, follows suit, chronicling the story of two friends, one black and one white. Sure, they are battling machines, with the future of the world at stake. Yes, they enter "our reality" through a computer program, and have holes all over their bodies. Nonetheless, the story is of male bonding, growth, and two men overcoming their (racial) differences to secure a single goal. Most importantly, it a story of redemption of a split white self and the reunification of Thomas and Neo into a single subject!

Huck Finn Fixation: Race, Redemption, and the *Matrix* Franchise

A theme related to the buddy formula has been that of redemption. Filmmakers repeatedly tell stories of interracial friendships resulting in the redemption or growth of the white protagonists. Whereas in the past, films presented the maturation of black characters through their contact with whites, recently, a role reversal has taken place within Hollywood. Several films have elucidated the ways that black-white friendships can improve the life experiences of whites, while ignoring what blacks gain from such relationships.

The career of Cuba Gooding, Jr., reflects this trend, in films like *Jerry Maguire, Men of Honor,* and *Radio.* In *Men of Honor,* Billy Sunday, the racist master diver played by Robert De Niro, evolves as a husband and a man because of his interactions with Carl Brasheer. Witnessing honor, dignity, and dedication in Brasheer, Sunday is forced to interrogate his own racism, anger, and alcoholism, and becomes a new man in the process.

Donald Bogle, borrowing from Mark Twain's classic *Huckleberry Finn,* describes this type of relationship as a "Huckfinn fixation," in which "the white hero grows in stature from his association with the dusty black" (140). Reflecting a liberal humanist positivity and the desire to counter both identity politics and the deleterious incidences of 1990s racism, the idea of redemption through friendship and integration infects a spectrum of films. Examples of films are endless as the wave of films employing the "Huckfinn fixation" increase with each year. Films like the *Die Hard, Lethal Weapon, The Shawshank Redemption, The Green Mile, Hardball,* and *Monster's Ball* all tell stories of honorable black men (children in *Hardball* and Halle Berry in *Monster's Ball*) teaching disreputable white men.

In each, a white character, limited by his own flaws—racism, drugs, anger, and laziness—grows merely by knowing his "black buddy," who serves as the catalyst for change and eventual redemption. The *Matrix* trilogy follows this formula precisely: the relationships between Thomas Anderson and Morpheus and the relationship between Neo and The Oracle, as well as between believers Neo and Sati, all conform to the model of the Huckfinn fixation.

As the first film begins, Mr. Anderson is lost within the ambiguity and uncertainty of the matrix. Stuck in an unsatisfying work situation, without a partner or friends, Mr. Anderson embodies the stereotype of a dazed and confused Generation X-er. Through Morpheus's tutelage (and a little red pill) and guidance, as well as that of The Oracle and Sati, Mr. Anderson is transformed, from a depressed and scared man to a Jesus-like savior. His relationships with a black man and two women of color provide meaning to his life, while providing his own redemption.

Even as we witness Neo's transformation, rendered with exacting detail, we are given very little information about his redeemers: Morpheus, The Oracle, and Neo's other compatriots are flat characters, without identity, history, or subjectivity. With *The Matrix* and its subsequent incarnations to a lesser degree, characters of color function purely in relationship to Neo, existing as his source of redemption and our evidence of the hopeful reality of integration.

Orientalism and the Limitations of the Black-White Paradigm

Many of the popular interpretations of the *Matrix* franchise have phrased their celebratory and oppositional readings in black-and-white terms (see Smith, "*Matrix* Diversity"). Such a formulation is terribly limited. The number of roles and the powerful images of African Americans make the trilogy quite positive. For other communities of color, however, the grounds for celebration prove to be unstable. Within the films themselves, Latino, Asian, and other characters of color are under-represented, if not wholly absent, reflective of their history of exclusion from Hollywood.

In a few instances, "other" people of color can be found in the shadows or background, existing as little more than voiceless and faceless scenery. The practice of reducing America's racial problems to black-white relations leads to celebrations of a superficial remedy that alters the perceived place of African Americans. While present in the films, these other communities of color are more emblematic of how racialized communities are used as peripheral displays, background scenery, and exotic evidence of the "revolutionary" structure and message of the *Matrix* franchise.

In spite of the limitations of the black-white paradigm, all associated media products of the franchise reduce Asian Americans and the Orient more generally to well-worn clichés. They rely on what Edward Said has termed Orientalism to fashion the Asian (American) other. The Wachowski brothers have an admitted fascination with things Asian (Corliss 68). The exotic, non-Western serves as an inexhaustible source of desire and inspiration, a supplement and alternative to the constrictions of Western civilization. Animé, Hong Kong, and Eastern thought, with several references to Karma, inclusion of Japanese lettering and Samurai weapons, clearly influenced the conception and execution of the various elements of the franchise.

More troubling is the Key Maker within *Reloaded*. Here, the long-standing stereotype of the wise, old Asian grandpa embraces the traditional racialized ideas of wisdom and heavy accents afforded to Asian characters. In preparing for an interview with Randall Duk Kim, a classically trained Shakespearean actor, Daniel Epstein confessed that he "expected a little wizened man who could barely speak English" (Epstein).

The Orientalism of the films extends beyond stereotypical renderings of East Asia to the Indian subcontinent. In the final installment of the trilogy, Neo encounters a family of programs, a South Asian couple and their daughter Sati, in the train station. The patriarchal father offers Neo a series of erudite and mystical reflections, peppering his comments with Eastern notions like Karma.

A more subtle demarcation of the Asian as exotic comes through the employment of Japanese characters that signify the unknown elements of the matrix. Seraph, Kung Fu master turned escort, reflects the mysterious wisdom of Asian characters, who is unable to "know someone until you fight them." Interestingly, none of the three significant Asian characters within the trilogy *exists in the real world*. The scripts of the films, as well as much of the *Animatrix* and *Enter,* unfold as a syncopated set of choreographed martial arts fights, reducing the Asian (American) once again to kung fu clichés. It is through a series of martial metaphors—sensei: student relationships, fighting styles, and stylized interpersonal combat—that the Asian (American) become discernible and meaningful.

Furthermore, *The Animatrix* appropriately begins with a sparing session between a black man and an Asian woman as part of their preparation to battle the matrix. Within these initial moments, neither speaks, allowing the camera (and viewer) to focus on their sexualized bodies. While the scene shows two freedom fighters training, these activities are peripheral to the sexuality displayed through their actions. With the glistening black male body in contrast to the exposed ass and heaving breasts of his Asian female combatant, the stereotypes are endless. The shape and significance of the Asian (American), then, like the African American, is materialized through stereotypes.

The Unbearable Whiteness of Power

The Matrix racializes power, invariably coloring dominance as white and oppression as black. In relating the historical background of the trilogy, *Animatrix,* "The Second Renaissance," uses revealing rhetoric to paint the predicament of machines in a human controlled world: "the machines worked tirelessly to do man's bidding ... though loyal and pure machines earned no respect from their masters." Indeed, the master:slave dynamic that structures "The Second Renaissance" clearly draws upon the painful history and unresolved legacies of human bondage in the United States, and with them references shared understandings of inferiority, property, constricted rights, and inhumanity.

In "Bits and Pieces," in *The Matrix Comics* (pages 015-016), the landmark trial of B1-66ER, the first robot who rose and killed his human owners, in turn, evokes slave rebellions and the Dred Scott case (Chief Justice Taney's belief that blacks were an inferior species is noted). The subsequent uprising of the machines recycles more contemporary events: the robots and their riot in urban areas are put down by phalanxes of predominantly all-white cops. Subsequently, they stage The Million Machine March, an obvious allusion to the Million Man March organized by the Nation of Islam. Although in "The Second Renaissance," human society is clearly multiracial and many of the robots lack skin or pigment, the animé short conveys their condition through the familiar moments of oppression and resistance in the African American experience. In stark contrast, the engineered world of the matrix completely reverses these arrangements: multiracial human insurgents fight the exploitation and enslavement by machines, the latter embodied most often by white Agents. In this context, it is more than a little ironic that a white, namely Neo, is at once the hope of humanity and their most potent force.

Conclusion

In *The Matrix,* Morpheus tells Neo, "The matrix is a world pulled over your eyes to blind you from the truth." Still confused about the essential meaning of truth, Morpheus poignantly reminds Neo his most important life lesson: "You are a slave, Neo. Like everyone else you were born into bondage." As with the films themselves and their critical reception, Morpheus's sermon reflects the dominance of color-blind ideology, as claims of bondage erase the racial significance of slavery (oppression, confinement). As a racial project, the trilogy reduces bondage to codes for power, subsuming issues of race superficially without any substance beneath the surface.

The trilogy, as well as its connected mediums, offers the opportunity to interrogate the meanings of race and racism in the contemporary United States. It simultaneously reveals the commodification of otherness and the erasure of difference. On another level, it uses racial bodies as a source of "appeal to domestic minorities and global markets." At another level, it "adds great value for the core audience, because ... future scientific rationalism and technology must eventually make race distinctions as we know them irrelevant" (Wynter 149).

Through popular cultural projects like the *Matrix* franchise, dominant discourses of racism limit conversations to positivity, inclusion and representation, thereby undermining our understanding of color-blind racism. In such a haze, the American tendency to pretend that race is not an important and visible construct, is like "the matrix, [it] is a world pulled over our eyes to blind us from the truth." As race holds meaning beyond the surface of spice and inclusion in forces of inequality, privilege, and oppression, we must all remember that it is there, and the *Matrix* franchise is one of the agents of its continuation.

Works Cited

Barnett, P. Chad. "Reviving Cyberpunk: (Re)Constructing the Subject and Mapping Cyberspace in the Wachowski Brothers' Film *The Matrix.*" *Extrapolation* 41/4 (2000): 359-374.

Bernardi, Daniel Leonard. Star Trek and History: Race-ing Toward a White Future. New Brunswick: Rutgers University Press, 1998.

Bogle, Donald. Toms, Coons, Mulattoes, Mammies, and Bucks: An Interpretive History of Blacks in American Films. New York: Continuum, 2001.

Greene, Eric. Planet of the Apes as American Myth: Race and Politics in the Film and Television Series. Jefferson, NC: McFarland, 1996.

Corliss, Richard. "Unlocking the Matrix." Time Magazine 12 May 2003: 64-74.

Guerrero, Ed. Framing Blackness: The African American Image in Film. Culture and the Moving Image. Philadelphia: Temple University Press, 1993a.

———. "The Black Image in Protective Custody: Hollywood's Biracial Buddy Films of the Eighties." Black American Cinema. Ed. Manthia Diawara. New York: Routledge, 1993b.

Haber, Karen, ed. Exploring the Matrix: Visions of the Cyber-Present. New York: St. Martin's, 2003.

Ho, Jeffrey B. "The Matrix: Using American Popular Film to Teach Concepts of Eastern Mysticism in the College Classroom." Reversing the Lens: Ethnicity, Race, Gender, and Sexuality Through Film. Ed. Jun Xing and Lane Ryo Hirabayashi. Boulder: University of Colorado Press, 2003: 197-211.

hooks, bell. Black Looks: Race and Representation. Boston: South End, 1992.

———. Killing Rage: Ending Racism. New York: Owelett, 1996.

Horsely, Jake. The Matrix Warrior: Being the One. London: Orion, 2003.

Irwin, William, ed. The Matrix and Philosophy: Welcome to the Desert of the Real. Chicago: Open Court, 2002.

Lavelle, Kristenea M. The Reality Within the Matrix. Wisconsin Dells: Saxco, 2002.

Lott, Tommy L. The Invention of Race: Black Culture and the Politics of Representation. Oxford: Blackwell, 1999.

"'Matrix' Diversity at odds with Sci-fi's White History." Duluth News Tribune 6 June 2003. Available online at <http://www.duluthsuperior.com/mld/duluthtribune/entertainment/6027288.htm>. Accessed 25 July 2003.

Omi, Michael, and Howard Winant. Racial Formation in the United States: From the 1960s to the 1990s. New York: Routledge, 1994.

Roberts, Adam. Science Fiction. New York: Routledge, 2000.

Seay, Chris, and Greg Garrett. The Gospel Reloaded: Exploring Spirituality and Faith in the Matrix. Colorado Springs: Pinon, 2003.

Smith, Lynn. "The Intellectual and 'The Matrix.'" Available online at http://www.calendarlive.com/movies/cl-et-smith20may20,0,4130850.story?coll=cl-movies. Accessed 28 July 2003.

Taylor, Chris. "It's Jada's Body, But You Can Use It." Time Magazine 12 May 2003: 74.

West, Cornel. Race Matters. Boston: Beacon, 1993.

Wynter, Leon. American Skin: Pop Culture, Big Business and the End of White America. New York: Crown, 2002.

Yeffeth, Glenn, ed. Taking the Red Pill: Science, Philosophy, and Religion in The Matrix. Dallas: BenBella, 2003.

Žižek, Slavoj. "The Matrix or Malebranche in Hollywood." Philosophy Today SPEP Supplement (1999): 11-26.

3

Religion, Community,
and Revitalization:
Why Cinematic Myth Resonates

RICHARD R. JONES

I n 1999, four professors, including myself, from a small, Christian, liberal arts university in eastern Tennessee, sneaked out of our hotel rooms
one evening, piled into one car, and hurriedly drove several miles to
see *The Matrix*. We were supposed to be reading and preparing for participation in a faculty seminar for freshman orientation the next day. Instead,
we stayed out late that night to see *The Matrix* and spent several hours after-
ward talking about it, which noticeably diminished our performance and
participation in the next day's activities. Two of those professors were biol-
ogists, one a chemist, and the last one (me) an anthropologist. Two of us
had already seen the movie, but wanted to see it again. The other two needed
very little prompting to go along.

In retrospect, this behavior raises some interesting questions. Why do
some movies inspire such interest, and others not? What is it about *The
Matrix* that captured the attention of four very serious academics in the midst
of a very hectic schedule of work? Why is the *Matrix* franchise so popular?
What about the animé short films, video-game tie-ins, comic books, and
books like this? What is it about Western society and culture that resonates so well with the *Matrix* films? In other words, how much of society
and culture are reflected in the films?

In order to answer these questions, I discuss the *Matrix* films from the perspective of religion. Two main ideas permeate this reflection. The first is an
understanding of religion as a system of symbols and purveyor of values in
the sense meant by Clifford Geertz (1-46) and Émile Durkheim, which is that
culture communicates a believable set of values that unites participants into
a moral community. The second is an understanding of religion as an agent of
socio-cultural change in the sense meant by Anthony Wallace (421-29). Those
two ideas will provide the basis for understanding how the *Matrix* universe

creates a kind of community and how it transforms participants' ways of thinking about the world by providing a system of collective values.

Why Examine the *Matrix* Universe from a Religious Perspective?

The religious symbolism is, on the surface, rather obvious, and it seems there is only so much that can be said about it. Buddhism, Hinduism, Christianity, Islam, New Ageists, and others, can all find something to relate to in this universe. It does not represent any one of those religions more than any other. By reducing important religious themes in the *Matrix* universe to general schemas, a new level of categorization arises that incorporates previous systems of categorization and creates a new truth. This parallels exactly what is happening to religion in the Western world. Many people are convinced their particular religious perspective is correct—those people could analogously be said to be in the matrix. Increasingly, however, more and more people are beginning to question their beliefs, and not just religious, but beliefs they hold about happiness, success, and the social order. This challenging of fundamental beliefs is brought about by the Western values of materialism, individualism, and freedom, by our increasing diversity, and by our increased access to information. This emerging group of people sees a new, and different, truth.

The way in which religious symbolism is portrayed is, however, very powerful, particularly when examined within the context of Western culture. What emerges from a closer look at the religious symbolism is the need to examine higher levels of symbolic classification in order to understand what it all means. Of course, the religious symbolism in the *Matrix* universe connects to contemporary religious symbols, but new levels of categorization also emerge as a result of those connections, which, in turn, reflect new ways that some Westerners are beginning to think about the world.

Why Neo Can Be Read as Christ or Buddha

Any serious religious discussion of *The Matrix* eventually comments on the fact that "God" is conspicuously absent. Yet the film has been an economic and popular success in a culture that is largely theistic in one way or another.

I suggest that this absence of God is an essential element of the film's myth and is central to what makes the movie popular in Western societies. If any particular version of God had been presented in *The Matrix,* I believe the movie would have had far less appeal to the Western public.

In order to understand why the "atheistic" religious symbolism of this alternate universe has such appeal to theists (as well as to atheists), it is necessary to provide a brief and very general overview of some aspects of religious history in the Western world. As Europeans colonized North America, they displaced—but did not totally replace—the native religions with several versions of Christianity. Roman Catholics, Anglicans, Lutherans, Presbyterians, Methodists, and various other Protestant groups dominated the emerging culture and nation.

Other established religious groups from around the world eventually became a significant part of the cultural landscape of America as well: Buddhists, Muslims, Hindus, Zoroastrians, followers of Shinto, Jews, and others. Of most interest here, however, are the groups that are truly "American." That is, those groups that came into being as a result of social processes at work in American society. For example, the Church of Jesus Christ of Latter Day Saints, various Pentecostal and Charismatic Christians, various fundamentalist Evangelical Christians, the Church of Scientology, the Nation of Islam, and numerous nature religions, spiritualists, and many others, seem uniquely American.

America is, undoubtedly, the most religiously sectarian nation in the world. Proverbially, Hinduism may have thirty-three million gods, and devotion within the religion is divided among those gods, but it is possible, at least in theory, for participants of one cult to participate in any another. This gives Hinduism a kind of unity that is nearly unimaginable in American religion. A good Southern Baptist would not worship in a Mormon Church, and some Seventh-Day Adventists believe that Christians who worship on Sunday are receiving the Mark of the Beast; certainly one would have a difficult time getting an Orthodox Jew to go to a mosque for prayer.

The unique events in the history of the settling of America—the mass immigrations of diverse groups, the westward expansion and settlement, the philosophical underpinnings of the political system—have all contributed to a set of values that emphasize individual rights and freedom. Very early in American history, those values produced an effect on religious belief. Mormonism and the movement that would become the Jehovah's Witnesses developed early in the nineteenth century. In the twentieth century, Spiritualism, the Holiness movement and Pentecostalism, Scientology, Nation of Islam, and the New Age movement became a part of American culture. That names just a few. The large number of sectarian schisms and other religious movements in America are far too numerous to discuss in detail here.

This proliferation of religion in America is all the more remarkable when you consider that Christianity did quite well for over four hundred years as, essentially, one church. From the first century until the middle of the fifth, there were three major spheres of Christian influence—Constantinople, Alexandria, and Rome—but only one Church. Ecumenical Councils were convened to settle theological and political differences. The first split came in 451 C.E., after the Council of Chalcedon, when the Alexandrian, or Coptic, Church left full communion with the others. The split has usually been attributed to theological differences but, in actuality, it was largely caused by significant cultural and linguistic differences (Jones 1997). Other splits followed, such as that of the sixteenth-century Protestant Reformation, but the total of all those schisms is far less than what happened to the Christian religion in America in the nineteenth and twentieth centuries.

Today there are hundreds of distinct, organized religious groups in America. Freedom and independence allow people to move easily from one religious group to another and, if none are available that meet the perceived need, it is easy to create a denomination or branch.

Much of contemporary religious practice and sectarianism in America has also adopted the capitalist consumer credo: Give the consumer what she wants. According to this model, many religious groups offer particular styles of worship, ministries that target specific demographics (e.g., child care for parents with children), and various versions of perceived truth.

A child born in Western society is faced with an almost overwhelming number of choices in life, among which is religion. The American elementary and secondary educational systems present religion as a matter of personal choice and only provide students an overview of the world's major religious systems. If the student goes on to a college or university, more familiarity with alternate religious views is obtained and the potential choices are multiplied.

Additionally, the entertainment industries, access to the Internet, and increased contact between diverse groups in our society have all heightened awareness of religious differences and diversity. It is nearly impossible for a child growing up in America not to have his personal religious views, whatever they are, challenged by the myriad alternatives that present themselves. In a society that values freedom and individualism above nearly all else, it is perhaps inevitable that fragmentation of all monolithic institutions and belief systems will occur. Such fragmentation works against the creation of a common shared culture and creates a tremendous cultural dissonance between the desires of the individual (to be free) and the needs of the social order (for individuals to conform to community standards). Consequently, as a result of seemingly endless choice and the difficulty of balancing the desires of self with the needs of society, fundamental questions about truth must necessarily arise.

Neo faced such fundamental questions. He was dissatisfied with things as they were and had a feeling that there was a deeper truth. His quest for truth was through the most advanced medium of information technology available to him—his computer. Given that *The Matrix* universe is a replica of 1999 American society and culture, Neo faces exactly the same doubts and concerns about the truth that many contemporary Americans face in their lives.

When Morpheus presents Neo with the choice of either the red pill or the blue pill, he is presenting Neo with the choice of reality as Neo currently knows it, with whatever religious symbols and cosmological explanations he currently possesses, or with a new reality, one with new symbols and new cosmological truths. Americans, regardless of ethnicity, understand this choice and relate to it. Some have made the choice to change the religion of their birth, to adopt a new religion, or to abandon religion entirely; they have, in a sense, taken a sort of "red pill." Others are still entertaining the choices, and some will never see that there is a choice.

Morpheus tells Neo that the world he knows will cease to exist, if he takes the red pill. Neo's choice ultimately involves a conversion, enlightenment, and redemption. Neo is made "new" and "old things pass away," as the Christian tradition puts it. This conversion does not, however, take place by means of one simple decision. There is a dialogue about truth, between Morpheus and Neo, and there is a physical and mental struggle throughout as Neo takes the red pill and looks into the mirror that soon reaches out and engulfs him.

His "New Birth" is quite traumatic for Neo, and those who have already been transformed must take care of him for some time. American Evangelical Christians have always had a view of crisis conversion much like Neo's and believe it is an essential part of their religious experience. Many other religious groups have similar ideas about conversion, enlightenment, and redemption and can relate in much the same way. For example, the devout Hindu will take up the ascetic life in old age and struggle to achieve escape from rebirth by practicing spiritual disciplines; the Zen Buddhist will struggle to lose desire and to get beyond the illusions of this world. Hindu and Buddhist alike must face the crisis caused by completely reordering their understanding of reality.

Once converted, Morpheus, the Prophet, tutors Neo, and reveals his prophecies, which he obtained from an other-worldly messenger, The Oracle. Such prophetic leaders have been common in Western society:

- Joseph Smith, founding prophet of Mormonism
- William Miller and Ellen G. White, founders of the Seventh-Day Adventists
- L. Ron Hubbard, founder of Scientology
- David Koresh, leader of the ill-fated Branch Davidians in Waco, Texas
- Aimee Semple McPherson, founder of the International Church of the Foursquare Gospel
- Jim Jones, leader of the People's Temple who died in Guyana with most of his followers in a mass suicide
- Mary Baker Eddy, Christian Science founder
- Baghwan Shree Rashneesh, guru of tantric yoga and head of a short-lived commune near Antelope, Oregon
- Benny Hinn, famous contemporary television evangelist
- and others.

The Trinity Broadcasting Network, widely available on cable television, has numerous prophets promising the truth if you take their "red pill," which is to subscribe to their particular beliefs, which usually involves sending money to them as evidence of your "faith."

The level of commitment the televangelists require is no less than that required of Neo. In both cases, the old life must be abandoned and the new life embraced. All the symbols and myths of the new life must be adopted by the convert, along with the appropriate behaviors. The temptation of the old life is always there, however. Cypher was tempted so much that he betrayed the crew of the *Nebuchadnezzar*. Like Cypher, many televangelists in the 1980s betrayed the cause they believed in. Although no one died in the case of the televangelists (at least no one that we know about), some followers did lose their faith. From the American religious perspective, particularly the Christian one, the matrix *is* the worldly system, and the religious world—the spiritual world—is perceived of as real and outside of it. Conversion is necessary to enter this spiritual world and conversion must happen by choice. In the *Matrix* universe, all the *real* prophets, messiahs, human society, truth, and apocalyptic visions exist outside of the world created by the machines.

In the *Matrix* universe, conversion is from a world of simulation to the real world—which is almost the exact opposite of what conversion entails in the universe familiar to most contemporary religionists. Religions in this universe demand a conversion from the real world to a world of myths and symbols. It does not involve waking up in a different world. But, in the *Matrix* universe, conversion involves leaving a simulated world of myth and symbol and waking up in the real world. This is a mirror transformation of the familiar orientation of the real and illusory worlds, and why we relate to the new transformation, is linked to the fundamental way in which our minds work to categorize things.

Converts, whether in this universe or in the real world of the *Matrix* universe, each perceive their group to be enlightened, separate from those who do not know the truth. In both universes, the systems of symbols embodied in the mythical themes of religion give purpose to the action and events encountered by the participants. So fundamental is this desire to know and embrace a transcendent truth that the transformation of the conversion process in the *Matrix* universe, which inverts the orientation of real and simulated worlds, still relates well to a Western public because of its familiarity with multiple perspectives and a fascination with "newness."

To return to the absence of direct references to God in the matrix, from the standpoint of people freed from the matrix, God would seem to be part of its delusion. Once free from the matrix, it is easy to see how the rebels would embrace an agnostic, if not atheistic, view in opposition to the predominantly theistic view of the illusory world from which they were delivered. Such a reversal of attitudes toward God is a natural extension of the human tendency to invert and transform mythical processes and symbols, as just discussed with conversion. Religious people in the Western world, especially Christians, perceive God as close and personal. However, in *The Matrix*, the rebels must necessarily perceive God as remote or non-existent, so that no direct references or appeals to God occur. The destination of the convert in the *Matrix* universe is the real world, not God's heaven.[1]

The *Matrix* films present a schematized view of religion that appeals to many Westerners, because such views embody the essence of how religion has developed in Western society and culture. The characters and symbols are generic enough to relate to nearly every major religious persuasion, yet specific enough to synthesize a new vision.

Thus, there is a Prophet, Morpheus, fully revealed as he speaks to the inhabitants of Zion in *Reloaded,* but not a Muhammad; there is a Messiah, Neo, who invokes the symbol of the cross in *Revolutions,* but not a Jesus Christ. We encounter evil in the form of Agent Smith, who enforces the oppression of the machines and ultimately dares to escape the matrix himself, but no Satan. There are other-worldly messengers, like The Oracle and the Merovingian, but no angels. Reincarnation is suggested by Agent Smith's offer to return Cypher to the matrix, but there is no Karma. The rebels dwell in a sacred city, Zion, but not in one named Jerusalem, Mecca, or Delhi. The rebels who live outside the matrix in the films are religious, but their truth exists outside of the confines of the world religions programmed into the matrix world itself. Inside the matrix, religions mirror the contemporary religious landscape in America and depict it as an illusion.

At the beginning of *The Matrix,* driven by his own doubts and questions, Neo is beginning to look beyond his everyday experience for a deeper truth. Many Westerners feel like Neo. They know something is not right, but they cannot quite articulate what it is. They search, like Neo, for the truth. Many search for answers in the same medium as Neo does: the Internet. Others find that pop culture offers a deeper truth, outside of formal political, religious, and economic institutions. For example, a large number of Americans are convinced that an extraterrestrial spaceship crashed in Roswell, New Mexico, in 1947. Also, despite overwhelming evidence to the contrary, those same people believe in an elaborate government conspiracy to cover up the occurrence.

Likewise, the popularity of the *X-Files,* speaks volumes about the suspicions Westerners hold about government, the military, business, and international organizations. Only Fox Mulder and his skeptical partner Dana Scully are able to ferret out the real truth about alien abductions, the JFK assassination, the United Nations, and a host of paranormal encounters. The loss of faith in the established institutions of our society, as portrayed in the *X-Files* and as instantiated in numerous conspiracy books, UFO groups, paranormal research groups, radical political groups, etc., has prompted the search for a new truth, and that new truth is being synthesized in the entertainment industry in the Western world. In the *Matrix* franchise, the new truth reveals that the real conspiracy is far greater than ever imagined, to the extent that even our perception of reality is a deception and our lives are merely fictions stimulated by electrodes implanted in our brains by machines.

Hence, the religious themes and symbolism in *The Matrix* relate well to Westerners because they synthesize elements of various religious traditions and produce new themes and symbols that are not specific to any one tradition. It is fashionable nowadays to be a Christian, or a Muslim, but there is an increasing tendency not to strongly affiliate with any particular established group. The proliferation of independent churches of many different faiths, and the growing tendency of churchgoers not to join formally the churches they attend are evidences of this.[2]

For the cultural elite of America—the educated middle and upper classes—a new level of religious categorization has emerged as a result of higher levels of education, increased diversity, and loss of faith in traditional institutions that generalizes across religious and cultural differences. This has led to a kind of cultural dissonance, where a growing number of people view traditional religious people as trapped by a delusion, while more traditional religious people view the emerging group as bound by their own delusion. To traditionally religious people, the matrix is the worldly system we live in now. To the cultural elite, the traditional religious and other institutional systems are the matrix. The *Matrix* universe allows the viewer to read it either way. The polysemous nature of the themes and symbols is part of the appeal. We see what we want to see when we take the red pill.

Community and the Matrix:
Why Morpheus's Prophecies Bring People Together

Since the time of Émile Durkheim (1858-1917), social scientists have realized that religion serves a vital collective function in human societies by helping to unite groups into a moral community. But today, it is not immediately clear that one can identify a common moral community. Values about what is right and wrong, or about what is good and evil, vary considerably. In fact, Westerners are deeply divided on issues such as abortion, homosexuality, sex, drug use, euthanasia, and cloning.

In such an instance, we have to inquire closely about what is collective about Western society. Where do Americans overcome their differences and form a united community? There is a common political system and economy, but neither of those provides sufficient motivation for moral behavior. The events surrounding the personal behavior of former president Bill Clinton show that Americans clearly separate moral behavior from political action and economic concerns. Likewise, most Americans uncritically accept the exploitation of poor people around the world for the growth of their own nation's economy. Retailers in America amass huge profits from the sale of clothing and athletic equipment manufactured cheaply abroad and bought at prices that rarely raise the standard of living above the poverty level for the workers who produce the items.

Traditional formulations of capitalism and politics alone cannot provide a basis or motivation for collective moral action. It is religion that provides the system of symbols, the myths, the moods, and the motivations that unite groups. As I have argued, America is religiously plural and its religious institutions and groups cannot provide any comprehensive moral unity for the nation. Yet America is a nation that, in spite of its differences, frequently acts in unity. After the destruction of the World Trade Center, the collective empathy and action of people across America was extraordinary. There is a collective moral community in America, but its source is not the churches, temples, mosques, and synagogues of our various religions.

The framework of our contemporary collective moral community emerged and coalesced in the early twentieth century along with the growth of the entertainment industry. The things Americans hold in common are almost all traceable to movies, TV, radio, music, books, magazines, and video games. Nearly all Americans participate somehow in this monolithic system of entertainment.

This is an entertainment culture. Consequently, I believe that the entertainment industry, not religion, now provides the shared symbols, myths, and the moods and motivations that instill in people tendencies to behave in certain ways. Mass-media entertainment cuts across all the religious, ethnic, political, economic, geographic, and social boundaries that divide us. A new social way of thinking—a new system of categorization—has been created by the entertainment media that links and unites Americans into a single moral community.

As the Hollywood studios in the 1930s began to turn out larger and larger numbers of films, it was quickly realized that certain kinds of films attracted large audiences. What is true for the cinema is also true of other media. Certain recorded songs sell well; others do not. It is not always a matter of quality or money spent, either. The film *Billy Jack* was, from the standpoint of script, cinematography, and acting, a terrible film, but it was immensely popular when released in 1971. Likewise, films like *Home Alone* and *A Christmas Story* cost very little to produce, but have enjoyed incredible box office success. All of these films, including the *Matrix* trilogy, have a generalized set of values that span a great number of cultural and ethnic differences.

In the music industry, it is what I call the "everybody songs" that enjoy the greatest success. Songs like *Love Me Tender, Lucy in the Sky with Diamonds, Paint it Black, Superstition, Bohemian Rhapsody,* and a host of other songs (I fear I date myself by this listing) have had wide appeal throughout our culture because the words can be interpreted either as reflecting nearly universal personal experiences and longings, as in *Love Me Tender,* or can be interpreted to mean just about whatever you want, as in *Bohemian Rhapsody,* or *Lucy in the Sky with Diamonds.* The *Matrix* franchise is a type of visual, religious, literary, and dramatic "everybody song."

The more generalized the themes and symbols in the songs, the greater the appeal to a wider audience. The trick for the moviemaker, songwriter, novelist, poet, and video game programmer is to set the generalizations within attractive framework (i.e., within a particular setting, melody, prose, meter, and/or simulation) and to provide the right transformation of the generalized mythic elements (the plot). If done well in cinema, the results are blockbusters like *Star Trek, Star Wars,* or the *Matrix* trilogy, which present us with generalized schemas of hero (and other) myths transformed in new and interesting ways.

A magnificent example of this process is seen in the recently successful film, *O Brother, Where Art Thou?,* a transformation of the story of Odysseus. Failure to take such transformations into account can result in disasters, like *Plan 9 from Outer Space,* the famously bad 1959 Edward D. Wood, Jr. film.

Because the financial success of media companies depends on products that appeal to a wide range of consumers, capitalism has driven entertainment industries toward products that generalize nearly everything, including the mythical and moral elements in entertainment products. This effect of capitalism does not reduce *The Matrix,* its sequels, and the video games to mere manifestations of capitalism, however. Because humans are creatures of culture, capitalist endeavors are only successful because we have inside of us a need to find and create community. Successful movies do not just function to serve the needs of a capitalist society, rather, they function to instill moods, motivations, and meaning in people's lives, which make people willing to pay to see them.

Granted, not all popular media productions include or emphasize strong mythical or moral elements, but what all media productions do have in common is stylizing and generalizing human interactions by various means of editing out the extraneous. The goal is usually to clarify the story being presented. Ordinary people, filmed doing ordinary things, are not very interesting—as anyone who had sat through hours of friends' home videos knows. Even so-called "reality" TV shows have to act out the reality within a highly structured and highly edited framework, usually one with numerous rules to guide some sort of competition. Consequently, there is very little "real" about them, in the ordinary sense of everyday human interaction.

When a moviegoer enters a theater, he or she enters a highly structured environment to view a highly stylized and generalized depiction of human interaction. For the two hours or so that the theater patron sits in front of the silver screen, she shares a common experience with millions of other people—especially if it is a very successful movie. The experience then becomes part of everyday conversation with other people.

Reviews are written about the movie in magazines and newspapers. It is mentioned on television in the news. The stars and performances become part of trivia games. As a result, people find everyday significance and relevance in such films, which offer a system of symbols that make up a network of communication for social interaction. In our society, we would consider it odd if people failed to recognize references to Darth Vader or *The Teenage Mutant Ninja Turtles*. Movies provide reference points for much creative use of language: "I am your father." "Do a John Wayne." "Go ahead. Make my day!" "If you build it, they will come." and "He is the One."

Mass entertainment media provide the system of symbols that unite us into one moral community. The symbols associated with films are used much as scripture and catechisms were used in the past. Films provide the proverbs for a new age. "Beware the dark side" from *Star Wars* and "Rosebud" from *Citizen Kane,* are just two examples of quotes that have become proverbial in our society.

Some films generate a greater sense of community than others. *The Matrix, Star Wars,* and *Star Trek* are notable examples of community-creating films. How so? Such films and their sequels go beyond the two hours of screen time and a little conversation. Those films develop loyal and avid followers who meet to discuss them. They generate commercial spin-offs and commercial tie-ins of all sorts. People write books about those films. People speculate and analyze them. People dress up as characters from those films and attend conventions. Video games are produced based on them. Computer screen savers, mouse pads, trivia books, T-shirts, and a host of other things are personalized with symbols from those films. Films with this kind of status create real communities of interactive participants who share the symbols, moods, and motivations of the films involved. They are truly "religions," in terms of the root meaning of the word: *religare,* "to tie fast."[3]

The *Matrix* universe unites the viewers into one moral community by giving them myths and cosmological explanations to which they can relate. It instills in them a sense of awe and wonder. It teaches that good will triumph over evil; that a person's actions do matter; that we are connected and dependent on each other; that treachery is always punished; that love has power to overcome; that one must believe to achieve; and that courage and persistence win the day. It also teaches that reality is not necessarily what we think it is, and that truth must be pursued. Finally, it teaches that most people never achieve an understanding of the truth, and that their "salvation" is dependent on the actions and understanding of the few who have achieved "enlightenment."

Revitalization: Public and Private Space

American society experienced many challenges throughout the twentieth century: rapid urbanization, large-scale immigration, two World Wars, the Great Depression, the Korean War, the Vietnam War, and the Civil Rights movement, just to name a few. The resulting stress experienced by individuals was exacerbated by many different factors such as high unemployment, financial losses, war deaths, and disabilities, Cold War fears, riots, rising costs, changing industries, and, in general, the overall rapid pace of social change. Such factors brought America, by mid-century, to a period of religious revitalization, and we are still in the midst of that revitalization process.

The many and varied prophets of religion (and their associated religious and entertainment institutions) of this period of revitalization, such as Paul and Jan Crouch, founders of Trinity Broadcasting Network, and Pat Robertson, founder of the Christian Coalition, are all in competition for our time, money, and allegiance. The biggest challenge to contemporary prophets of religion and, to those of entertainment as well, is to synthesize a cosmological and moral system that will appeal to a large enough group of people so that it creates a sense of community and helps people find meaning in their everyday lives.

The prophets of religion tend to argue for absolute values and an otherworldly cosmology. Consequently—and because they usually disagree with each other so much—they are only successful in appealing to a fraction of the larger population. The prophets of entertainment, however, have taken a different approach. They offer a set of values that are more general and relative, and a cosmology that is very much this-worldly, as in *The Matrix*. Not surprisingly, the prophets of entertainment are capturing the larger collective audience.

Most people participate in both sets of values and cosmologies. People buy into the prophets of religion and into the prophets of entertainment simultaneously, with little or no cognitive dissonance, because the values of the two sets operate at different levels. One's personal religious values and cosmology tend to get acted out in private spaces among close social relations; one's more collective values and cosmology tend to get acted out in public spaces among more distant social relations.

Organized religion has largely lost the battle over public, or collective, space in America and is now largely restricted to private spaces, such as homes and churches, as evidenced by the banning of compulsory prayer from schools and by restrictions upon government-sponsored display of religious symbols such as (Christian) nativity scenes or the Ten Commandments. On the other hand, entertainment "religion" has dominated the public and collective space of Western culture, because it more effectively creates a sense of moral community across all the pluralistic divisions of our society.

Unless a person is employed by a religious institution, most of the metaphors, themes, symbols, and references used in the workplace to provide vision and positive and negative sanctions are derived from the entertainment media. "Show me the money!" from the 1996 film *Jerry Maguire,* is more likely to be the theme of a business convention than "money answereth all things."[4] Likewise, an employer is more likely to chastise an employee with, "O.K., Gilligan," a reference to an incompetent sailor in the TV series *Gilligan's Island,* than with, "Get thee behind me, Satan!" spoken by Jesus to Peter in Matthew 16.23.

When one enters a theater to see *The Matrix* films or, for that matter, any other movie, one enters a collective space where many ordinary rules of public behavior are restricted and/or prohibited: no talking, no smoking, remain seated unless coming in or exiting, and turn off all cell phones and pagers. The space one enters is reserved for the spectacle of light and sound about to take place, and, in the case of *The Matrix,* for the mythic story that is about to be told.

In many ways, the cinematic experience is just like the experience of going to a church, synagogue, or mosque. It is religious practice that conveys values; therefore anything that conveys values must be religious practice. I am aware of the tautological nature of that statement, and am not troubled by it, because culture itself is a tautological system that always refers to itself to generate meaning.

The cinematic experience is just the beginning, however. When the movies are released on video and DVD, we get "extras," such as "the making of" and "behind the scenes" add-ons. Fan clubs generate websites and other publications. In addition, there are comics[5] and *The Animatrix.* All of these things constitute a kind of devotional and hagiographic literature that exegetes, or explains, the original films more fully, and provides a much more detailed background of the characters and the production of the film/s.

The iconography of the *Matrix* films is also widely available: one can purchase highly detailed figures of Neo, Trinity, Morpheus, Agent Smith, Niobe, and Tank, some outfitted and posed to depict various important mythic events such as "Martial Arts Neo," "Martial Arts Morpheus," "Bullet-Dodge Neo," and "Neo Vs. Agent Smith."[6] Screen savers, mouse pads, and movie posters keep us constantly aware of the *Matrix* universe, while Powerade and other products have used iconographic representations of the *Matrix* mythos to generate sales.

Of course, traditional religious iconography is used in much the same way, although sometimes irreverently: St. Joseph helps sell aspirin for children; Madonna has invoked various religious symbols in order to sell her music; Blue Nun wine has been around for a while; and I still feel a greater emotional affinity to hospitals and schools that are named after various saints.

Perhaps the most interesting innovation of the entertainment industry is the video game tie-in. The ability to simulate aspects of a myth allows for the interaction to go far beyond what liturgies and rituals allow in traditional religious services. Traditional liturgies and rituals typically recite the creed and symbolically reenact certain important mythic events, but seldom use the sophisticated imagery and variable outcomes of actions to simulate events in the way that video games, such as *Enter,* do. Also, video game simulation is not dependent on the immediate cooperation of a community in order to reenact mythic events. Video games take the "public" of the films and allow us to place it in our "private" sphere and to experience it as we choose. In many ways, the identification of the participant with the characters and storyline of the myth in video games is stronger than in traditional religious rituals. It seems one can only go so far with lighting, music, incense, reciting the creed, and rhythmic recitations and prayers. The world of simulation extends the religious experience in a new dimension. The participant now has a script with a large number of (electronic!) variables and can act out many variations of the myth, entering *Enter* as either Niobe or Ghost, for instance.

In *Enter,* all the major characters of *The Matrix, Reloaded* and *Revolutions* are included. One can fight Agents. Or do all the things Neo can do, such as defy gravity and dodge bullets. The player becomes, essentially, the One, who will fight to save enslaved humanity. This video game has become a sophisticated kind of vehicle for a more total and complete communion with our myths and heroes than traditional religious rituals ever allowed. As electronic and gaming technology develops in newer and more complex ways, we may one day be able to generate a simulated world nearly indistinguishable from reality, as Mizelle and Baker suggest in this volume.

Considering where we are headed culturally and technologically, I am left with two questions I cannot answer:

What happens when the new religion becomes "that real?"
Can both the real and simulated worlds then peacefully co-exist?

Notes

1. Paul Fontana offers a more in-depth discussion of God in *The Matrix* in his article, "Finding God in *The Matrix.*"

2. The claim here that Westerners have a tendency to identify but not formally affiliate is based on my own ministerial work over the last eighteen years (I am a credentialed Protestant clergyperson) and on my own ethnographic investigations among various Christian groups in Chile, the Philippines, Jordan, Egypt, and the United States (including immigrant Egyptian Christians).

3. *The American Heritage Dictionary of the English Language,* 3rd edition.

4. Ecclesiastes 10.19, King James Version.

5. Some comics are currently only available online at http://www.TheMatrix.com.

6. From the website http://www.toysnjoys.com.

Works Cited

Durkheim, Émile. *The Elementary Forms of the Religious Life.* New York: Free Press, 1915.

Fontana, Paul. "Finding God in *The Matrix.*" *Taking the Red Pill: Science Philosophy and Religion in The Matrix.* Ed. Glenn Yeffeth. Dallas: Benbella, 2003: 159-184.

Geertz, Clifford. "Religion as a Cultural System." *ASA Monographs 3: Anthropological Approaches to the Study of Religion.* Ed. Michael Banton. New York: Tavistock, 1985: 1-46.

Jones, Richard R. "An Ethnohistory of Coptic Monasticism." Ann Arbor: University of Michigan Dissertation Services, 1997.

Wallace, Anthony F. C. "Revitalization Movements." *Reader in Comparative Religion: An Anthropological Approach.* Eds. William A. Lessa and Evon Z. Vogt. 4th ed. New York: Harper and Row, 1979: 421-429.

4

Story, Product, Franchise:
Images of Postmodern Cinema

BRUCE ISAACS AND
THEODORE LOUIS TROST

Introduction

Adistinctly postmodern sensibility pervades the *Matrix* franchise, a "text" that is constructed by various postmodern discourses even as it seeks to repudiate them thematically.[1] As film franchise, the *Matrix* demands to be read as a postmodern resuscitation (or "reloading") of prior mythologies, Christian and otherwise, that recolors the past as text and, perhaps more significantly, as contemporary product. Today, popular cinema "construct[s] the significance of the past only as [it] *frames* it in the present" (Collins 280, our emphasis).

The *Matrix* franchise is framed *textually* (as a play of intertextual components) and *formally* (transgressing the traditional boundary of textual homogeneity). Thus, to offer a reading of an entire "franchise," as opposed to a single film, one needs to "play" across its entirety, immersing oneself fully in the whole *product:* the trilogy of movies; the homage to Japanese animé, *The Animatrix;* the computer game *Enter;* the inevitable comic book tie-in; and the plethora of marketed merchandise—Neo's sunglasses are already available for purchase! And for many of us "plugged into" the matrix of contemporary popular culture, this is only a beginning.

The Matrix as Redemption Narrative

"You've been down that road before, Neo; you know where it leads."

—Trinity, in *The Matrix*

The narrative at the center of the *Matrix* franchise begins with Thomas Anderson, a.k.a. Neo, an alienated young man (a lone hacker in the void; a virtual Steppenwolf of cyberspace) who is called out of the obscurity of his corporate cubicle to lead a band of rebels against the ubiquitous foe, Artificial Intelligence. In his role as messiah, Neo's ultimate mission is to bring peace, an abiding harmony between "Zion," the subterranean city where the remnant of humanity is gathered, and "0-1," the surface city and realm of the machines.

Neo's unrelenting nemesis is the evil Agent Smith—a cyber-generated "mass man" (literally, in *Revolutions*) in the tradition of the 1950s "organization man" personified by Sergeant Joe Friday from the television series *Dragnet*. When Smith catches up with Neo in room 303 in the Heart O' the City hotel at the end of the first *Matrix,* Neo dies in a simulated cyberworld. His body remains docile, strapped to a chair, while the mind is "plugged in"—functioning spatially and temporally only in the simulation.

When the messianic Neo rises from the corridor floor, we see the matrix through new eyes, the eyes of the arisen One, who now decodes the data that forms the simulation. In reading and decoding the matrix, Neo transcends the world of illusion.

A number of interpretations have treated this death and resurrection according to theological, particularly Christian, patterns, often in a peculiarly American mode.[2] For example, John Shelton Lawrence suggests that *The Matrix* re-enacts "a stirring performance of America's most reliable pop narrative—the American monomythic tale of redemption by reluctant, unelected heroes" (Lawrence in this volume). Elsewhere Jewett and Lawrence discuss the monomyth as a "secularization [of] the Judeo-Christian redemption dramas that have arisen on American soil" in which "the supersaviors in pop culture function as replacements for the Christ figure" (*xx*).

Certainly this classic American myth is at work in the *Matrix* franchise. At the end of *The Matrix,* Neo's gravity-defying leap backed by Rage Against the Machine's song, "Wake Up," signals both an ascension into heaven along orthodox Christian lines and (as he exits a phone booth) a Clark Kent-like transformation into Superman, now engaged in a never ending battle for freedom.

Suggestively, Neo is not alone in his mission to redeem humanity. Morpheus, Trinity, and Neo form an unconventional Christian trinity: Morpheus as the surrogate father to Neo, the Son, with Trinity as a feminized Holy Spirit. Interestingly, this formula of three-in-one, or three-as-one, reoccurs throughout the (coincidence? we think not) *trilogy*. In *Reloaded*, for example, Morpheus remarks to a gathering of rebels intent on ensuring Neo's safe visit to the Source: "I see three captains and three ships; this is not a coincidence."

When Seraph, Morpheus, and Trinity enter the gothic Hel Club in *Revolutions*, they form a triangle with their backs to each other, a tripartite protective force. In the fifteen-minute Zion battle scene, the three primary Armored Personnel Units (APUs), headed by Mifune, draw up into the same formation. Before reaching the machine city, Neo and Trinity follow three power lines that guide their path. Beyond the limitations of zero and one in the digitalized world, then, the *Matrix* franchise offers up an alternative numerology, a triune possibility suggesting, perhaps, a reordering of power in ways that resonate with Christian speculations about the three persons of the Deity.

From Morpheus's "religious" point of view, at least, a notion of predestination shapes all events. Faith in this destiny—what was "prophesized" [sic], as Morpheus tells Neo shortly after his retrieval from the matrix in the first installment—is the key to knowing how to act in the present. Thus Neo must "believe" he is the One before he can become it. "You're waiting for something," The Oracle tells him in *The Matrix*, "Maybe your next life." Being the One is knowing it "balls to bone": knowledge based on an inward, even a physical, "feeling," or faith in an evangelical Christian (Schleiermacher) or even "born again" sense.

Morpheus's "Now do you believe?" after Neo rescues Trinity from a falling helicopter, and "He's beginning to believe" from the subway station duel in *The Matrix*, reinforce this necessity for faith. Characters such as Commander Lock—connoting a closed mind, and perhaps bearing a symbolic attachment to the materialism of the philosopher, John Locke—stand outside the circle of true believers. They have no time for "religion," which Lock calls "Morpheus's bullshit."

As a Christ figure, Neo dies and is resurrected. He also performs a number of miracles including the resurrection of Trinity at the end of *Reloaded*—which parallels the resurrection of Lazarus in the Gospel of John. After Neo's final "death" in *Revolutions*, the Deux Ex Machina says "It is done!" echoing John 19.30. In *Reloaded*, upon jacking in to the matrix, Neo is dressed in a priestly cassock with a neck collar, prompting The Oracle to say, "My goodness, look at you, you turned out all right." Shortly before he meets The Oracle, Neo casually strolls by a market window cluttered with cheap

Christian paraphernalia—the camera pauses momentarily on a figure of Christ painted on a decorative plate.

As Jewett and Lawrence observe, the Christ motif is the most easily recognized and accessible of the various narrative tropes inscribed by popular films. Perhaps this is still the case, since a uniquely Christian symbology resonates more clearly and transparently for a popular audience than periodic doses of Greek heroic myth (*O Brother, Where Art Thou?*), Buddhism (*The Legend of Bagger Vance*), Gnosticism (some of the dialogue in the first two *Matrix* movies before the franchise turns Johannine and orthodox in the third film), or Hinduism (as in the depiction of the paradoxically "Mobil"—or, by anagram—"Limbo"—way station where Neo is trapped at the beginning of *Revolutions*). It is precisely this resonance, according to Lawrence, that provides fertile ground for the growth of the American monomyth.

The traditional performance of myth is recuperative, turning a gaze upon a distant past, a prelapsarian Eden that must be "re-established in a happy ending" (Jewett and Lawrence 170), or, along the lines of Herman Melville's *Billy Budd,* a redemptive death and the dawn of a new day (see Lewis). The Marxist theorist, Fredric Jameson, has written of a postmodern aesthetic that reflects obsessively on the idyllic past, forming an abiding and overarching nostalgia in its cultural and textual practices. He cites *Star Wars, American Graffiti,* and *Chinatown,* among others, as examples of postmodernist "pastiche," "imitation[s] of dead styles" and the "longing to experience them again" (*Cultural Turn* 7-8).

Contemplating *The Matrix,* Laura Bartlett and Thomas Byers speak of its (nostalgic) return to an ideology depicting the triumph of liberal humanism over post-structuralist postmodernism, that is to say of rationalistic (logocentric) metanarratives, over what Roland Barthes calls a "network," or a "combinatory systematic" (161). Certainly the *Matrix* trilogy can be read as redemptive myth. To some extent we perform such a reading in our rendering of mythical, particularly Christian, elements in the films. We do not wish to deny the significance of the narrative, but wish to emphasize that a reading focused exclusively on this aspect of the franchise is inadequate and unsatisfying. For instance, even if references to the Christian concept of trinity are made explicitly in the film, what (if anything) is the significance beyond the referential?

In our estimation, the postmodern subject is a textual "hacker," that is to say, a natural transgressor of the mythical reading, who is implicated by the interpretive frame of the movie itself. Such a subject need not stumble over concepts such as Jameson's disparaging "pastiche," implying a superficial rein-vestment of some image or condition. Instead, she or he can invest in a proj-ect of textual *re-presentation*. Hence we offer a conceptual model of a fran-chise that demonstrates simultaneously an awareness of a perennial narrative in popular culture, a myth as *metanarrative,* and at the same time, a profound ambivalence toward metanarratives (huge mythic patterns—we restrict our discussion to the Christian myth) as part of liberal human discourse. To explore this play of and within a textual franchise, we turn to two iconic postmod-ern figures, the protagonist cohering *only as detached from a prior form,* namely "Neo," and the French philosopher Jean Baudrillard.

The Matrix as Intertextual Site and Product

"He is the One."

—Morpheus in *The Matrix*

Neo is Christ*like,* but he is not Christ; he is not an avatar, descended (or arisen) into a simulated and fallen world to save humanity from its own sins. It only *appears* this way from a monomythic, particularly Christian, perspec-tive. *The Animatrix* (in "Second Renaissance, Part I") establishes that human-ity has been instrumental in its own defeat: "Then man made the machine in his own image. Thus would man become the architect of his own demise."

Thenceforth, humanity is born (literally, rather than metaphorically) into bondage, and only the elect (those who reject a program installed by an "intuitive" machine, The Oracle) are awakened from passivity. Fewer still—indeed, there have been only six—constitute an anomaly in a system of otherwise "mathematical precision," "facilitating the function of the One."

In classic myths, the chosen are always just a few; the agency of a multitude might easily steer the narrative from individualist to collective, which would defeat the purpose entirely. Consider, for example, *Star Wars, Lord of The Rings,* and *The Terminator,* sagas that chart the narrative of a lone figure emerging from relative obscurity. In *Revolutions* we discover that indeed there is only one Neo, the true Savior, who fosters an abiding (though, it appears to us, fragile) peace between humanity and machines.

Thematically, the tropes of the classic hero monomyth are out in force here. The name Neo, in fact, has a certain archetypal resonance. Con-sider the (anti)heroes of Sergio Leone's *Dollars* trilogy (*Fistful, Few, Good*) and

Once Upon a Time in theWest. These are all veritable "men with no name." In both instances, regardless of the ostensible depiction of hero or antihero, a man with no name takes on the reflection of an iconoclastic figure. He is, on the one hand, the original Adam, and his plight the plight of all. On the other hand he is the epic hero, Odysseus, who escapes from his captor the Cyclops Polyphemos as a result of his crafty self-reference: "'Nobody' is my name. My father and my mother call me 'Nobody,' as do all the others who are my companions" (*Odyssey* IX.366-67—Lattimore 146).

In the *Matrix* franchise, we witness both a thematic and an aesthetic upon mythic structures. Neo is also a man with no name, but instead of the Leone gunfighter, his role is that of an iconoclastic postmodern character, both everyman and no-man. In this sense, *The Matrix* represents immersion in what Jameson calls "a perpetual present" (*The Anti-Aesthetic* 125). De-historicized and lacking a contextual reality, this One is an apotheosis of the re-presented image, "Neo."

Rather like the greater part of popular, late-capitalist culture, the *Matrix* franchise is very much concerned with appearances, and particularly with *images* of objectified forms.The postmodern aesthetic, according to Jameson, depends upon making fetishes of parts of a forgotten past, an a priori (but now irretrievable) ideal (*Cultural Turn,* 8-9). Indeed, shortly after swallowing the red pill, Neo confronts the reflected image of himself in a mirror that contorts his image as he moves toward it.

Dino Felluga suggests that this scene represents Neo's negotiating of a mirror-phase of character-development (familiar from the theory of Jacques Lacan), which is merely one in a sequence of other phases, notably the Christian concept of rebirth (80). But the distorting image that ultimately fractures also makes metaphoric Neo's confronting the simulated image as a distorted reflection: he realizes for the first time that what he has thus far known of himself has been *merely* an image, or more precisely, a perpetually unchanging image-*construct*. In this sense, a vital subtext of the franchise engages with this postmodern dilemma: How does one deal with the realization that life has been an image (on a screen)?

In what follows, we offer an alternative to a harmonious "metanarrative" (or monomythic) reading of the grand finale of *Revolutions*. In so doing, we are less interested ostensibly in what the films "say," and indeed whether they are saying anything at all along the lines of what Bartlett and Byers call "a neo-Romantic version of the liberal-humanist" project (30). Instead we contend that the battle between Neo and Smith (the Burly Burly Brawl on the film set) constructs a *simulation* of a traditional (hence, made-nostalgic) textual frame founded on stable, and staple, mythologies. We conclude that the *simulation* ultimately empowers the postmodern subject and a dominant postmodern aesthetic.

The Matrix as Franchise

In one of the opening sequences of *The Matrix,* we are offered a fleeting shot of a hollowed-out copy of Jean Baudrillard's (in)famous *Simulacra and Simulation,* in which the protagonist, whom we later learn is alienated (literally) from the Real, stores illicit software. The fact that the book is represented as depthless, and thus non-contextual inside the simulation (the concluding chapter of Baudrillard's book, "On Nihilism," appears to have rewritten itself into the middle section of the book!) offers a second order signification of what Roland Barthes terms the "play" of the text. How are we to locate Baudrillard's seminal work if it does not locate itself?

To classify the Real in dialectical opposition to the matrix, Morpheus refers to a "desert of the Real," a Baudrillard*ism* that establishes this particular work as foundational to the matrix construct. In this radical brand of post-structuralist theory, we are not dealing with a matrix, but *the* matrix. The Wachowskis are aware that the notion of a matrix of simulation components—"miniaturized cells, matrices, and memory banks, models of control" (Baudrillard 2)—is used by Baudrillard in *Simulacra and Simulation.*

It is disappointing to read Baudrillard's comments on *The Matrix Reloaded* (Lancelin), in which he suggests that the Wachowskis ultimately conflate simulation with illusion. After all, Baudrillard suggests, illusion is nothing new; Plato mentions it more than a few times. But *simulation,* and its concomitant *hyperreality,* is something unique to the postmodern condition. A similar reading by Bartlett and Byers suggests that *The Matrix* is a film that tries for some inimitable postmodern *chic,* but attains only a neo-conservative dichotomy that esteems transcendental truth over a system of authoritarian-controlled lies (30).

Simulation is a performance of a once-indissoluble truth that simultaneously erases that truth through its performative aspect. Accepting the performative aspect reveals that there remains only the apparition, the phantasm. "'The simulacrum is never what hides the truth—it is truth that hides the fact that there is none. / The simulacrum is true'—Ecclesiastes"

(Baudrillard 1). Of course, Baudrillard has had the last laugh at the expense of the true believer: this epigram appears nowhere in the Bible!

Illusion, on the contrary, is precisely that which brings the truth into greater relief, thereby reinforcing the eternal dichotomy between truth and lie, object and simulation. To "free his mind," Neo must actively contemplate the antithesis between reality and the matrix. Appreciating the illusion for the prison that it is allows him to escape, to "know" the parameters of the lie, and thus to transcend them. The greater part of published critical analysis of *The Matrix* posits the essentialist notion that ultimately, and resoundingly, the matrix is subordinated to the Real.[3]

While we would take issue with this notion, even on a thematic, narrative level,[4] we should recall that Baudrillard's simulacrum *contaminates* the Real in its very existence, that is to say, in its *performance* of the real. This is why his comments on *Reloaded,* and Bartlett and Byers's suggestion that *The Matrix* is "pomophobic" [avoidant of postmodernist tenets], are unsatisfying. After all, postmodernism is not *merely* a literary or philosophical theory. It is, to quote Francois Lyotard's now classic formulation, a "condition," a state of being that contaminates the whole (Introduction and 37-52). To suggest that the *Matrix* franchise somehow transcends, and thus evades, this contamination, dropping anchor at a neo-Romantic conservatism is anachronistic, whether we follow Baudrillard's or Lyotard's conception of postmodernity.

A subversion of traditional and a singular metanarrative occurs at the point of the *inception* of the text. Barthes classically formulated a continuum between a "work" and its discursive "textual" forebear—what Barthes calls "decant[ing]," a pouring of the textual into its molded, or *framed* form (Barthes 162). In this case, Barthes's "textuality" relies upon a free play of meaning, while the work places a restrictive boundary on that play. While the text coheres in the realm of language, the work resides in tactile form—for instance, in a library.

The phenomenon of the Hollywood franchise sets in motion an additional interpretive frame. The franchise aesthetic, in contrast to traditional film aesthetic, is a broad and discursive system of cultural production and consumption. Interpretation (in this sense, the term feels vaguely anachronistic) takes place at the point of consumption—upon the purchase of an action figure, for example—just as significantly as it does in a viewing of the film. The critical and analytical response to the franchise relies not only on playing the game *Enter* (The Oracle's mystifying reference to her "new shell" in *Revolutions,* and Smith's contemplation of how she "escaped," makes little sense without playing the game that forms a vital part of the narrative) but on the act of *consumption*.

Each product purchased, each viewing of a film, or, for that matter, each chapter in a book that deals with the subject of the *Matrix* franchise, implicates and welcomes the consumer into the franchise fold. The matrix has us, and we welcome it. To criticize the textual franchise only on a viewing of the films, to deconstruct the franchise *outside* of the franchise construct, is to be what the nameless narrator of Chuck Palahniuk's *Fight Club* calls a "faker" (Palahniuk 201). The reader of the franchise is implicated in the operation of the text at the point of initial consumption.

Of course, none of what we suggest is especially new in critical theory. Adorno and Horkheimer's famous formulation of the "culture industry" appeared in the mid-forties, and has been around ever since in various Marxist readings of popular culture and consumption (Horkheimer 121). Jameson is particularly intent on establishing a depthless postmodernity, a reader/viewer passivity, and a popular culture that is ever popular but light on culture ("Postmodernism" 69-71). Neither Adorno and Horkheimer nor Jameson identifies a driving aesthetic beneath the play of culture production and consumption. But what if the aesthetic of consumption is as significant a part of the postmodern condition as traditional content-based interpretive practices? If, as Lyotard argues, the metanarratives of Western civilization have fragmented before a sustained "incredulity" (Lyotard *xxiv*), how do postmodern cultural artifacts prove their worth? The question simply asks whether consumption can be its own aesthetic reward.

We use the term "consumption" in a two-fold sense. Traditional textual analysis founded upon a harmonious reading stands in stark contrast to Barthes's post-structuralist conception of "playing the text." In our formulation, the act of playing is a form of consumption that installs the consumer as an active participant in the consumption process. Our second usage describes a trend in contemporary cinema founded upon textual appropriation, essentially a re-presentation of a once "sacred" cinematic past. In this sense, the word consumption refers to playing a range of intertextual components. Though often discussed as occurring simultaneously with the dawn of the postmodern aesthetic (thus, in some critical models, constituting that aesthetic), textual appropriation is also nothing new. But to our minds, acknowledging and celebrating that spirit of appropriation, of rendering the past anew as a functioning simulacrum, is exemplified in relatively few texts, of which the *Matrix* franchise is a particularly fine example.

Consider the momentous climax of the *Matrix* franchise as a Baudrillardian simulacrum of cinematic text and myth (though it should be stressed
that to discuss "texts" as linear is operating on a contradiction in terms: is the
franchise complete when the "Zion Archives" appears in the *Matrix* comic
books and the "canon" closes? Or is the canon always open to revision, revelation, and future revolutions?). The romantic hero says good-bye to his love
in an excruciating and wonderfully sentimental exchange, demonstrating
what Jewett and Lawrence call the "sexual segmentation" of the monomythic
hero (59). This segmentation is necessary to establish the plight of the One
as heroic-individualist. Physically blinded, he confronts a heavenly simulacrum, a realm of "white on white" (Palahniuk 201), or in this case, light on
light. Heaven is a machine construct. The artifice is maintained in the quasi-
God figured Deus Ex Machina, also a construct of component sentinel parts.

Upon jacking in to the matrix, the traditional hero dons the cinematic
ethos of the classic anti-hero in a second re-presentation of a Sergio
Leone Western showdown (the first takes place in a subway station at the
conclusion of the *The Matrix*). The Wachowski brothers tip their hats to
Leone's "texts," particularly the films in the *Dollars* trilogy. Neo's flowing
coat is as suitably a religious cassock as the dust jacket of the Cheyenne
"romantic bandit" in Leone's *Once Upon a Time in the West*.

The anti-hero is further inscribed by the mirror-shades of William Gibson's cyberpunk protagonists, Case and Molly, in his seminal *Neuromancer*.
The camera that rests on Neo's black boots (the boots are configured
elsewhere in the series as sexual fetish, particularly as they are worn by the
quasi-androgyne Trinity, in *The Matrix)* and ascends his body (a recognizable cinematic trope of contemporary popular cinema) recalls James Cameron's
Terminator, a film that looms gargantuan over this franchise. The shot that
opens on Neo in the final showdown in *Revolutions* replicates a shot of the
entrance of Schwarzenegger in *The Terminator,* and is the crucial indication
that we are watching a performance of a prior cinematic piece.

Performance as an aesthetic value permeates this sequence. Indeed,
Reeves as actor steps aside to admit *Neo* as actor. The new age sentimental-
ism of the contemporary leading man ("Trin, you can't die!") is *refigured into*
a stoic, transcendental heroism. "It ends tonight" acts as a depthless (to be
sure, hollow, as in Baudrillard's bible of the simulacrum, and infinitely
regressing, as in Barthes's conception of the freedom of the text) reverber-
ation of every line prefiguring a climactic confrontation. The archetypal
good versus evil showdown is reconfigured as a highly stylized homage to

Hong Kong kung fu cinema of the 1970s; the viewer recalls Neo's "imper-sonation" of Bruce Lee in a sparring duel with Morpheus in a simulated dojo. The silhouetted shot of the fighters in an abandoned warehouse is a familiar trope of classic Hong Kong cinema, and, incidentally, is used to astonishing effect in Tarantino's recent *Kill Bill*.

Three other cinematic references are significant and operate to con-struct a discursive, performative frame of reference. The mid-air tussle between Neo and Smith is reminiscent of the climactic fight between Super-man and General Zod in *Superman 2;* the Christ figure partakes of the Mar-vel Comics pop heroic tradition. The second, and a more obvious hom-age, is the circular energy field that explodes from the confrontation between Neo and Smith, replicating the shot of a nuclear explosion in *Akira* that leads to the formation of the futuristic dystopia of Neo-Tokyo. More distantly, the general visual style recalls *Dragonball Z,* a cult animé series popular both in Japan and the United States.

Crucially, Morpheus's rhetorical final question "Is it real?" in *Revolutions,* uttered while gazing upward at a heavenly glow, subverts any notion of a resolution to the postmodern dilemma with which we began: can one resolve the psychical, metaphysical, and existential crisis that informs the contem-plation of the Real as constructed image?

Morpheus's rhetorically empowered question is virtually a pastiche of Schwarzenegger's final line in Paul Verhoven's *Total Recall*. Standing beneath a Mars sunrise that recalls an image from a classic Hollywood Technicolor epic, he utters: "What if I'm dreaming?"; to which his love replies: "Then kiss me before I wake up!" The textual fabric that touches the *Matrix* fran-chise and *Total Recall* draws also on the classic metaphysical conundrums of the sci-fi writer, Philip K. Dick, who authored "We Can Remember It For You Wholesale," upon which *Total Recall* is loosely based. Dick's open-ended, often self-effacing metaphysics (as seen, for instance, in *The Three Stigmata of Palmer Eldritch* and *Ubik*) pervade the textual play of the *Matrix* franchise.

This reading of a sequence in *Revolutions* offers a conception of the fran-chise as a cinematic simulacrum that inscribes Neo simultaneously as the apotheosis of the monomythic figure *and* its redundancy. As postmodern text, the franchise consumes its textual precursors, gorging on a "sacred" past, so to speak, but without the disparaging and debilitating recourse to what Jameson calls cinematic "pastiche." Instead, the redundancy of the mon-omyth takes place at an acceptance of the postmodern text as discursive *and* constructed—a functioning simulacrum.

The image of Neo as a re-presentation of Christ on the cross performs an *absence* rather than a presence of the Christian story. A driving aesthetic of postmodern cinema is image-consumption, an appreciation of text as a fractured mirrored reflection, aware of its constructedness, its component parts, its radical self-conscious artifice. It is a cinematic aesthetic divested of the burden of cultural myth as originary, instead re-historicized at the core of that aesthetic. Rather than seeking the "new" Christ in an eternal return, it seeks a new Christ *image,* a new incarnation of an originary mythic form that has been re-presented into obsolescence. Neo is only Christ insofar as he coheres in a simulated matrix "with a set of quotation marks that hover above [him] like an ironic halo" (Collins 286).

Conclusion

What coheres ultimately in the internal logic of the franchise is a panorama of residual mythic images. The tools required to decode these images are a part of postmodern consumption practices as much as traditional textual interpretation. The postmodern textual critic is aware of the parameters of the construct in which the text is played. There is thus a necessary ambivalence in aesthetically responding to texts as *artificial.* A hope always lingers to see the original, the true One whose replication is that which Plato considered a "familiar," merely the paltry reflection of an ideal form.

The nostalgic meditation on the "really real" informs a major part of the critical writing on popular contemporary culture that is, to our minds, reductionist. We argue that traditional myths resonate discursively rather than harmoniously, challenging the integrity of the original mythic tale, whether religious or secular. Underscoring this resonance is the perpetual contemplation of the construction of the image. But this contemplation is not necessarily a-historical nor hyperreal, theoretical paradigms (the first drawn from Jameson, the second from Baudrillard) that divest postmodern culture of aesthetic and descriptive value. It might be, as Jim Collins suggests, "icons, scenarios, visual conventions [that] continue to carry with them some sort of cultural 'charge' or resonance that must be reworked according to the exigencies of the present" (Collins 286). Just what that charge is, in an ever more complex and diverse popular culture, is increasingly difficult to evaluate and, indeed, to conceptualize.

Notes

1. For a discussion of *The Matrix* as "pomophobic" (rejecting the central tenets of post-modernism, particularly the politics of pluralism), see Bartlett and Byers.

2. For two readings of the function of the Christian narrative in *The Matrix,* see Seay and Garrett, and Fontana. Fontana offers a particularly lucid account of the concurrent play of various mythological systems.

3. For a reading of the Matrix/Real dichotomy, see Gordon and Baudrillard's comments in Lancelin.

4. One can only read the return of Neo to the "Source" at the conclusion of *Revolutions* as ambiguous and subversive of the monomythic drama. The Source is a machine main-frame, an organic-mechanical being at the core of human originary myths. The realization of Neo as a synthesis of machine and organic human offers a postmodern cyborg intrusion into the traditional monomythic ontology—the image in the machine city of a flesh-like organic tube attached to a mechanical womb installs a similar postmodern mythology espoused by the seminal sci-fi film, *Aliens.* Consider that in *Alien: Resurrection,* Ripley is an alien-human hybrid, much as Neo appears to be a symbiosis of human and machine at the conclusion of *Revolutions.*

Works Cited

Barthes, Roland. *Image—Music—Text*. Trans. Stephen Heath. London: Fontana, 1977.

Bartlett, Laura, and Thomas B. Byers. "Back to the Future: the Humanist Matrix." *Cultural Critique* 53 (2003): 28-46.

Baudrillard, Jean. *Simulacra and Simulation*. Trans. Sheila Faria Glaser. Ann Arbor: University of Michigan Press, 1981.

Collins, Jim. "Genericity in the Nineties: Eclectic Irony and the New Sincerity." *The Film Cultures Reader*. Ed. Graeme Turner. London: Routledge, 2002: 276-290.

Dick, Philip K. "We Can Remember It For You Wholesale." *Preserving Machine and Other Stories*. London, Gollancz, 1971: 129-49.

——. *Ubik.* Garden City NY: Doubleday, 1969.

——. *The Three Stigmata of Palmer Eldritch*. St Albans: Triad, 1978.

Felluga, Dino. "*The Matrix:* Paradigm of Post-Modernism or Intellectual Poseur? (Part I)." Yeffeth 71-84.

Fontana, Paul. "Finding God in *The Matrix*." Yeffeth 159-84.

Gibson, William. *Neuromancer.* Glasgow: HarperCollins, 1993.

Gordon, Andrew. "*The Matrix:* Paradigm of Post-Modernism or Intellectual Poseur? (Part II)." Yeffeth 85-102.

Horkheimer, Max, and Theodor W. Adorno. *Dialectic of Enlightenment*. Trans. John Cumming. London: Allen Lane, 1973.

Jameson, Fredric. *The Cultural Turn: Selected Writings on the Postmodern, 1983-1998*. London: Verso, 1998.

———. "Postmodernism, or the Cultural Logic of Late Capitalism." *Postmodernism: A Reader.* Ed. Thomas Docherty. New York: Harvester Wheatsheaf, 1993: 62-92.

———. "Postmodernism and Consumer Society." *The Anti-Aesthetic: Essays on Postmodern Culture.* Ed. Hal Foster. Seattle: Bay, 1983: 111-25.

Jewett, Robert, and John Shelton Lawrence. *The American Monomyth.* New York: Anchor-Doubleday, 1977.

Lancelin, Aude. "Baudrillard Decodes *Matrix.*" Trans. anon. *Le nouvel Observateur* No. 2015 (19 June 2003); posted in trans. 8 Nov. 2003. <http://www.teaser.fr/~lcolombet/empyree/divers/Matrix-Baudrillard_english.html>. Accessed 24 Nov. 2003.

Lattimore, Richard, trans. *The Odyssey of Homer.* New York: Harper, 1991.

Lewis, R. W. B. *The American Adam.* Chicago: University of Chicago Press, 1955.

Lyotard, François. *The Postmodern Condition: A Report on Knowledge.* Trans. Geoff Bennington and Brian Massumi. Minneapolis: University of Minnesota Press, 1993.

Palahniuk, Chuck. *Fight Club.* New York: Norton, 1996.

Seay, Chris, and Greg Garrett. *The Gospel Reloaded: Exploring Spirituality and Faith in* The Matrix. Colorado Springs: Pinon Press, 2003.

Films

Akira. Dir. Katsuhiro Ōtomo. Animated. Prod. Shunzo Kato. 1988.

Alien. Dir. Ridley Scott. Perf. Sigourney Weaver, Tom Skerritt. 1979.

Alien: Resurrection. Dir. Jean-Pierre Jeunet. Perf. Sigourney Weaver, Winona Ryder, Dominique Pinon. 1997.

Aliens. Dir. James Cameron. Perf. Sigourney Weaver, Michael Biehn. 1986.

American Graffiti. Dir. George Lucas. Perf. Richard Dreyfuss, Ron Howard, Mackenzie Phillips. 1973.

Chinatown. Dir. Roman Polanski. Perf. Jack Nicholson, Faye Dunaway, John Huston. 1974.

Dragonball Z. Dir. Minoru Okazaki. Animated TV Series 1989-96.

A Fistful of Dollars. Dir. Sergio Leone. Perf. Clint Eastwood, Marianne Koch, Gian Maria Volonte. 1964

For a Few Dollars More. Dir. Sergio Leone. Perf. Clint Eastwood, Lee Van Cleef, Gian Maria Volonte. 1965.

The Good, the Bad, and the Ugly. Dir. Sergio Leone. Perf. Clint Eastwood, Lee Van Cleef, Eli Wallach. 1966

Kill Bill: Volume 1. Dir. Quentin Tarantino. Perf. Uma Thurman, David Carradine, Lucy Liu. 2003.

Lord of the Rings: The Fellowship of the Ring. Dir. Peter Jackson. Perf. Ian Holm, Ian McKellen, Christopher Lee. 2001.

The Matrix. Dir. The Wachowski Brothers. Perf. Keanu Reeves, Carrie-Ann Moss, Laurence Fishburne. 1999.

Matrix Reloaded. Dir. The Wachowski Brothers. Perf. Keanu Reeves, Carrie-Ann Moss, Laurence Fishburne. 2003.

The Matrix Revolutions. Dir. The Wachowski Brothers. Perf. Keanu Reeves, Carrie-Ann Moss, Laurence Fishburne. 2003.

Once Upon a Time in the West. Dir. Sergio Leone. Perf. Charles Bronson, Claudia Cardinale, Henry Fonda. 1968.

Star Wars. Dir. George Lucas. Perf. Mark Hamill, Harrison Ford, Carrie Fisher. 1977.

Superman II. Dir. Richard Lester and Richard Donner. Perf. Christopher Reeve, Margot Kidder, Jackie Cooper. 1980.

The Terminator. Dir. James Cameron. Perf. Arnold Schwarzenegger, Linda Hamilton, Michael Biehn. 1984.

Terminator 2: Judgment Day. Dir. James Cameron. Perf. Arnold Schwarzenegger, Linda Hamilton, Edward Furlong. 1991.

Total Recall. Dir. Paul Verhoeven. Perf. Arnold Schwarzenegger, Rachel Ticotin, Sharon Stone. 1990.

Music

Rage Against the Machine. "Wake Up." *The Matrix: Music from the Motion Picture.* Warner Brothers, 1999.

5

Fascist Redemption or Democratic Hope?

JOHN SHELTON LAWRENCE

"Comprehension is not requisite for cooperation."

—Councilor West in *The Matrix Reloaded*

"[*The Matrix Reloaded*] is suspicious of salvation narratives. It's deeply anti-dogmatic. The critics haven't figured that out yet, but the scholars will get to it."

—Cornel West (Agger AR15)

Despite millions of words about the *Matrix* franchise, popular commentary has said little about the politics of the trilogy's imagined world. Critics have lamented the long battle scenes, the platitudinous capsules ("Whatever has a beginning has an end"), and the weary acting of *Revolutions*. But even for these unenthusiastic voices, the embedded political values seem negligible—if not entirely benign. The literate insider Cornel West, correctly anticipating that scholars would find an all-too-familiar hero story, has challenged them to "figure out" the "anti-dogmatic" suspicion of "salvation narratives" that lies within the trilogy.

I have tried that and mostly failed, finding this to be one case where, for popular audiences, appearances = reality. On its face the *Matrix* franchise is a salvation tale that appeals to faith in superheroes who distance themselves from their institutions. The miracles that make the heroic acts possible are beyond the grasp of the average leader in Zion. Hence "comprehension is not requisite for cooperation" in the world where we witness liberating, mystically inspired deeds.

I will put my diagnosis severely: the *Matrix* narratives strike me as celebrating a mythology with anti-democratic implications; its narratives are sketched with a chiaroscuro of elements that thrilled the millions who cheered early-twentieth-century fascisms. These affinities for fascism, combined with the grand success of *The Matrix,* heighten my anxiety about the depth of democratic attitudes in the West. I don't question the popularity or inventive artistry of the films. I have watched them all, read *The Matrix Comics,* and parsed the scripts for *Enter the Matrix,* recognizing the attractions of the imagery and technical innovations.

If cultural democracy means nothing more than delivering products that quench popular tastes, the *Matrix* franchise reigns as supremely as *Star Wars* and Walt Disney. However, democracy should mean more than merely satisfying markets.

Realizing that there is no universally recognized "essence of democracy," I offer the characterization that underlies my judgment.[1] (The problematic term "fascism" will receive its description later.) By "democratic spirit" or "democratic way of life" I mean a social atmosphere in which each person feels accountable for community well-being and works at building institutions that foster shared responsibility. Borrowing Robert Putnam's well-known metaphor from his *Bowling Alone* book, a democratic community is one that bowls—and rules—together. Against Councilor West's maxim, it is also a society where "comprehension IS required for cooperation."

A democratic political order aspires to policies that seem reasonable to those compelled by law to follow them. Why shouldn't this be so in this imagined world? One answer comes early in *The Matrix* when Morpheus offers to Neo a pessimistic assessment of the average human being. As they stroll through the illusionary city in "the Construct," looking at its inhabitants, he remarks:

> What do you see? Business men, teachers, lawyers, carpenters. The very minds of the people we are trying to save. But until we do, these people are still a part of that system, and that makes them our enemy. You have to understand, most of these people are not ready to be unplugged. And many of them are so inert, so hopelessly dependent on the system that they will fight to protect it.

This view certainly punctuates the need for the heroic few and becomes important at the end of *Revolutions* when we learn that only a few human beings have been liberated as a result of the war.

In sections that follow, I show how the American mythic and European fascist strands flow together in the anti-democratic mix of the matrix. In some final remarks, I qualify my harsher judgments by pointing to several democratic elements scattered incoherently among the narrative strands of the *Matrix* franchise. If new stories lie waiting in the pipeline at Warner Brothers Pictures—an eventuality suggested by the inconclusive ending of *Revolutions*—the democratic spirit, and with it the repudiation of fascist elements I describe, may come to stronger display.

The *Matrix* as American Monomyth

Redemption

Within the U.S. cultural context the *Matrix* series offers stirring variations on America's most reliable pop narrative—the American monomythic tale of redemption by reluctant, selfless superheroes. The American version of "monomyth" evolved out of story patterns identified by world mythology's great scholar, Joseph Campbell. His renowned study, *The Hero with a Thousand Faces,* offers a provocative description of the archetypal plot for heroic action. The *classical monomyth,* as Campbell called it, offers this recurring pattern:

> A hero ventures forth from the world of common day into a region of supernatural wonder; fabulous forces are there encountered and a decisive victory is won; the hero comes back from this mysterious adventure with the power to bestow boons on his fellow man. (Campbell 30)

One finds examples of this plot in the stories of Prometheus stealing fire from the gods to benefit mankind, of Aeneas visiting the underworld to discover the destiny of the nation he would found, of St. George and the dragon, and of Hansel and Gretel.

Campbell plausibly suggests that this classical archetype is partly inspired by traditional rites of initiation, through which persons depart from their community, undergo trials, and later return for integration as mature adults who can serve others. In several ways the transformation of Thomas Anderson to Neo—from criminal hacker/corporate slacker to savior at Zion—conforms to this older model. He must choose to leave his more comfortable pedestrian existence, permitting the programs orchestrated by Morpheus to develop the frightening powers needed to liberate suffering humanity.

As this classical heroic paradigm was reshaped on the American continent, it became less about maturing for leadership in community institutions and more a story of redemption in which heroes defy their own institutions to save the community. It thus acquired an intensely individualistic flavor. Restating Campbell's model to reflect the American attitudes toward community institutions, it can be rendered as follows:

> A community in a harmonious paradise is threatened by evil; normal institutions fail to contend with this threat; a selfless superhero emerges to renounce temptations and carry out the redemptive task; aided by fate, his decisive victory restores the community to its paradisiacal condition; the superhero then recedes into obscurity. (Lawrence and Jewett 6)

Whereas the classical monomyth reflected rites of initiation, the *American monomyth* shows features from stories of redemption by others. In its particulars it secularizes the Judeo-Christian dramas of community salvation that arose on American soil during the conquest of Native Americans. The Puritans living in a hostile environment often found themselves in situations where they called upon their Lord to deliver them from the evils around them. The heroic character model, taking its cues from the Bible that was central to colonial interpretations of history and deliverance, combines elements of the selfless servant who impassively gives his life for others (as does the saintly, lion-taming Daniel in the Book of Daniel) and the zealous crusader who destroys evil (as with the image of the sword-wielding Jesus in the Book of Revelation).

When *The Matrix* develops this American character scheme for its hero, Neo's earliest training for being super requires him to resist interest for "the woman in the red dress," an interest that his male colleagues on the *Nebuchadnezzar* evince in a heroically unworthy manner. Neo thus joins Clark Kent, whose sexual passion for Lois Lane is thwarted, and the celibate Batman, Spider-Man, other fantasy superheroes whose jobs as community saviors do not allow for the interferences of intimacy and domestic life. In their celibate commitment, they too join into the priesthood of Jesus. Neo's holy aura is conveyed by the priestly cassock that he wears for his trips to the matrix world. In the grungy world of Zion, however, he is permitted intimacy with Trinity in a significant love relationship.

These superpowered saviors in American pop culture often act as direct replacements for the Christ figure. *The Matrix* makes this symbolic identification several times, having Neo rise from the dead, and twice rendering him in cruciform pose, once during his rebirth as a superbeing and again in the final scenes of *Revolutions*. The voice of the Deus Ex Machina forges the Christ link one final time in pronouncing the benediction on Neo's death with the New Testament's words for the expiration of Jesus: "It is done" (John 19.30). As a pop Christ figure, Neo makes a pair with the Arnold Schwarzenegger character (Jericho Cane) in the millennial *End of Days* (1999). Satan has Cane strung up on a cross to die in an alley. At the tale's conclusion, Cane, who managed to escape from his cross, self-sacrificially impales himself on the sword of St. Michael to save the entire world from Satan's destruction. Reflecting on the characteristic ending in the American monomyth, the deaths of Cane and Neo are the ultimate disappearance from the community's scene. Rather than maturing to lead, they die to redeem.

We cannot say that every feature of the *Matrix* franchise neatly matches at every point the archetype of the American monomyth. Like most cyberpunk genre stories, *The Matrix* dispenses with any prior Eden that is under attack by outside evil. The hell that became the living present for human beings is the product of human tactics in the war with machines. And that inhumanity was compounded by faith in colossally powerful weapons that destroyed the earth's atmosphere. Eden may be the goal in the future, but the happy times for human beings are located in a past so distant that it is not part of the story. In the stories of "Second Renaissance Part I" and "Second Renaissance Part II" that provide detailed information about these destructive wars, we find anti-stereotypical moral premises at odds with the stark stereotypes that introduce us to the moral landscape of the matrix-controlled world. The failure of humanity is also treated in the Wachowski brothers' story, "Bits and Pieces of Information" in *The Matrix Comics*. But the subtlety of those films and the comics treatment (to be discussed in the final section) is not part of the trilogy itself.

Spiritually Perfect Violence

In addition to its redemptive dimension, the American monomyth is a recurring dream of "regeneration through violence" (Slotkin 1973) that begins with the Puritan conquests of the native peoples. In secularizing Judeo-Christian dramas of salvation, the tale endows its heroes with unsurpassed physical and mental powers—while assigning to them a defensive stance of complete moral innocence. This lack of material interest or aggressive intent in the heroic characters creates a license for idealized punishment; relatively unlimited power can be used to neutralize evil. And because those powers are so precise, they can be employed without injury to the innocent.

The development of Neo's capacity for a savage form of flying kung fu is the most conspicuous transformation away from his life as an office drudge. The powers of kicking, chopping, and flying that he acquires fit this model of spiritually perfected violence that is both precise and innocently motivated. The moral characterization of Neo's ultraviolence is shared with Zion's leading team players Morpheus, Trinity, Niobe, Ghost, and Seraph, but distinguished from theirs by his greater speed, focus, and lethality in battles. Given the paranoid reality for those who live in Zion and the metaphysics of evil that permeates their existence, they have the moral license to enter buildings, clubs, and kill everyone without hesitation. The "lives" they destroy are "unreal" because they are only simulated creations of the matrix's organization Artificial Intelligence, although they occupy the virtual "bodies" of those "jacked in."

In the spiritual innocence of their violence, the *Matrix* heroes join the Lone Ranger, whose silver bullet can wound but never kills. They join powerful Simba of *The Lion King,* whom even the most vulnerable jungle critters beg to come back and eliminate the torturous regime of his Uncle Scar—a lion who actually wants power. (The sensually perverse Merovingian is the Uncle Scar of the matrix.) The commandos of Zion join Luke Skywalker, a man with an utterly clear conscience as he destroys the Death Star with a Force-guided nuclear missile—a moment in cultural history that helped restore a nuclear pleasure earlier dampened by the grim awareness that hundreds of thousands of Japanese were incinerated at Hiroshima and Nagasaki. The final task of Zion's teams in each of the first two films is to blast apart great skyscrapers, deeds that link them symbolically with Timothy McVeigh as he coldly destroys the McMurrah Building in Oklahoma City, and with Al Quaeda's warriors who smash the structures that symbolize Western capitalism and military power.

These ecstatic visions of destruction carry with them no vision of a reconstructed world after its evils have been purged by violence. In this the narratives echo the political vagueness in the Book of Revelation. There

Armageddon's final battles take humanity beyond the need for political responsibility; the defeat of Babylon's beast means that Christ himself can return and rule for a thousand years, apparently making political institutions unnecessary or wholly subordinate to spiritual rule. This feature of Revelation, such an important source for the American mind, may help explain the monomyth's peculiar inattention to the aftermath of destroying evil, a feature it shares with Marx's vague apocalypse of "the dictatorship of the proletariat." Similarly at *Revolutions*'s end, we only know that a peace (temporary?) has resulted from Neo's return to the Machine City and his final battle with Agent Smith. There is no suggestion of a plan for Zion to transform itself from a paranoiac war-all-the-time existence to a more tranquil period. Such schemes remain in limbo—or in future sequels of *The Matrix*, should the Wachowskis rethink their claim that the trilogy is complete.

The Matrix Reverberates with European Cults of the Heroic Leader

The man! The deed! Thus pine both people and
   High Council.
Do not expect the one who dined at your tables!
Perhaps one who for years sat among your murderers,
Slept in our cells, will rise and do the deed.

        —from Stefan George's prophetic poem of 1907
                 (Haffner 16)

Credire, Obbedire, Combattere! (Believe, obey, fight!)

    —the motto of Mussolini's National Fascist Party in Italy
                   (Payne 215)

To bring themes from European fascism to the *Matrix* series is an admittedly unwelcome intrusion. Zion, after all, is fighting for freedom, the goal of every democratic movement. It is further complicated by the circumstance that the term "fascism" notoriously lacks precision since it has come to function as a condemnation of any kind of authority or exercise of power that is disagreeable to the speaker. An extra obstacle to clarity today is that twentieth-century Europe offered so many national flavors of fascism, with differing social, economic, military, religious emphases. For example, while the Nazis admired Mussolini's movement and theory of heroic leadership, it differed with the Italian fascists significantly in policies on the persecution of detested social groups such as Jews and the handicapped. After 1945, the defeats of Germany and Italy drove the label underground, creating a superficial appearance of death.[2]

America and Fascism

America quickly forgot that William Randolph Hearst's newspapers employed both Mussolini and Hitler as regular columnists in the Sunday section "March of Events" during the 1930s, offering them as much as $1,750 per article. The Italian invasion of Ethiopia and the intervention in the Spanish Civil War in 1935 only increased Mussolini's attraction for the Hearst papers (Nasaw 470-74). America also forgets that one of Columbia Pictures' most successful releases in 1933 was *Mussolini Speaks*. Columbia's screen dedication disclaimed any objectivity: "To a man of the people whose deeds for his people will ever be an inspiration to mankind—Mussolini" (Krueckeberg). Mussolini was so pleased with this film's propaganda value that he invited Harry Cohn, President of Columbia Pictures to Italy for an award, an invitation that Cohn accepted (Dick 71-72).

Nevertheless, to the extent that fascism is represented in popular stories, it is typically coded as Nazi and totally evil. *Star Wars*, for example, presents its imperial leaders in Nazi and Stalinist dress, giving them exaggerated, authoritarian mannerisms. American fans thus bristle quickly at the idea that stories like *Star Wars* or *The Matrix* have a kinship to fascism, particularly with self-effacing heroes like Luke Skywalker and Thomas Anderson/Neo.

Fascism as Providential Leadership

In getting a sense of what fascism is, we need to step back and recall that before fascism fully materialized in its concentration camps, enslaved populations, death factories, etc., it was a theory of providential leadership. The guiding power for heroic leaders would allow destiny's hero—"the One" chosen—to permit the rebirth of their threatened civilizations.

Moreover, it was not merely the silent majorities of those countries but also respected social theorists like Robert Michels in Italy or philosophers such as Martin Heidegger in Germany, who hailed the Nazis as heroic

Nietzschean leaders asserting "the will to power." Even after the Nazis had murdered citizens in the streets, burned books, suspended civil liberties, German philosophers identified themselves with the party (Rockmore 33, 39-40). In his famous rector's address at Freiburg in 1934, Heidegger focused on "The One" who would save Germans by giving commands. He told his students, "Not doctrines and 'ideas' should be the rules of your existence. The Führer himself, and he alone is the German reality, present and future, and its law" (Sluga 144).

This spirit of surrender to the leader's heroic will is echoed in the dedication of Morpheus to whatever Neo chooses to do. In *Revolutions* he responds to Roland's assertion that Neo's plan to take a single ship to the Machine City proves that "he was totally out of his goddamn mind." Morpheus's faithful reply expresses his unreasoning faith:

> Neo is doing exactly what he believes he must do. I don't know if what he is doing is right and I don't know if he will reach the Machine City. And if he does, I don't know what he can do to save us. But I do know that as long as there's a single breath in his body, he will not give up. And neither can we.

Morpheus's surrender of his own judgment goes beyond Heidegger's leap toward the Führer principle, because Hitler was at least the nation's leader. Neo is merely a savior recruited on the initiative of Morpheus.

In another gesture symptomizing his intellectual subservience, Heidegger joined fellow academicians in the Leipzig Declaration, which envisioned a rebirth in declaring that "the National Socialist revolution ... brings with it the total transformation of our German being." The statement ended with the loyal "Heil Hitler!" (Ott 205). The culturally transforming leap away from reason is given a metaphysical foundation in Heidegger's gnostically themed *Being and Time* (1927). There he looks backward to the rationalistic errors of the Greek systematic philosophers whose abstractions made Being "go away."

In Heidegger's political sense of his time, someone would have to break through the old, overly rational categories so that Being could return again in a self-revealing way to the consciousness of human beings. Hitler's heroic Nazis would thus, in Heidegger's scheme, repair the permanent deficit in awareness caused by those first thinkers who took philosophy too far away from its mythic roots. Evincing his sincerity, Heidegger himself was a Nazi party member and remained so until the end of World War II (Rockmore 112).

The Natural Heroic Aristocracy

Another German fascist theme, that of a natural aristocracy composed of martial heroes, was shared with Italian fascism, where it had received some of its most striking formulations. Nations were to be led by heroes who had attained personal power by mastering their wills, instinctively moving where their visionary souls guided them. The Italian Fascist thinker Palmieri described such warriors as partaking of the divine to a measure impossible for ordinary mortals. Such persons are capable of "that magic flash of a moment of supreme intuition" that comes "to the hero and none other" (Cohen 346). Mussolini extolled war as the moment of supreme moral clarity in writing that "war alone brings up the highest tension of all human energy and puts the stamp of nobility upon the peoples who have the courage to meet it" (Mussolini 1935). And disdaining the parliamentary style of decision in liberal democracies, Mussolini proclaimed, "We think with our blood" (Cohen 314).

Neo too has transcended ordinary rationality, an intuitive-based surpassing that permits him to say, "I see the digital rain behind the mendacious reality." And his final actions in fighting with Smith are confessed as equally devoid of reason. "You can't win. It's pointless to keep fighting. Why, Mr. Anderson? Why? Why do you persist?" Neo replies, "Because I choose to," a pure affirmation of will. This final choice is consistent with Neo's brooding silence, the film's way of signaling that he is more intuitive and attuned to action than to thought.

By focusing so intently on Neo's will as "the One" and investing him with uniquely redemptive powers for all of humanity, *The Matrix* feels pitch perfect in its attunement to popular instincts enabling the European heroic leader ideologies commonly labeled as fascist. Within that framework, the heroic leader is appointed and assisted by Providence and finds his true fulfillment as a warrior. Such leaders have special powers of knowing "the metareality of the past and the absolute goal which would be realized in the future" (Payne 215). These political heroes, according to the fascist myth, uniquely carry the destructive power needed for the regeneration of decadent, demoralized, and victimized people who have been seduced by liberal doctrines of equality, materialist comforts, and the futile processes of parliamentary democracy.

Drawing upon the same feelings of dissatisfaction, *Reloaded* and *Revolutions* several times show us the inadequacy of group judgment in Zion's councils. In order to save their community, Morpheus, Niobe, and Neo all take heroic actions that defy the insight and authority of figures like Lock, whose ability to command is impaired by his demand for evidence. The rebel commandos stand for belief and decisive action rather than rational calculation or policy.

In the poem quoted above, Stefan George reveals himself as just one of many who expressed hope for a single, powerful figure who would rescue Germany. He yearned for the type of leader that Hitler seemed to be: a decisive man, always ready with "the deed." Confirming George's apparent prophecy about the leader's criminal background, Hitler had restarted his career in jail for having participated in the November 1923 attempt to overthrow the government; there he wrote his best-selling *Mein Kampf* (1925, 1927).[3] Echoing this theme of criminality as credential, both Neo and Trinity share backgrounds as hackers-for-hire until receiving the prophetic call from Morpheus.

In his book *The Hitler Myth*, Ian Kershaw quotes numerous politicians and theologians who fantasized about transferring their sense of national responsibility to an individual of unsurpassed power. In the words of one frustrated writer, he would be the "bearer of godly power and destiny and grace." "In our misery we long for the Leader. He should show us the way and the deed" (18). Joseph Goebbels, Hitler's fawning minister of propaganda, wrote "that Fate has chosen him to show the way to the German people" (28).

Hitler himself apparently came to believe with sincerity this myth of destiny. The references to Providence and his acceptance of the role dictated by it were frequent in his speeches (Kershaw 82). For the Nuremburg Nazi party rallies of 1934, he commissioned Leni Riefenstahl to make the grand propaganda film, *Triumph des Willens* (*The Triumph of the Will*). It shows Hitler descending upon the city from the air with filmic overlays of Christian symbolism. Roger Eatwell has astutely described the film's iconography of this scene:

As the plane swoops down over the sleepy medieval city, its shadow forms a cross, "blessing" the disciplined columns of marching men along which it flies. When Hitler descends from the plane's door, backlighting creates a halo effect around his head. As he makes the journey from the airport to his hotel, vast crowds line the streets in order to express their worship for the New Christ who has been sent to save Germany. (145)

Whatever Hitler may have privately thought about the Christian symbolics of his staging, he knew how to manipulate the messianic expectations that Germans brought to politics. On stage, he could project a shy modesty, embarrassed at the attention his oratory brought. As a sign of his selfless-ness, he lived a very spartan, secluded existence with minimal material comforts. It was only the total defeat of German in war and Hitler's ignomin-ious suicide that finally destroyed the credibility of faith in the genius of a single leader.

Fascism, Heroics, and Democracy

Even if one doesn't see even an implicit political recommendation in *The Matrix,* the parallels between its heroic values and the ideals of European fascism should give us pause. Karl Popper, a victim of Austrian fascism in the 1930s, has suggested that democratic thinkers shun the traditional, authoritarian question "Who should rule?" because it presupposes we can identify the "good ones." Experience indicates the difficulty of finding persons in whom total powers can be entrusted, and our most perceptive tradition about human nature informs us that power inevitably corrupts.

Therefore, Popper argues, "We must ask whether ... we should not pre-pare for the worst leaders, and hope for the best." He suggests replacing the question of who should be empowered with "How can we so organize polit-ical institutions that bad or incompetent rulers can be prevented from doing too much damage?" (119-20). The premise of the *The Matrix* is that singu-lar heroes can overcome a monumentally corrupted reality. Although people of Zion deliberate their policy and work as a team, in the end they depend upon an visionary Christ-like redeemer whose incomprehensible and suicidal mission is required to save them. It is smashingly good box office, but it can hardly qualify as a democratic story.

Fragments of a Counter-story

To this point, my exposition has emphasized the striking conformities of the story with the American monomyth and some potent ideals of European fascism. But one can't be fair to the *Matrix* vision without also mentioning some fragments that don't fit this larger pattern. These may point to deeper messages that the Wachowskis had in mind—without sufficiently shaping their stories for the popular audiences that have consumed their stories with such gusto.

How Long the Peace Will Last

Among the heroic defenders of Zion, Neo is the subject of adulation. At the conclusion of *Revolutions,* The Oracle affirms, "I believed." Niobe gives a prayer-like incantation, "Neo, wherever you are thank you." And the Kid proclaims enthusiastically: "He saved us. It's over! He did it! It's over! He did it!" The calmer, puzzled Councilor Hamann wants to know what he did, and the Kid shouts in response, "He ended the war, the machines are gone." But the film leaves us with the question whether this is an illusion. The Architect, who clearly had intended a different mission for Neo in *Reloaded,* is skeptical, posing this question for The Oracle: "Just how long do you think this peace is going to last?" She replies with her usual indeterminacy "as long as it can." This is at odds with Morpheus's hot declaration that "the war ends tonight."

As best as we can judge at the conclusion of *Revolutions,* Neo has not liberated all of humanity, only "the ones that want out" according to the promise of the Architect. But Morpheus had stated in *The Matrix* that "as long as the matrix exists, the human race will never be free," and he has also expressed the view that most people are part of the enemy's system and "are not ready to be unplugged." If this ironic juxtaposition expresses "the critique of salvation narratives" that Cornel West has in mind, we must concede his characterization. However, such a subtle undermining of the idea of redemptive leadership will doubtless remain hidden to those whose view its story through the most popular frames. It may even look like the entrée for a sequel—consonant with the comic book superhero tradition—in which a more complete liberation is effected.

With its persistent emphasis on violent battle, the *Matrix* franchise may receive its cultural identification through products like the widely sold *Enter the Matrix* game, which is principally a series of violent capers in driving and shooting at the swarming enemies who are part of the matrix system. The sneering presence of Niobe, aggressively projecting two guns into the face of the player, may be the icon activating the hands and stirring the spirits in our culture of first-person shooters.

A Message of Peace and Compromise?

Some final considerations relate to the character of Neo's final mission, one that embodies significant ambiguities about dramatic closure in the trilogy. Neo has been trained as a killer and becomes the best. But in the end, he loses his will to destroy the matrix. Instead he goes to the Machine City to offer his services in neutralizing Agent Smith. In the words of Neo to the godly presence of Deus Ex Machina, renegade Smith "has gone beyond your control ... and you cannot stop him. I can." Neo has agreed thereby to serve the interests of the matrix by stabilizing its system of control

Yet he is not quite equal to the physical destructiveness of Agent Smith. In the end, he "defeats" Smith by letting him kill him. In the scheme of salvation that operates in *The Matrix,* Neo's violent, sacrificial death accounts for the peace that suddenly descends upon Zion. When Smith makes the mistake of trying to appropriate his shape by thrusting his hand into Neo's body, every one of Smith's snarling selves shatters into fragments. Judging the sequence of events by Morpheus's standard, Neo has sold out to the interests of the matrix. But Neo did save Zion, which was within minutes of being destroyed by the relentless Sentinels.

How might the usually taciturn Neo explain why he has acted as he did? One clue lies in a conversation he has with Councilor Hamman at the engineering level in Zion. Reflecting on all the machines, Neo remarks, "If we wanted, we could shut these machines down." Hamann replies, "Of course, that's it. You hit it. That's control, isn't it? If we wanted, we could smash them to bits. Although if we did, we'd have to consider what would happen to our lights, our heat, our air" (*Reloaded*). Neo replies, "So we need machines and they need us. Is that your point, Councilor?" Although Neo is hostile here, the truism he utters regarding interdependence may be the germ of a pragmatic compromise that leads to his accommodation with Deus Ex Machina at the end.

It is one mark of democracy that its institutions for resolving conflict allow adversaries to confront issues without destroying one another. The end of the war may begin an era in which Zion and the Machine City talk more and war less. However, one must remember that the violent, mutual destruction of Neo and Smith is what makes peace possible. In that regard, peace is simply produced by the exhaustion of the fighting forces. We are left without ambiguity about whether it was a victory for zealous warfare or compromise? Perhaps the commercial genius is to have it both ways.

Let us also consider a final complication of vision that comes to us through the short, powerful *Animatrix* films of "The Second Renaissance." Unlike the original film, which offers stark stereotypes of human innocence as against matrix cruelty and brutality, these shorts powerfully articulate a much more balanced vision on the sources of human bondage. We learn, for example, that humans were murderous in their brutal exploitation of the sentient machines. The butler B1-66ER is yelled at for not cleaning a toilet fast enough; its owner openly discusses discarding it as scrap. The owners refuse to honor their robot's plea that he is not just property and that his owner cannot destroy him. Clever visual echoes of slave labor on the pyramids, racist violence, the Holocaust, Vietnam, Tiananmen Square flash past as we see the mistreatment of intelligent machines. In "The Bits and Pieces of Information" version of the story in *The Matrix Comics,* fragments of the famous Dred Scott Decision of 1856 are cited (on pages 16-17). In that case the United States Supreme Court stripped African Americans of existing rights, asserting that they are "so far inferior, that they had no rights which the white man was bound to respect" (Wachowski 15).

"Second Renaissance" also shows another dark side of humanity with its depiction of human faith in weapons during "Operation Dark Storm." Humans arrogantly disregard the consequences of using them, sanctifying them with religious piety as they march toward their own self-destruction. Of the savage war that finally darkens the sky and results in human enslavement, the narrative voice intones, "May there be mercy on man and machines for their sins." This part of the matrix is an unmistakable critique of the holy war mentality, and it is hard to miss the finger pointing at the United States.

Does Neo possess an articulate understanding that all-out war to the finish with the matrix will be just that—the end of human life in Zion? If so, we see another ray of democratic enlightenment in the notion that polarized stereotypes of the other stand prevent the compromises that survival may require. If we can see both sides clearly, with both their virtues and their faults, the resulting accommodation serves human interests better than a war of annihilation. Yet the *Matrix* franchise wants to have it both ways—Neo fights the apocalyptic battle against Agent Smith to produce peace.

Is it all over? I hope that the *Matrix* franchise will continue and use its enormous cultural influence to play more explicitly with these democratic themes that have yet to be highlighted for the public. Like Neo, and so many critics of the franchise, I became weary with its wars, exploding buildings, and car chases. I would like to see more creativity expended on the ideas that bear on the survival of democracy.

Notes

1. The tension between the superhero genre and democratic values has been worked out in *The Myth of the American Superhero* (Lawrence and Jewett). *Captain America and the Crusade Against Evil: The Dilemma of Zealous Nationalism* (Jewett and Lawrence) discusses superheroic themes and holy war ideologies. My purpose here is to reflect upon *The Matrix* using characterizations of democracy that reflect some common understandings of democratic ideals.

2. Martin Lee's *The Beast Reawakens* is just one of many books that establishes the continuing vitality of fascist tendencies.

3. At the end of his life when Hitler was assuming full dictatorial powers within the Reich, George had the good taste to flee from Germany and die in Switzerland—where he was secure from the honors that the Nazis wanted to bestow upon him (Haffner 17).

Works Cited

Agger, Michael. "And the Oscar for Best Scholar." Interview, *New York Times* 18 May 2003: AR15.

Campbell, Joseph. *The Hero With a Thousand Faces.* New York: Meridian, 1956.

Cohen, Carl. ed. *Communism, Fascism and Democracy: The Theoretical Foundations.* 2nd ed. New York: Random House, 1972.

Dick, Bernard F. *The Merchant Prince of Poverty Row: Harry Cohn of Columbia Pictures.* Lexington: University Press of Kentucky, 1993.

Eatwell, Roger. *Fascism: A History.* New York: Allen Lane-Penguin, 1995.

Haffner, Sebastian. *The Meaning of Hitler.* London: Weidenfeld and Nicolson, 1979.

Jewett, Robert, and John Shelton Lawrence. *Captain America and the Crusade Against Evil: The Dilemma of Zealous Nationalism.* Grand Rapids: Eerdmans, 2003.

Kershaw, Ian. *The Hitler Myth: Image and Reality in the Third Reich.* Oxford: Clarendon, 1987.

Krueckeberg, John. "The Limits and Extremes of Imaging a Fascist Presidency: *Gabriel Over the White House* and the 'Strong Leader' Films of 1933." Unpublished paper from the President on Film Conference of the Film and History League, Nov. 10-14, 2000, Westlake Hills CA.

Lawrence, John Shelton, and Robert Jewett. *The Myth of the American Superhero.* Grand Rapids: Eerdmans, 2002.

Lee, Martin. *The Beast Reawakens.* Rev. ed. (original version 1997). New York: Routledge, 2000.

Nasaw, David. *The Chief: The Life of William Randolph Hearst.* Boston: Houghton Mifflin, 2000.

Popper, Karl. *The Open Society and Its Enemies.* Princeton: Princeton University Press, 1950.

Putnam, Robert. *Bowling Alone: The Collapse and the Revival of the American Community.* New York: Simon and Schuster, 2000.

Payne, Stanley. *A History of Fascism: 1914-1945.* Madison: University of Wisconsin Press, 1995.

Rockmore, Tom. *On Heidegger's Naziism and Philosophy.* Berkeley: University of California Press, 1992.

Seay, Chris, and Greg Garrett. *The Gospel Reloaded: Exploring Spirituality and Faith in the Matrix.* Colorado Springs: NavPress, 2003.

Slotkin, Richard. *Regeneration Through Violence: The Mythology of the American Frontier, 1600-1860.* Middletown, CT: Wesleyan University Press, 1973.

Sluga, Hans. *Heidegger's Crisis: Philosophy and Politics in Nazi Germany.* Cambridge: Harvard University Press, 1993.

Wachowski, Andy, and Larry Wachowski. "Bits and Pieces of Information," in *The Matrix Comics.* New York: Burlyman Entertainment, 2003.

Films

Riefenstahl, Leni. *Triumph des Willens (The Triumph of the Will)* 1936. Available in video formats with English subtitles.

6

Stopping Bullets: Constructions of Bliss and Problems of Violence

FRANCES FLANNERY-DAILEY AND RACHEL L. WAGNER

I n the film *The Matrix* (1999), a hacker named Neo finds that the world in which he has been living—an urban landscape of office buildings, rave clubs, and restaurants with good noodles—is actually a neural net interactive software program designed by futuristic sentient machines to keep him and other humans ignorant of their imprisonment for use as bio-electric fuel. Although patently fictional and chillingly Dickian in its articulation, the film resonated soundly and unexpectedly within our culture.[1]

The movie initially grossed over $460 million worldwide and became Warner Brothers' most successful film up to that point. Its wildly popular reception enabled the Wachowski brothers to craft 2003 as the year of the *Matrix* franchise, succeeding *The Matrix* with the sequels *Reloaded* and *Revolutions,* the series of Japanese animé shorts dubbed the *Animatrix,* a series of graphic comics, and the video game *Enter.* In large part, audiences have eagerly consumed this blitzkrieg of *Matrix* media, along with its storm of violent images.

Journalist Adam Gopnik put it well when he stated, "The first film struck so deep not because it showed us a new world but because it reminded us of this one" (73). But the series not only mirrors culture; it creates culture. As a result of the popular reception of the films, the concept of the illusory matrix has been woven into the fabric of our own postmodern media-saturated culture, appearing in advertisements, hundreds of articles, thousands of fan websites, fashion, and copycat media (see for instance <http://www.themeatrix.org>). In part, the resonance of the franchise stems from its syncretistic blending of aspects of world religions. Scholars and fans have noted the intentional presence of Gnostic, Buddhist, Hindu, Christian, Taoist, Manichean, Zoroastrian, Platonic, Neo-Cathar, Rosicrucian, and Jewish mystical motifs and structures throughout the trilogy, and many of these themes also appear in *Enter* and *Animatrix.*

No single religious system controls the overarching worldview of the series; rather, selective elements are taken piecemeal from various religions and woven into a new religious expression. The films gesture towards a transcendent realm and age to come, drawing on concepts such as the Christian concept of heaven, the Platonic world of the Forms, Buddhist *nirvana*, Hindu *moksha,* Jewish *tikkun olam,* and the Gnostic *pleroma* to create a pastiche of religious and philosophical referents. However, the ultimate realm of bliss (heaven, *moksha, nirvana,* etc.) posited by world religions is, in the *Matrix* series, never left intact. Rather, when considered beyond a superficial reading, the notion of an attainable plane of bliss is complicated until it falls apart and no longer functions on a single level.

Whatever the ultimate structure of reality in the *Matrix* franchise, every level is intertwined with violence. The selective appropriation of motifs and structures from world religious traditions, unhinged from ideals of an ultimate realm as well as from the non-violent core of those traditions, creates a dangerous element in the cultural reception of an otherwise thoughtful endeavor. Although an argument may be made that on one level the Wachowskis intend a critique of violence in their films, the popular reception of the franchise resonates foremost with violence, reflecting the failure of their critical stance.

Archetypes and Architects

From its self-consciously postmodern perspective, the franchise layers numerous religious archetypes, one upon the other, so that there is no single vantage point from which viewers may orient themselves. Some of the most fruitful lenses through which to interpret the films include Christianity, Gnosticism, Buddhism, Hinduism, and Buddhism, although this list is by no means exclusive.[2] The Wachowski brothers avoid serving as interpreters of the films, denying viewers any definitive sense of their views on the role of religious ideas in the films, but when a viewer asked which of the multiple allusions from religious traditions were purposeful, the brothers responded, "All of it" ("Wachowski Chat").

Christianity

Neo's cruciform position at the end of *Revolutions* may tempt viewers to embrace Christianity as the most essential lens through which to interpret the films, and indeed there are overt Christian references throughout the trilogy. From the prophesied birth of Neo, "the One," to his self-sacrificial death for humankind in *Revolutions,* Neo is obviously crafted as a Christ figure. He functions as an exorcist who expels the possessing Agents from the bodies of those in the matrix (Mark 1.25); has foreknowledge of future events such as the death of Trinity (e.g., Mark 13, Matthew 24); travels in the hovercraft called the *Logos* (cf. John 1.1-18, the Greek *logos* normally translated as Word); has supernatural powers (e.g., Mark 4.35, 6.30, 6.45; cf. Mark 8.11); is resurrected (Mark 16, Matthew 28, Luke 24, John 20); and is transfigured into light, his face shining like the sun (Matthew 17.1-8, cf. Mark 9.2, Luke 9.28).

The response others have to him confirms their belief in this Christ-like identity, since Link, Niobe, and Morpheus all seem to pray to him while looking up (*Revolutions*). Crowds throng around Neo, as they did around Christ, asking for protection of loved ones and rendering him offerings. In the *Animatrix* short feature "Kid's Story," a teenager nicknamed "Kid" even sacrifices his own life for his belief in Neo as Savior, recalling Jesus' statement that "those who want to save their life will lose it, and those who lose their life for my sake will find it" (Matthew 16.24-26).

Gnosticism

Neo's name in the matrix, Thomas Anderson, is a clue that an especially apt lens for understanding the films is Christian Gnosticism, which competed with traditional Christianity for hundreds of years and is still practiced today (see Pagels 1979 and 2003). Thomas, the brother of Jesus, who traveled to India, is an important hero of Christian Gnosticism (*Gospel of Thomas; Acts of the Holy Apostle Thomas*)—there may be a link between Gnosticism and the Hindu and Buddhist frameworks of the films.

Since Anderson is code for "son of man" (the Greek *andras* meaning, in English, "man"), the name Thomas Anderson indicates that it is a Gnostic Christ who is a son of man. Thomas/Neo functions as a classic Gnostic Redeemer figure who comes from the *pleroma* or heavenly realm (i.e., the "real world of Zion"). He repeatedly enters the material realm (the matrix), saving others by imparting transcendent *gnosis* or knowledge that our material bodies imprison the divine spark within.[3]

Other characters from the basic Gnostic myth appear as well. In the original myth, an inaccessible and transcendent god spawns numerous pairs of gods and goddesses. At one point in mythic time, a goddess named Sophia (the Greek word for wisdom) decides to give birth to a lesser god without the aid of her consort, thereby producing an aberrant being who mistakenly believes himself to be the highest deity (*Apocryphon of John*). Hurled out of the *pleroma* or divine realm, this godling becomes an ignorant Creator, forming the illusory material universe, the humans within it, and a host of semi-divine "archons" or "aeons," beings who police the imprisoned humans.

The *Matrix* franchise plays on this basic myth in multiple ways, most evidently in the character of the Architect of the matrix. Like the ignorant Gnostic Creator or demiurge, the Architect apparently has created an illusory material realm, the matrix, as well as the Agents who watch over the enslaved humans within it. There are also hints that Agent Smith, whose name suggests he is a forger, is another architect figure who seeks to remake the matrix in his own rotten image. Appropriately, Bane cries out upon seeing Smith, "Oh, my God," to which Smith replies, "Smith will do" (*Reloaded*).

In terms of this analogy, The Oracle is Sophia, who has knowledge of the transcendent realm outside of the matrix, and perhaps outside of the "real world" as well. Just before Smith attempts to take over The Oracle in *Revolutions,* she says to him, "You are a bastard," recalling the bastard offspring of Sophia. Smith suggestively replies, "You should know, mom."

The Oracle may also be seen as "the Mother" of the matrix, an idea introduced in the conversation between the Architect and Neo in *Reloaded*.[4] Together with the "Father" Architect and Neo, these three comprise the "Father, Mother and Son" trio that is a typical Gnostic depiction of God (Pagels 1979: 48-69; e.g., *Apocryphon of John* 2.9-14). However, as is the case with referents from other religious traditions, the films' characters are not constructed in simple one-to-one parallelism with Gnostic characters; rather, images are drawn from Gnosticism and transformed in a rich intertextual layering.

Buddhism

The deliberate incorporation of Buddhist ideas is apparent in the repeated images of complex religious patterns known as mandalas in *Animatrix;* by the inclusion of the Zen Garden in *Enter;* by the appearance of Buddhist monks in *Animatrix* "Second Renaissance, Part II"; by Buddhist references in the associated comic by Dave Gibbons called "Butterfly"; and by Seraph's (Collin Chou's) initial Buddha-like posture in *Reloaded*.

The Wachowski brothers openly admit that Buddhism is one of several worldviews that inform the films ("Wachowski Chat"). Buddhism teaches that ignorance of *samsara*—the complex interconnected sensory illusions that lock human beings into a repeating cycle of birth, death, and rebirth— is the fundamental problem of human existence.

Humans suffer when they cling to a notion of identity that is dependent upon this illusory construct. The title of the first film evokes this notion of *samsara,* presenting a picture of life within the matrix (*samsara*) as dependent upon interlocking neural perceptions that leave humans trapped within a miserable and false existence. Thus, in Buddhist fashion, Morpheus instructs Neo that he should not trust his senses as a reliable way of knowing (*Matrix*). Trinity, Neo, Morpheus, and others serve as *bodhisattva* figures (those who are close to attaining *nirvana* but willingly remain in *samsara* in order to save others) when they re-enter the matrix to teach about its illusory nature and liberate those inside.

At the same time, the films defy a simplistic view of enlightenment and *nirvana*. Although the matrix itself can be seen as an analogy for *samsara,* escape from the matrix hardly dissolves the individual ego, nor does it allow for perfect awareness of interconnection. Life for the crew of the *Nebuchadnezzar* is not *nirvana,* but a dingy, dirty struggle for survival, where one is condemned to eating *TasteeWheat,* "a bowl full of snot" (*Matrix*). Indeed, those who escape the matrix are riddled by the same self-doubt, the same suffering, and the same need for spiritual nourishment as those still enmeshed within it.

Hinduism

The *Matrix* franchise also clearly draws on Hindu traditions, as signaled by the presence of Hindu iconography on sale outside Seraph's chamber in *Reloaded.* Neo, as "the One," can be seen as a type of Vishnu, since he, like the Hindu god, has appeared among humankind numerous times before. Vishnu has female consorts, as do all of the Hindu gods, who embrace sexuality as a potent expression of creativity. Thus, Neo's sexual relationship with Trinity, expressed so vividly in *Reloaded,* can be understood by viewing it as an echo of Vishnu's relationship with a powerful consort (Fielding).

In addition, the conviction that the world of the matrix is a vast illusion would also be familiar to Hindus, especially those who embrace the philosophical school of Advaita Vedanta, based heavily on the *Upanishads* and best articulated by Shankaracharya, an eighth-century philosopher and author of numerous commentaries on Indian texts. Shankaracharya describes the entire universe as an expression of Brahman, the foundation of all being.

The universe only seems finite and discrete due to ignorance (*avidya*) and illusion (*maya*). The seeming multiplication of gods and goddesses in Hindu mythology can be explained by seeing these divinities as different facets of Brahman. Even humans share in the divine realm, since each human being's *atman* (real Self) is identified with Brahman. The films draw on this monistic perspective when the Key Maker advises the rebels that in order to achieve their goal in allowing Neo access to the Source, "All must be done as one" (*Reloaded*). Indeed, when viewed in Hindu terms, Smith and Neo's enmity is rooted in ignorance of their fundamental identity and connectedness, not only with one another, but with all beings (humans and machines) in the universe.

The repeated creation and destruction of Zion and the matrices also echo Hindu beliefs about recurring cycles of successive universes. Each universe begins with peace and morality, but gradually declines to the point that destruction is the only means to renewal. In Hindu belief, the god Brahma creates each universe, Vishnu sustains it, and Shiva destroys it. This trinity appears in new incarnations as the Indian family in the Mobil Avenue train station in *Revolutions,* where they imperfectly reflect the divine relationship of the Hindu divinities.

The name Rama-Kandra, Sati's father in *Revolutions,* points to Rama, one of the incarnations of Vishnu. But, as with other religious systems, the referents in the films are multi-layered. Rama-Kandra identifies himself as a "recycler" of programs; thus, he can be viewed as a destroyer, a creator, and a sustainer all by himself. His wife in *Revolutions* is Kamala, whose name means "lotus." She is said to be "very creative," and thus may be viewed as a type for Brahma the creator, who in Hindu myth emerges from a golden lotus that emerges from Vishnu's navel.

The child exile Sati has a name that also resonates with the triad, since the goddess Sati was the consort of Shiva the destroyer. Whereas in Hindu myth she threw herself on Shiva's funeral pyre, in *Revolutions,* Sati is given a creative purpose (to control the sun) and her birth itself is a creative act of love by her program parents. Also, since she is born of Kamala (lotus) and Rama-Kandra (Vishnu), she too can be seen as a type for Brahma. Fittingly, it is this young Indian girl Sati who survives the destruction of the matrix and who plays a crucial role in the dawn of the new matrix.

Taoism

The most fundamental symbol of the flow of the eternal Tao or energy in the universe, the yin-yang, appears on the earrings donned constantly by The Oracle throughout *Revolutions*. This timeless symbol depicts the constant harmonious cycling of yin (female, dark, earthy, passive, and intuitive) and yang (male, bright, heavenly, active, and rational) in all things, and its constant movement is perhaps echoed in the very name *Revolutions*. An expression of the harmony of opposites, the yin-yang is manifest in at least two major relationships in the third film, The Oracle with the Architect, and Neo with Smith.

The Oracle herself seems to construe the Architect as her opposite. While he "balances equations," she "unbalances them." Accordingly, he represents the yang and is male, dressed in white, found in a heaven-like Room, actively engaged and so rational he appears in the guise of Sigmund Freud. She, on the other hand, is the perfect manifestation of yin in both her incarnations: female, black, incarnated inside the gritty matrix (an earth to the Architect's heaven), and the epitome of intuitiveness that brings wisdom.

If the yin-yang is in fact an important structuring device in the third film, the viewer may understand in Taoist terms the significance of The Oracle's explanation to Neo that Smith is his antithesis (*Revolutions*). Accordingly, we see the two of them cycling in a tornadic spiral in the climactic conclusion of the trilogy. The catalyzing moment for Neo occurs when the voice of The Oracle speaks through Agent Smith proclaiming, "Everything that has a beginning has an end." This in fact is a classic statement of Taoism: "things arise and she [the Tao] lets them come; things disappear and she lets them go" (*Tao Te Ching* 2). Thus, Neo sacrifices himself and is "possessed" by Smith, a personal ending that must result in the eventual balancing of the equation: the antithetical Smith may thereby be overcome.[5]

Religious Syncretism

Overall, the various religious traditions we have discussed here—Christianity, Gnosticism, Buddhism, Hinduism and Taoism—find expression in a number of polyvalent symbols in the films. This syncretistic symbolism perhaps finds its zenith in a scene in *Revolutions,* when Neo and Trinity, aboard the *Logos* and on their way to the Machine City, momentarily emerge above the scorched sky and view the sun directly before plunging back into the darkness of the "real world." The ethereal sunlight simultaneously evokes heaven, the pleroma, *nirvana, moksha,* and the unspeakable eternal Tao, not to mention the Platonic Form of the Good (*Republic* VI.507-8, 514-18). Perhaps it is also a symbol for the "Providence" to which Niobe refers in *Revolutions.* In many ways, these multiple "centers" and frameworks of truth may accurately reflect our own global and postmodernist culture (Aho 65-7), allowing the individual viewer to create new meaning with each viewing. Whatever lens each viewer finds to be most relevant, we sense that beyond the "real world" of Zion and Machine City, there is perhaps more.

At the same time, the films never secure the existence of an ultimate realm. Is the "Source" identical with the Deus Ex Machina face that appears in the machine world, or is this simply one manifestation of an ultimate Source from a transcendent realm? The films are not clear on this issue. However, most world religious traditions agree that the ultimate realm cannot be shown visibly; thus ambiguity and seeing for oneself may be precisely where the Wachowski brothers mean to leave the audience.

The Smoking Gun

Unfortunately, the momentary bliss of the sunlit realm, which registers in Trinity's awe-struck face and the rare moment of relative quiet in the soundtrack, is by no means the overriding image of the films. Instead, most viewers likely walk away saturated with images of "guns, lots of guns" (*Matrix*). Indeed, the franchise's piecemeal appropriation from global religious traditions creates a troubling distortion. When the stance that the material realm and our bodies are illusory is unhinged from the context of the traditions from which it is drawn, the very core of the religious traditions may be lost, including the compassion, cessation of suffering and *ahimsa* (non-injury to all living beings) that are central to Buddhism and Hindu traditions, the harmony that is the goal of Taoism, Jesus' ethic of non-violence, and the peaceful bliss of Gnostic enlightenment.

By contrast, the dominating image of the *Matrix* franchise may be evident in a piece of media prominently displayed in the initial flight sequence in the first film. While fleeing the police, Trinity runs past a billboard with a gigantic, literally smoking gun; the ad simply reads "G U N S / ammo." The media image of the "smoking gun" is a metaphorical signpost for the centrality of violence within the film, especially given the Wachowskis's avid interest in Baudrillard and his arguments that media manufacture "reality" in our postmodern age (Baudrillard 76).

The films even seem to suggest that violence is necessary for reaching higher states of reality. Morpheus tells Neo that although they strive to free minds within the matrix, every person still trapped in the matrix is a potential entry point for the Agents. Thus, killing Agents—which results in the deaths of real people in the "real world"—is justifiable and, in a larger sense, redemptive for others.

One scene in *Enter* poignantly reflects the problematic relationship between violence and repose that exists in the *Matrix* franchise. Players can select to complete the game within the persona of Ghost, whom Wong dubs "a gun wielding Zen Buddhist assassin" who "can handle any gun with ease and deadly precision" (Walsh 188-9). At one point in the game, Ghost is found meditating in a Zen garden, where he is disturbed by a stone flung at him by Trinity.

The official guidebook for the game describes the garden as "beautifully landscaped" with "a wooden bridge, rock statues, and even a gong" (Walsh 151). This layout is typical for Zen gardens, which are intended to be areas of quiet meditation on the nature of reality. However, players of *Enter* are advised that these objects are all "breakable." Players are instructed to watch them "crumble to the ground by throwing Trinity through them" (Walsh 150-1). Despite the guide's proclamation that this is a "friendly sparring contest" that is "penalty-free," the juxtaposition of destruction with Zen Buddhist meditation is problematic for viewers unfamiliar with the sanctity of Zen gardens and the peaceful enlightenment that is the goal of Zen Buddhist meditation.

When asked his opinion on the ideal gaming experience, Wong replies that he hopes gamers will "feel like they were actually inside the *Matrix* universe" and then switch off the game, "heart pumping, brow glistening with perspiration" to "return to the real world" convinced that the gaming experience was "a dream." He says, "I don't want to see any Ghost-wannabes walking the streets shooting people and running up walls! It's not nice!" (Walsh 189). However, the name of the game itself, *Enter the Matrix,* encourages gamers to see their own world as a level within the matrix. Thus, some players may have difficulty drawing the line between the "dream" of the game and the world of the gamer, or between the peaceful reality of Zen meditation and the game's association of religious traditions with violence.

In addition, the many religious frameworks incorporated in the films often stand in tension with an overarching apocalyptic view that understands reality as a cosmic war between good and evil, destined to climax in a final violent battle as a prelude to peace (see Juergensmeyer 145-163). In this sense, *Revolutions* is evocative of the biblical book of Revelation, with at least one essential difference: in Revelation, the fundamental problem of evil, as well as its solution, takes place through the activity of divine beings.

The role of the faithful is a pacifistic one, and they are martyrs rather than warriors, who do not themselves engage in battle but who must wait on divine agency in the fight against evil (Revelation 6.9-11, 7.9-14, 13.9-10, 20.4). Historically, there have also been alternate interpretations of Revelation that construe the role of Christians to be physical combatants against identifiable earthly enemies (Juergensmeyer 28), and it is on these violent interpretations that the *Matrix* grounds its worldview. The *Matrix* franchise transforms religious traditions that embrace non-violence and envelops them within a stunningly violent, apocalyptic structure.

This violent translation of world religious traditions within the *Matrix* franchise has serious implications for our own violent culture with which it resonates. Already there have been a troubling number of copycat murderers who, legitimately or not, have cited the films as inspiration for their crimes. Studio executives strenuously deny any link between the films and real acts of violence.[6] However, they appear to have recognized some of the public criticism that might stem from the release of the *Animatrix* "Kid's Story," which ends with a positive portrayal of teenager's suicide in the matrix, since plans to make the segment available on the Warner Brothers' website were abandoned (Robischon 33).

The direct association of violence with religion in the films can result in some troubling simplifications by those interpreting the films. In an article detailing some of the most prominent Hindu elements in the first two films, Julien Fielding argues that "even if the movie audience feels uncomfortable at how quickly and without remorse Trinity and Neo blow away the policemen," this choice must be understood as a product of Hindu ideas about *dharma,* and should not concern us further.

Fielding blithely justifies the violence of the films in Hindu terms, ignoring the foundation of compassion, patience, non-violence, and self-control that are articulated repeatedly in Hindu texts such as the *Manusmriti.* Dharma is, properly understood, fulfilling one's duties to society, which only in the most extreme of circumstances involves violence. The classic articulation of the relationship between *dharma* and violence may be found in the *Bhagavad Gita,* where the god Krishna urges prince Arjuna to kill enemies in a battle.

However, the violence is qualified by Arjuna's responsibility to his caste (*kshatriya* or soldier), by his overwhelming reluctance to harm anybody, by the unfortunate but occasional necessity of violence as a means to justice, and especially by Arjuna's direct access to the god Krishna, who personally sanctions Arjuna's participation in the war. Moreover, there is a history of Hindu interpretation, exemplified best in Gandhi's commentary on the *Gita,* that entirely rejects violence and which interprets the text as a spiritual metaphor for conquering evil within. Clearly, any justification for violence based on precepts in world religious traditions must be approached with extreme sensitivity to the traditions' internal debates and critiques regarding the complexities of violence.

The Matrix Has You

The philosopher Jean Baudrillard's opinions about our media-saturated world provide a hermeneutical key to much of the films' perspectives on violence and religion, a point that is made clear by the copy of his *Simulacra and Simulation* in the first film, and by that fact that the work was required reading for cast members.

According to Baudrillard, our current "era of simulation" is characterized by "a liquidation of all referentials" (Baudrillard 2). That is, reality has become indistinguishable in many ways from the media's construction of reality, such that "the medium is the message."[7] In this sense, the simulation of violence, Baudrillard argues, is "infinitely more dangerous" than actual violence, since simulated violence "always leaves open to supposition that, above and beyond its object, law and order themselves might be nothing but simulation" (Baudrillard 20).

If one plays a game like *Enter,* in which one is drawn into the plot of the movie and the game as an active participant who blows away cops and security guards without consequence, then one might be tempted to see violent acts performed in our world as equally devoid of consequence. The collapse of a clear distinction between the real and the simulated causes confusion "between the sender and the receiver, thus sealing the disappearance of all dual, polar structures that formed the discursive organization of language" (Baudrillard 41).

The result is that discourse is circular, and the entire system is simply an "uninterrupted circuit without reference or circumference" (Baudrillard 6). Baudrillard describes the postmodern awareness of this process as an "anti-Copernican revolution," because it is characterized by "no transcendental instance either of the sun or of the luminous sources of power and knowledge—everything comes from the people and returns to them" (Baudrillard 42). If the franchise indeed inhabits a Baudrillardian universe, there is no transcendent realm, either of truth or of divinity, and the scene where Trinity glimpses the sun is a false sign.[8]

Instead of tolerant syncretism, Baudrillard and the *Matrix* franchise arrive at a relativism in which "all content can be invoked pell-mell," so that "all previous history is resurrected in bulk," and "everything is equivalent and is mixed indiscriminately" (Baudrillard 44). The only possible result is the meaningless multiplication of images and the extinction of difference, so that all world religions are copied indiscriminately onto media just as Smith replicates himself onto whatever unwitting subjects he can find. Smith himself is a simulacra, a copy without an original, and as such he embodies "the abolition of all alterity and of any imaginary" (Baudrillard 97). Any conviction in ultimate reality is dissolved in the circuitous recycling of other competing simulated realities, the proliferation of levels such as the films, the game, the internet site, the advertisements, the billboards, and even our own world that serves as simply another level in the *Matrix* myth.

Even for those who do not read Baudrillard, the blurring of the viewer's reality with the images on-screen is an integral part of the franchise's design. The entire trilogy is a self-referential universe sprinkled with clues that call into question the accuracy of the historical construction of reality initially recounted by Morpheus to Neo in the construct program (*Matrix*). As Morpheus narrates the recent history of humankind and the war with the machines in *The Matrix*, the visual depiction of these events places the viewer within a "Deep Image" brand television. As our point of view passes through the surface of the television screen, the image ripples, indicating that the rendition of reality offered by Morpheus (whose name is the same as that of the Greek god of dreams) is suspect.

In *Reloaded*, the Architect's Room is furnished with multiple television screens, each of which represents a vector of the space-time continuum, thereby deconstructing the viewer's notion of linear time.[9] The viewer's reference point shifts repeatedly along with Neo's, who is successively immersed within multiple television screens, a symbol of manufactured (un)reality.

The orienting image for the viewer's relationship to the franchise might well be found in a scene from *Animatrix* "Second Renaissance, Part II." Troops engaged in cosmic battle against machines kneel devoutly before a religious procession in which a television broadcasts the message of a televangelist. The television itself is encased within an ornate box that evokes the Ark of the Covenant, suggesting in Baudrillardian fashion that media has become religious reality.

Indeed, the matrix *PowerAde* ads support such a reading of the franchise's complex relationship with media. The ads are self-conscious evocations of the "power" of media, "aiding" in the commodification of reality. When the fictional Agent Smith and his look-alikes urge viewers to "Drink More" of a real product that they can buy, the ads at once express the fervent desire of the *Matrix* producers for consumers to consume more, while implying that the consumer's world is part of the larger system of the matrix.

Drawing viewers in and demanding that they acquiesce to consumption, the ads also remind viewers that they are consumed *by* media. Viewers both imbibe "power" and also serve as the power supply for the system of media itself. This idea is impossible to ignore when *PowerAde* ads appear as advertisements within the Mobil Avenue train station in *Revolutions* and are shown before the films in theaters. Such clues indicate that the Wachowskis may be engaging in a complex and deliberately crafted critique of their own production, inviting viewers to be critical of the very system that enables the *Matrix* to exist. Baudrillard acknowledges that "the confusion of the medium and the message is the first great formula of this new era" (30).

Too Much Yang

If one message the Wachowskis intend to send is a critique of media and violence, that message is largely lost in the medium that conveys it, namely, a franchise saturated with violence. As Margaret Miles has argued, "A film cannot use violent images to communicate a different message" (66). Moreover, according to Miles, some films function like religious icons for some people, meaning that some viewers are more inclined to imaginatively identify with a protagonist "by imagining the smells, the tastes, the touch the film character experiences" (188-89).

Although she maintains that this response is not typical, it is more likely when media attempt to collapse the spectatorial distance between viewer and image, as is the case with the *Matrix* franchise. For instance, gamers' egos are immediately drawn into the mythic world of the *Matrix* when the video game invites them to play a pivotal role in the unfolding of the matrix myth by taking on the persona of Niobe or Ghost, characters who appear in the films. In their new identity, gamers actively participate in parallel plot lines that dip and weave into the main story of the films, integrating the gamers' individuated experiences within the larger collective myth. The weapons gamers must employ (eight types of handguns, ten shotguns and rifles, a crossbow, 40mm grenade launcher, poisonous gas launcher, and various explosives) have real-life referents, as do many of the enemies (including security guards, police officers, police SWAT, SWAT sniper, military SWAT, armored military SWAT) whom gamers attack and kill in ways specific to the weaknesses each possesses (Walsh 7-10 and 24-25).

Even if one never "enters" the video game, the films themselves blur the distinction between the viewers and the matrix myth, by the product placement of real consumer goods (*PowerAde*) within the Mobil Avenue station, by depicting the contemporary world of the late 1990s and early 2000s as the setting of the matrix, and by drawing on motifs from real religious traditions and interweaving them into a new syncretistic myth.

This blurring of universes calls for a careful and critical evaluation of the *Matrix* franchise. Overall, there is simply too much yang. The film trilogy ends with obvious evocation of the yin-yang, symbol of universal harmony of opposites, worn by The Oracle in the closing scenes. Yet instead of offering balance between yin (passivity, femaleness, darkness) and yang (activity, maleness, brightness), the franchise is heavily weighted toward yang. On the whole there is an excess of violence, maleness, and whiteness.

In fact, the Wachowski brothers have revolutionized the onscreen depiction of violence. They demanded "Bullet Time" of their special effects producers before such a technique was even possible (Silberman 120). Convinced that a 360-degree view of kung fu action was necessary, they insisted that the technology be developed for the first film that would enable viewers to watch Neo smash his foot into the face of an opponent from all angles, as the camera seemingly pivots around the scene. In *Reloaded*, this technology was advanced to include CGI (Computer Graphics Imagery) and "virtual cinematography," since scenes like the Burly Brawl (in which Neo fights hundreds of Agent Smiths) are physically impossible to capture, even with multiple cameras (Silberman 120-121). Obsessed with producing more violence from more angles with more and better technology, the Wachowskis enact the advice of one of the Agents who, in one of the *PowerAde* ads, simply utters, "More!" The fourteen-minute-long car chase scene in *Reloaded,* and the proliferation of Smiths in the Burly Brawl, are both instances of the Wachowski brothers' dedication to more crashes, more fights, and more explosions, lasting for longer amounts of time.

The imbalance in favor of yang is also evident in the maleness and whiteness that ultimately serve as the default gender and ethnicity in the films (see King and Leonard, in this volume). Certainly, the Wachowskis appear to recognize the heavy weighting of yang in the first film in these respects by including more female characters in the subsequent films as well as numerous actors of various visible ethnicities. Even the first film includes more diversity than many Hollywood films of a similar genre. Nevertheless, just as it is problematic to subsume a pastiche of world religious traditions under the framework of violent, apocalyptic Christianity, it is similarly troubling when a multicultural and gender inclusive universe is repeatedly portrayed as pinning its hope for salvation on one white male. Although actor Keanu Reeves has a multicultural ethnic background, he reads onscreen as white to most viewers.

As the "Source" of the *Matrix* franchise, the Wachowskis craft a mythic, postmodern universe with multiple religious frameworks, ethnicities, gender constructions, and interpretive possibilities. It is no surprise that so many viewers are taken with this richly textured endeavor, which in so many ways resonates with our own complex, global cultures. The brothers may even intend a convoluted Baudrillardian critique of media and violence.

Nonetheless, the very medium of film problematizes the relationship between the illusion of image and the real world, such that film can easily perform a religious function, presenting what John Lyden calls "an alternate reality in which we participate during the viewing experience," and which "offer[s] ritualized experiences with religious power for the viewer" (Lyden 4). The Wachowskis' association of violence with selective motifs and structures from actual world religious traditions implicitly legitimizes the violence within the *Matrix* universe, which in various ways intertwines with our own. As viewers, then, we must engage in a conscious critique of the substance of the media that we consume and reclaim the non-violent core of these religious traditions, if we are interested in stopping bullets.

Notes

1. Articles on the series consistently cite the works of science-fiction writer Philip K. Dick as a seminal influence on the Wachowski brothers. Dick's many works (see Works Cited) often explore the theme of robot consciousness and the problems of trusting our memories.

2. For an examination of Gnosticism and Buddhism in the first *Matrix* film, see our article entitled "Wake Up! Gnosticism and Buddhism in *The Matrix*" at the Warner Brothers' Official Matrix Website, <http://www.whatisthematrix.warnerbros.com/> or in The Journal of Religion and Film 5:2 (October 2001), University of Nebraska at Omaha, 15 December 2003 <http://www.unomaha.edu/~wwwjrf>. Donna Bowman has also written a compelling treatment of anti-Gnostic Pauline theology in the second film. See also Fielding for its initial treatment of Hinduism in the films, and Ford.

3. *Gospel of Thomas* 1, 3, 7, 11, 24, 29, 47, 56, 112, 113. Fielding asserts that the lens of Gnosticism is problematic since we never literally see Neo imparting knowledge to those within the matrix. However, this view is unnecessarily literal in a trilogy that layers metaphor upon metaphor. At the end of the first film Neo clearly asserts his intention to free those in the matrix by freeing their minds. Moreover, the "Kid" in the *Animatrix* short "Kid's Story" credits Neo with his realization that the matrix life is illusory, repeatedly declaring, "You saved me Neo," as he likewise declares in *Reloaded* and *Revolutions*. Since *gnosis* (knowledge) involves self-realization, Neo replies, "You saved yourself," echoing *Gospel of Thomas* 3: "If you know yourselves, then you will be known, and you will know that you are sons of the living Father." See Pagels 2003.

4. As the "mother of the matrix," The Oracle may control the course of events even more than it seems. Each time we see her in her home, she is baking cookies. "Cookies" are small programs that remember one's identity, thus they may serve to remind characters in the film of important information, and may even direct their choices accordingly. Astute viewers will pay close attention to all substances ingested in the films, since every item within the matrix is a program in and of itself, with discrete functions. Thus, when The Oracle teaches Sati to bake cookies, this is more than a domestic scene—she may in fact be training Sati as a programmer and a creator.

5. Moreover, if there is a constant cycling of yin-yang opposites, both Neo and his "antithesis" Smith will arise again. Since Neo vanquishes Smith in essentially the same manner as in the first film (by infusing him with exploding light), Smith's subsequent demise at the end of *Revolutions* should similarly prove to be temporary. Hence, as the trilogy concludes we see The Oracle and Architect—one layer of the yin-yang—discussing the temporary peace and suggesting that Neo will be back. The suggestion seems to be then, that Smith too, in one form or another, will eventually return as some part of a cycle, or a *revolution*.

6. In February 2003, Josh Cooke, who frequently dressed like Neo, gunned down his parents in the basement of their Virginia home. In April 2000, Vadim Mieseges, a college student, dismembered his landlord. In July of the same year, Tonda Lynn Ansley, of Ohio, murdered her professor. All claimed to be imprisoned in the matrix, and saw their violent acts as justifiable for that reason. Lee Boyd Malvo, the teenager convicted in the Washington sniper attacks, scribbled notes from his jail cell about being stuck in the matrix. Eric Harris and Dylan Klebold, the teenagers responsible for the Columbine shootings, are also big fans

of the films, and committed their murders twenty days after the release of the initial film in 1999. When interviewed by the *Washington Post* earlier this year, the studio denied any causal connection, claiming adamantly that "any attempt to link these crimes with a motion picture or any other art form is disturbing and irresponsible." See Jackman.

7. Cultural critic Marshall McLuhan (1911-1980) coined this famous phrase, which is actually a misquotation of the title of one of his books, *The Medium is the Massage.* McLuhan's punned title suggests that the "message" is lost in the "mass-age."

8. Indeed, in the films, "seeing" is not literal. In *Revolutions,* Neo is blinded like the seers Tiresias and Orpheus of Greek tradition, and, like them, he is able to see with his mind. Yet true prophecy does not entail foretelling the future. Although Smith believes he has the "eyes of The Oracle," it is Neo, although blinded, who ironically has the true "eyes of The Oracle," since he can perceive the underlying structure of reality both within the matrix and outside of it.

9. Another troubling aspect of the incorporation of our world as a level within the matrix is the wholesale integration of traumatic events from our history into the myth, such as the recasting of the war with the machines in terms of the Holocaust in *Animatrix* "Second Renaissance, Part II."

Works Cited

Aho, James. "The Apocalypse of Modernity." *Millennium, Messiahs, and Mayhem: Contemporary Apocalyptic Movements.* Ed. Thomas Robbins and Susan Palmer. New York: Routledge, 1997: 61-72.

Baudrillard, Jean. *Simulacra and Simulation.* Trans. Sheila Faria Glaser. Ann Arbor: University of Michigan Press, 1994.

Bowman, Donna. "The Gnostic Illusion: Problematic Realized Eschatology in *The Matrix Reloaded.*" *Journal of Religion and Popular Culture* IV (Summer 2003). University of Saskatchewan, <http://www.unomaha.edu/~wwwjrf>. Accessed 15 December 2003.

Cartlidge, David, and David Dungan, eds. "Acts of the Holy Apostle Thomas." *Documents for the Study of the Gospels.* Minneapolis: Fortress, 1994: 30-48.

Dick, Philip. K. *Do Androids Dream of Electric Sheep?* New York: Del Rey-Balantine, 1968.

———. *The Simulacra.* New York: Ace, 1964.

———. *The Three Stigmata of Palmer Eldritch.* New York: Doubleday, 1965.

———. *Valis.* New York: Bantam, 1981.

———. *Divine Invasion.* New York: Simon and Schuster, 1981.

———. *The Transmigration of Timothy Archer.* New York: Simon and Schuster, 1982.

Fielding, Julien. "Reassessing *The Matrix/Reloaded.*" *The Journal of Religion and Film* 7:2 (October 2003). University of Nebraska at Omaha. <http://www.unomaha.edu/~wwwjrf>. Accessed 15 December 2003.

Ford, James. "Buddhism, Christianity, and *The Matrix:* The Dialectic of Myth-Making in Contemporary Cinema." *Journal of Religion and Film* 4:2 (October 2000), University of Nebraska at Omaha, <http://www.unomaha.edu/wwwjrf.> Accessed 15 December 2003.

Gibbons, Dave. "Butterfly." Digital Comic. Warner Bros. <http://www.whatisthematrix.warnerbros.com>. Accessed 13 December 2003

Gopnik, Adam. "The Unreal Thing: What's Wrong with the Matrix?" *The New Yorker* (19 May 2003): 68-73.

Jackman, Tom. "Escape the Matrix: Go Directly to Jail." *The Washington Post* (May 17, 2003): A01.

Juergensmeyer, Mark. *Terror in the Mind of God: The Global Rise of Religious Violence.* Berkeley: University of California Press, 2000.

Lyden, John C. *Film as Religion: Myths, Morals, and Rituals.* New York and London: New York University Press, 2003.

McLuhan, Marshall, and Quentin Fiore. *The Medium Is the Message.* New York: Random House, 1967.

Miles, Margaret R. *Seeing and Believing: Religion and Values in the Movies.* Boston: Beacon, 1996.

Mitchell, Stephen, trans. *The Tao Te Ching: A New English Version.* New York: First Perennial Classics, 2000.

Pagels, Elaine. *The Gnostic Gospels.* New York: Vintage, 1979.

———. *Beyond Belief: The Gnostic Gospel of Thomas.* New York: Random House, 2003.

Robinson, James, ed. "The Gospel of Thomas," "The Apocryphon of John." *The Nag Hammadi Library.* San Francisco: HarperSanFrancisco, 1990: 104-138.

Robischon, Noah. "The Fast Picture Shows." *Entertainment Weekly* 705 (18 April 2003): 32-33.

Silberman, Steve. "Matrix2." *Wired* (May 2003): 113-121.

"Wachowski Chat." Online Chat Session with Andy and Larry Wachowski. "Matrix Virtual Theatre." 9 November 1999. <http://www.whatisthematrix.com>. Accessed 15 December 2003.

Walsh, Doug. *Enter the Matrix: Official Strategy Guide.* New York: Pearson Education, 2003.

7

The Déjà Vu Glitch in the *Matrix* Trilogy

MICHAEL SEXSON

These our actors,
As I foretold you, were all spirits, and
Are melted into air, into thin air——

—William Shakespeare, *The Tempest*, Act 4: Sc.1 148-150

Recently, while teaching the first day of an introductory course in literature, I used the term "déjà vu.""Does anyone know what this phrase means?" I asked, with the kind of condescension that comes with decades of teaching freshmen. A student in the front row, with confidence and a twinkle, replied, "Yes. It's a glitch in the matrix." There was a ripple of laughter.

I paused and said, "Yes. And can you tell us how you know this?""Of course," my front-row student said. He then proceeded to recount how, in the first of the *Matrix* films, Neo is walking into a building and notices a black cat stroll by. A moment later he looks back and sees what he assumes is the same cat repeat precisely the movements of the previously seen cat. He announces to the others who have descended into the world of the matrix that he has had a "déjà vu" experience. Seriously worried, Trinity explains to Neo that a déjà vu episode typically means that there is a "glitch" in the matrix. "It happens," she says, "when they change something."

I let this definition of "déjà vu"—"a glitch in the matrix"—stand. I could have imposed my own understanding of the term, but at this moment, with such an unexpected remark from a student, the class was moving in a more interesting direction than the more conventionally academic one I intended to map, and, more, the students were all optimally attentive.

"What," I asked, "is a glitch, and who is the 'they' that Trinity is referring to, and (portentously) what, after all, is the matrix?" They explained with the good-natured patience of persons talking about red and blue to the color blind that the matrix is a computer-simulated world; that the "they" is a race of machines who created the matrix and were fueled in part by the energies of human bodies kept in vats; and that the "glitch" is a readjustment or almost undetectable rebooting of the computer program.

Noting my slight lack of comprehension, one woman said, "It's like when you shut off your VCR and then you turn it on again and it starts up a few frames before when you turned it off so you can better remember where you were." "Why is this a glitch?" I asked. "Well, with the VCR it's not, but with the matrix, it means that people who are taken in by the computer simulation might wake up to the fact that it's all an illusion."

"And what happens when one wakes up to the realization that all this (wide sweeping gesture) is all an illusion?" First-row student chomps at the bit: "You go tumbling down the rabbit hole and find yourself in the desert of the real."

"Nice phrase. Yours?"

"No. Morpheus says it when he shows Neo that the real world is a wasteland that came about after a war between the humans and the machines."

"What about the reference to a rabbit hole?"

"Morpheus offers Neo a blue pill and a red pill. If he takes the blue pill he stays in the matrix and thinks no more about it; but if he takes the red pill, he finds out how far the rabbit hole goes. Morpheus is referring to *Alice in Wonderland*. He even says to Neo that he must feel a little bit like Alice."

"Thereby discovering the world beyond illlusion?"

"Yes, reality."

"And one gets to this reality because an imperfection, or 'glitch' in the design and operation of what one had heretofore thought to be real makes one think that something is wrong?"

"Yes, a splinter in the mind. Morpheus says that Neo is talking to him because all his life Neo has felt that something was wrong with the world but he doesn't know exactly what it is. It's like a splinter in the mind."

"And so?"

"So Neo has to learn that he is the messiah who will lead people out of their dreamworld into reality."

"And reality is … ?"

"Zion, a city at the center of the earth populated by awakened people and threatened by attacking machines."

"This is preferable to living obliviously in the matrix?"

Noisy debate.

STUDENT A: "It's supposed to be but frankly, I think life on the space ship pretty boring, and the food is described as snot."

STUDENT B: "Reality is always preferable to illusion even if it isn't pretty."

STUDENT C: "I'm with Cypher in the first movie. He made a deal with the agent to betray the others because a steak tastes better than snot even if it's a computer simulation. All he wanted was to forget that he had ever left the matrix in the first place."

STUDENT D: "Then you and Cypher deserve each other. You're both believers that ignorance is bliss. Ignorance isn't bliss, it's oblivion."

TEACHER: "Clearly the film has been provocative for everyone. In our discussion we raised questions of remembrance and forgetting, of mind splinters that urge us to question what we see and think and feel; of glitches in the illusion-making mechanism that exposes it as unreal; of whether 'real' reality is preferable to simulated reality. This is a good prologue for discussing the nature and meaning of literature, but before we leave the *Matrix* trilogy, let me ask what seems to be a very simple question, but will likely be the most complicated one we've addressed so far."

Captive Audience.

TO REPEAT: "What *is* the matrix?"

FIRST-ROW STUDENT: "To repeat: It is a computer simulated world created by machines who want to enslave humans."

STUDENT HITHERTO SILENT: "*The Matrix* is a movie."

Silencio.

FIRST STUDENT: "That's what I call taking something literally."

TEACHER: "By literally I assume you mean taking it at face value, a term, which by the way, is figurative. Like saying you should let the facts speak for themselves. In other words, being literal is one of the ways we have of acting figuratively. But there are occasions when it is instructive to act as if things were literal, as in saying, it's a movie. Notice she didn't say 'it's only a movie,' or 'it's just a movie,' minimizing its imaginative value. What's at stake when we say *The Matrix* is a movie rather than a simulated world created by malevolent machines?"

STUDENT WITH HAT: "It means the matrix is a simulated world created by malevolent machines otherwise known as Hollywood interested in making obscene amounts of money by keeping people sitting in chairs watching unreal images on a screen."

HITHERTO SILENT: "That's ironic."

TEACHER: "Irony is a rhetorical term, a term of figuration, at the other end of the continuum of the literal. What's ironic?"

HITHERTO: "That a movie whose message is we should wake up from a dream world created by machines is itself a machine that creates a dream world that keeps us in the dark."

FIRST-ROW STUDENT: "I don't think so. After seeing the sequels, which complicates things a lot, especially about the relationship of humans and machines, I rather think that the whole trilogy wants us to develop our intelligence about what illusion is."

TEACHER: "You mean to say that the filmmakers, who may or may not be malevolent, but who are clearly in charge of the machinery that generates the illusions we call the *Matrix* trilogy, are concerned that the audience recognize the irony of their situation and engage the contradictions and complications with a deeper and more refined sophistication."

FIRST-ROW STUDENT: "Well put."

TEACHER: "Thank you. Is it now possible to sum up what we've been saying so far? May I suggest we go back to the beginning and remember what was said about glitches and déjà vu? When we watch a movie—the *Matrix* trilogy or any other movie—we might have a déjà vu experience, a sense that we've been there, done that, seen this already. This might be seen as 'glitch' in the system because it alerts us to the fact that what we are watching is literally untrue—a series of celluloid frames or digital reproductions which are variations on typical themes and issues.

"The more familiar we are with these themes and how they operate in a variety of imaginative contexts, the more sophisticated we then become with respect to the nature and meaning of illusion. We come to understand that while watching the film, we have suspended our disbelief and have come to regard Neo, Trinity, Morpheus, and the whole crew as characters assembled from reality.

> "Once we leave the theater, however, and, most importantly, once we increase our sophistication with regard to the ways in which illusions are generated and employed, we come to see that these people are merely actors, who, after the film is over, vanish into thin air. They are, we come to see, cinematic conventions, and our recognition of them as such is tantamount to a enormous shift in how we relate to the world, or to speak metaphorically, it is a like waking up from a long sleep or confusing dream. The next difficult step perhaps is to see ourselves as also cinematic conventions, or to shift the metaphor, computer programs, or 'software.' But we're not there yet."

Now you might think it is not just simple but positively simpleminded to point out that *The Matrix, Reloaded,* and *Revolutions* are movies. If so, it's a simplemindedness that most of us share. The artist René Magritte once created a "realistic" (Vladimir Nabokov once said that he was waiting for the time when he could write the word "reality" without the quotation marks it wears like claws) painting of a smoker's pipe and underneath it wrote the words "This is not a pipe." Most of us, when asked what we saw when we viewed the Magritte painting, would say, "It is a pipe." Magritte's text beneath the painting, however, reminds us that of course this is not a pipe but simply (simply!) the representation of a pipe. A simulacrum.

I once drew on the blackboard a series of geometric shapes—a square, circle, triangle, etc.—then asked the class to describe what they perceived. All but one in the class wrote something like: "I see a square, a circle, a triangle. . . ." But one clever student simply (simply!) reproduced the figures she saw on the blackboard. She didn't write about the pictures; she re-presented them. Much like our clever student who said *The Matrix* is a movie.

Again, we need to ask, Why is this important? Don't we all know that the pipe is not a pipe, the word is not the thing? Well, yes, we know it, but we don't *know* it. The cinematic convention named Morpheus says, and the line is endlessly quoted, "Unfortunately, no one can be told what the matrix is. You have to see it for yourself." There is a great difference between conceptual understanding and the shock of existential experience. Between saying, "of course it's not a pipe," and realizing, to quote The Oracle in the first film, "from balls to bone," that we've lived our whole lives thinking unreal things were real.

One of the great virtues of the *Matrix* trilogy is that, no matter what we may think of it as a work of art, it brings richly to mind countless other imaginative investigations into the relationship between reality and illusion. It not only reminds us, it *re-minds* us. The film is not just suggestive, it is, to use Freud's term, powerfully *overdetermined*, alerting us not only to what the filmmakers intended, but of what they were unconscious. To take a single example, early in *The Matrix*, Morpheus explains to Neo that the red pill is part of a trace program that will permit pinpointing his location within the matrix. Neo asks, "What does that mean?" Cypher, the betrayer, responds: "It means buckle your seat belt, Dorothy, 'cause Kansas is going bye-bye."

No one is going to have trouble recognizing Cypher's reformulation of a famous line from *The Wizard of Oz*, but only a handful are going to catch the reference to the film *All about Eve*. In that movie, Bette Davis famously says: "Fasten your seatbelts, it's going to be a bumpy night!"

Now it may be that the Wachowski brothers when they wrote that line for Cypher did not consciously intend the reference, but in the masterfully overdetermined world they have created, it doesn't matter. It works. *All About Eve* is a movie about the most infamous of dream-making machines— Broadway. Its ironic genius is in showing how the actors, directors, and writers of movies are peculiarly suspectible to being duped by people who understand better than they how illusions can be manipulated for their own malevolent ends.

This possibly unintended reference to *All About Eve* then opens a Pandora's box of associations with movies about movies, a box with examples which may shed more light (even better, deeply resonating darknesses) on the Matrix trilogy than the list of usual suspects (a term which in itself is worth a mini-essay on filmic referencing).

The usual suspects among films would include (to mention merely recent and well-known examples) *The Truman Show, eXistenZ, Dark City, Total Recall, The Thirteenth Floor, Solaris, Waking Life, Vanilla Sky*, and others. These films are demonstrably similar in theme and have been discussed often brilliantly, but perhaps to exhaustion, on various websites and books concerned with the Matrix series. I would like to suggest a film which to my knowledge has never been mentioned in the same breath with the *Matrix* series, and has probably been seen by few of the trilogy's fans: *Last Year at Marienbad*.

Made in 1961 by two enigmatic Frenchmen, Alain Resnais and Alain Robbe-Grillet, *Last Year at Marienbad* is the movie most people mention when they discuss the incomprehensibility of art films. Black and white, severely formal, repetitive and monotonous, it is about a man at an aristocratic resort who tries to convince a woman that they had met the previous year there and planned to run away together the following year. The woman seems not to remember the previous liaison and most of the film consists of the man's persistence in awakening the woman to recollection of the decision.

For decades the film has been either praised or dismissed as a formal cinematic meditation on the themes of time and memory. Then, recently, an English professor named Thomas Beltzer published an online essay on the film which helps to clear up its obscurity (sensesofcinema.com/contents/00/10/marienbad.html). The essay recounts how Beltzer discovered, after reading the dust jacket of a novel by the Argentinian writer Aldofo Bioy Casares, that the film was based on Casares's novella, *The Invention of Morel*. In the novella, a fugitive escapes to an island where he sees people strolling about, dancing, and carrying on like vacationers at a resort like Marienbad. He discovers that the people are actually holographic representations, created by a diabolical machine that converts flesh-and-blood people to mere filmic representations.

What Beltzer suggested was that the people in *Last Year at Marienbad* are *literally* film creatures, bloodless, bodiless, who have their existence in the play of light and shade. Caught in a seemingly endless loop of repetitious dialogue and action within an architectural encasement that can best be described as an elaborate matrix, these beings are unaware of the immateriality of their own existence and of the world about them.

Partially awakened to this horrifying truth, one man seeks to leave the matrix and take with him a woman steeped in forgetfulness and oblivious to her dream-like state. He seeks to re-mind her of the past, of a universe beyond these illusory walls and corridors, this world of simulation and simulacra.

What makes this film (and the novella on which it is based) more relevant to a discussion of the *Matrix* trilogy than the usual suspects is in the use of a similar cinematic metaphor. The world of illusion in which we find ourselves is like that of a film. Films are composed of frames of images and actions which, when run through a machine at a certain speed, create the illusion of actuality. Engrossed in this deception, the spectator forgets that it is a film and comes to accept it as reality. Occasionally, however, something goes wrong with the machinery—the image is blurry and needs adjustment, or, in the good old days, the film in the projector breaks or burns—and the viewer is jolted out of a satisfying stupor.

The principal metaphor in *The Matrix* is that "reality" is actually a film generated by machines and watched by people in dark places. It is interesting to note here that the chief suspect among the usuals as far as the philosophy and literature is concerned is Plato's *Allegory of the Cave (RepublicVII)*. Plato's depiction of a group of prisoners chained together watching shadows flicker on the wall of a cave is eerily prophetic. Had the technology of the cinema been available in Plato's time, he would most surely have used it as the basis for his famous allegory.

Now we come back to where we began—with a discussion of déjà vu as a "glitch" in the matrix.

However sophisticated the inventor of the matrix is, he doesn't seem to have freed it from glitches that would seem unlikely and unforgiveable in a world of sophisticated computer programming. Apparently, when Agents get word that the rebels have entered the matrix, the keepers of the machinery need to alter the simulation, or as Trinity says, "change something."

This adjustment evidently involves the repetition of a single frame, such as a black cat walking by. Someone witnessing the repetition will likely dismiss it as *mere* déjà vu, something already seen. Someone, however, who already is suspicious that something is wrong—*ontologically* wrong—with the world of experience—someone, that is, with a "splinter in the mind," is already primed to see this as an exposé of the system, a glitch that exposes the illusion-making machinery and possibly its maker, the "man behind the curtain," or, as we discover in *Reloaded*, the "Architect."

The widest and deepest sense of déjà vu, however, then involves the notion that this machine entails exposure to nothing less than the entire history of representations of reality, along with the mind-boggling complications and contradictions which attend such a history. A full-blown déjà vu experience amounts to a baptism in significant forms of repetition. Would not another satisfactory metaphor for such an experience be "matrix"?

Plato's name for this was *anamnesis*, complete and full recollection of the primal forms, an experience which he says (speaking metaphorically of course) is akin to having regrown wings so that one can fly (*Phaedrus*, 57). Perhaps like Neo?

If it is valuable to think of the *Matrix* trilogy as a cinematic experience capable of helping us to engage the issue of reality and illusion on a sophisticated level, then we are going to have to put into the background a lot of concerns that people have over these movies, such as whether it is possible for a computer simulation to replicate both the individual and collective memories of humans, or whether the human body really generates enough energy to be worthwhile harvesting. Questions such as these arise when we forget that the movie is a movie, an elaborate set of metaphors and images which are not the things they stand for.

In *The Matrix*, Neo, on his way to see The Oracle, finds himself in a waiting room filled with people who possess special psychic gifts. Among them is a young boy, head shaved in the Buddhist fashion, who is occupying himself with the telekinetic exercise of spoon bending.

THE CHILD SPEAKS: "Do not try and bend the spoon. That's impossible. Instead only try to realize the truth."
NEO: "What truth?"
SPOON BOY: "There is no spoon."
NEO: "There is no spoon?"
SPOON BOY: "Then you'll see that it is not the spoon that bends, it is only yourself."

A quick study in telekinesis, Neo bends the spoon easily. Later in the film, while rushing into the matrix, he repeats the phrase as if it is a mnemonic or mantra.

In *Reloaded,* Neo is accosted by a minor character who alerts him to the fact that he has forgotten something important. It is the spoon from the first film. It is almost as if the filmmakers are saying that in all the perverse complications of the sequel, the one significant thing to remember is the spoon.

The spoon episode is far more than a lesson in Buddhism, as several commentators have tried to make it. It is, I suspect, the cornerstone of the movie. To understand that there is no spoon is to understand with Magritte that there is no pipe.

There is *in fact* no Neo or Morpheus or Trinity or Agent Smith. These are all actors, and at the film's end, vanish into thin air, until we see them the next time, repeating lines and gestures as only filmic beings can do enabling us to see them against a broader and deeper background of other fictions who help us to enhance our understanding of how imagination works. That is to say, who enable us to wake up. I think we're there now.

There is no matrix. It is all real.

TEACHER: "The assignment for the next class is to read the first act of Shakespeare's *Tempest*. Be prepared to deal with the question, 'Why is the title of this play by Shakespeare ironic?'"
HITHERTO SILENT STUDENT: "I think I know why already."

"Why?"

"Because there is no tempest."

"As the Oracle said to Neo in *The Matrix:* 'Bingo!'"

Works Cited

Beltzer, Thomas. *LastYear at Marienbad: An Intertextual Meditation.* October 2000. Online. <sensesofcinema.com/contents/00/10/marienbad.html>. Accessed 18 December 2003.

Plato. "The Allegory of the Cave." *The Republic.* Trans. Benjamin Jowett. NewYork: Modern Library Classics, 2001; book VII.

———. *Phaedrus* and *LettersVII andVIII.* Trans. Walter Hamilton. NewYork: Penguin, 1973.

Shakespeare, William. *The Tempest.* Ed. Stephen Orgel. New York: Oxford University Press, 1987.

Film

All quotations from *The Matrix* come from the online screenplay of the film found at <ds2.pg.gda.pl/~colan/screenplay.htm>.

8

Visions of Hope, Freedom of Choice, and the Alleviation of Social Misery: A Pragmatic Reading of the *Matrix* Franchise

STEPHANIE J. WILHELM AND MATTHEW KAPELL

When we first saw *The Matrix* in 1999, it became apparent that this was not just another Hollywood movie packed with dazzling special effects, a beautiful woman in tight vinyl, and a few waxing philosophical dialogues to fill in the gaps between action sequences. No, there seemed to be something familiar in the brooding scowl of Morpheus, the determination of Trinity, and even in the skepticism displayed by Cypher.

What was it about the movie and its subsequent units that moved millions to see them over and over again? In our essay we posit that the popularity of the franchise, and even more importantly, our need as fans, scholars, and movie critics to pick apart its meaning, is due to the fact that the Wachowski brothers have not only represented the core fears of Western civilization's past and present, but also our hopes for a better future.

From a classical era that focused almost exclusively on myth, religion, and tradition, to the notions of progress that came with the Renaissance, the Enlightenment, and the Industrial Revolutions of the modern era, humanity has been consumed with striking a balance between the control and release of power. Our obsession with having power over machinery, over our governments, but most of all, over ourselves, has pushed us past the ages of reason and discovery and back again. Through that balance of power all of our greatest fears and hopes seem to have been answered. The convenient way of life produced by modernity, i.e., electricity, weaponry, assembly lines, has also produced the massive destruction of two world wars and the proliferation of nuclear devices.

It seems then that the Wachowski brothers created the *Matrix* franchise as an example of our world, one that has, as Morpheus describes in *The Matrix,* "marveled at its own intelligence" while ignoring its failings. It is because the *Matrix* franchise offers this familiar vision that scholars are consumed with understanding intellectual and philosophical underpinnings of the films, hoping that by applying the "right" terms, the "right" schools of thought, we can better understand our own world, our own matrix.

Conceptualizing History and Interpreting the Franchise

Most previous interpretations of the franchise have been undertaken by dividing the Western history of humanity (and its representations in the films) into three distinct eras, that of a mythological distant past, a recent "modern" past, and a postmodern present. These groupings are wholly arbitrary and suggest that there is a series of "sharp breaks" from one era to the next. This is not actually the case. As the American intellectual historian Richard Tarnas notes in *The Passion of the Western Mind* when he divided the history of Western thought into similar groups, "any division of history into 'eras' or 'world views' cannot in itself do justice to the actual complexity and diversity of Western thought."

In delineating the three distinct eras of western thought we follow Tarnas's model. But, where he calls them "classical," "medieval," and "modern," we term them:

1. The classical era (the age of myth, traditional societies, prior to the emergence of science: roughly from the beginning of recorded history until the fourteenth century in Europe).
2. The modern era or modernism (from the beginning of the Renaissance in the fourteenth century through the Enlightenment in the eighteenth century and developing further until about 1970).[1]
3. The postmodern era (sometime recently, characterized by the rejection of modernism and the idea that "reason" and "science" can explain everything).

If we accept these groupings, as most previous critical interpretations of the franchise imply they have, then determining which era of intellectual thought the *Matrix* franchise relies upon for its meaning is largely an exercise in applying a working definition of the terms to the franchise. It is important to note, however, that we believe it is impossible to label the *Matrix* franchise as belonging to only *one* specific school of thought, like "modern" or "postmodern." It is our contention that to understand all the subtle nuances of the franchise, one must consider them through the lens of pragmatism, a perspective that incorporates all the positive attributes of past worldviews and offers what William James calls "a method of settling metaphysical disputes that otherwise might be interminable" (1997, orig. 1907).

To settle our own "metaphysical disputes" over the meanings and interpretations of the *Matrix* franchise, we will first apply what we see as the most positive attributes from each of the three distinct eras of Western thought to the films, beginning with the classical age and ending with postmodernism. By doing this we hope to show that by using a pragmatic perspective, many of the difficult-to-answer questions about the *Matrix* franchise suddenly seem more understandable. Instead of questioning the meaning of "truth" and "reality" (questions and concepts that are both difficult to comprehend and central to many readings of the franchise), pragmatism concerns itself with issues of social hope, increased freedom, and choice (issues that have come to be understood and embraced by all of Western civilization).

In The Beginning, It Was Good

The mythological underpinnings of the *Matrix* franchise are both obvious and extensive. While the Christian aspects of the film seem the most noticeable, we think that the entire corpus of human mythology is, in one way or another, presented or implied in the *Matrix* franchise. As many of the contributors to this volume note, the *Matrix* franchise intentionally incorporates previous mythological structures in ways that resonate with viewers. We believe that the Wachowski brothers do this because they agree with William G. Doty, the co-editor of this volume, that myths remain "devices to reenergize cultures, even those as apparently blasé as our own" (Doty 68).

It is impossible simply to state that one group within the franchise represents one type of thought (the humans as "classical," and the machines as "modern," for example). Instead, the *Matrix* franchise represents all of the eras of Western thought through each perspective it brings to the foreground.

The most obvious reading of the film would paint the machine intelligences as strictly modernist, yet this is not entirely the case.

In *Reloaded,* the Architect explains the age of the matrix by telling Neo, "I prefer counting from the emergence of one integral anomaly to the emergence of the next." The Architect tells Neo that he is not the first "One," he is the sixth. This is indeed a strange way of considering time, especially for a machine. It is not based on a constant "unit" like a second or day or year, as is the modernist conceit. It is based on the return of "The One" to "The Source" and thus the Architect seems to divide time by what the noted scholar of myth, Mircea Eliade, calls, "rituals that govern renewal" (Eliade, *Eternal Return* 51). In short, the Architect and "father" of the matrix does not, himself, use a "mechanistic" and modernist conception of time, he uses a mythological one!

Such a concept of time, Henri and H. A. Frankfort suggest, is "qualitative and concrete, not quantitative and abstract. It does not know time as a uniform duration or as a succession of qualitative indifferent moments" (Frankfort and Frankfort 23). In other words, for the Architect it does not seem to matter if the period between the second and third "One" was twenty years or two thousand; it is the period between "renewal" that is important, not the number of years.

This mythical underpinning is expanded in *Reloaded* when the Architect tells Neo he is to "select from the matrix twenty-three individuals, sixteen female, seven male, to rebuild Zion." Eliade might be writing about this aspect of the films when he says that this understanding of mythic time is one in which "a new regenerated humanity is born, usually from a mythical 'ancestor' who escaped the catastrophe" (Eliade, *Eternal Return* 87).

Such a mythological manner of thinking about time clearly suggests that the Wachowski brothers are not attempting to show the *Matrix* films as being purely modern or postmodern, especially when we look at the most "classical" of characters, Morpheus. His position in the series seems to be one who lives not by "reason" but by "faith." His professions of faith, based on what was said to him by another mythological figure, The Oracle, are based on what Cornel West calls a "tradition [that] may serve as a stimulus rather than a stumbling block" (*The American Evasion of Philosophy* 230). Morpheus's belief that Neo is "The One" in *The Matrix,* and that one man can fight for all of humanity in *Revolutions,* embraces religious tradition while rejecting humankind's complete dependency for survival on reason, science, and technology.

The Logical Culmination of Progress

The representation of modernism and its progress in the *Matrix* franchise can most readily be seen, ironically, in "The Second Renaissance Parts I and II" of *Animatrix*. Just going by the title, one might think that this Second Renaissance was much like the first historical Renaissance, and that this sequence was depicting yet another rebirth of human civilization. We find, however, that this is not the case. This is not a sequence showing a *re*birth, but rather *the* birth of the machine civilization.

In "Second Renaissance" the machine intelligences are the "moderns," much like their human counterparts were during the period of Enlightenment in eighteenth-century Europe. Philosophers such as John Locke argued that by employing "reason" and "observation" one could arrive at an improved, if not yet quite perfect, understanding of reality. The machines, by accepting a grand design and a certain level of control, come to an understanding of human reality through the use of science and technology. Their products, like flying cars, are faster and more efficient than those produced by humans, and their production methods are the epitome of "modern industrial techniques."

These techniques are perfected in the creation of the matrix itself, a creation that is, as the narrator of "Second Renaissance Part II" states, "The very essence of the second Renaissance." These ideals of efficiency rely upon the concept that with the right ideas and understanding of "reality" it is possible to produce, and then reproduce, products (*and people!*) perfectly.

The question then is not "what is the matrix?" It is "what is modernism?" The answer, however, remains the same: control. The "pure, horrifying precision" that Morpheus describes in *The Matrix*. The fields of growing babies, the powerhouse holding and drawing energy from people, the matrix construct itself, are all the end results of the machine intelligences' understanding of science, reason, and progress.

You Cannot Search for Truth if there is No Such Thing

Since *The Matrix* so prominently features the book *Simulacra and Simulation* (the seemingly empty book that Neo pulls his illegal software out of to give to Choi in the first film), a work by the eminent postmodern French sociologist Jean Beaudrillard, many critics have labeled the entire franchise postmodern in theory and design. The American scholar Frederic Jameson has proposed one definition of postmodernism. He defines postmodernism in the works of history and arts as a "random cannibalization of all the styles of the past [and] the play of random stylistic allusion" which he also calls a "pastiche" (Jameson 18).

As applied to the franchise, this sort of "random cannibalization" of styles in all the films does seem to apply. At times they appear to be "Hong Kong martial arts films," while at other points they resemble old "American Westerns," Japanese animé, romantic dramas, "cyberpunk works," or many other genres of world cinema. Jameson even goes so far as to call this kind of postmodernism "the increasing primacy of the 'neo'" (Ibid.)!

British sociologist Anthony Giddens also defines postmodernism in a way that seems to apply nicely to the *Matrix* franchise. He calls it the idea that "we have discovered that nothing can be known with any certainty, since all pre-existing 'foundations' of [knowledge] have been shown to be unreliable; that 'history' is devoid of ... 'progress'" (Giddens 46). What he meant by this is that there was a time in the history of the Western world in which people sought to explain everything through a single "grand theory" which contained a certain notion of historical progress.

Karl Marx applied a "grand theory" to the notion of historical progress with his concepts of materialism and communism, much as Sigmund Freud did with his idea of the unconscious. In other words, analysts contended that if you understood the idea of "class conflict" (Marx) or "sexuality and the unconscious" (Freud), you could then understand the "truth" of why the world was the way it was. Marx believed that understanding why there was conflict between members of different social classes explained all historical change. Freud thought this conception of the "unconscious" explained *all* human behaviors.

These are just two examples of what is meant by a "grand narrative," or what Jean Francois Lyotard calls a "metanarrative," and is exactly what postmodernists and postmodernism claims to reject (*The Postmodern Condition* xxiv). The use of grand narratives as a way of explaining the world has been part of Western thinking since at least the eighteenth century. It was then that Enlightenment philosophers argued that "reason" would allow for a perfect understanding of reality (some would argue that this idea goes all the way back to Plato).

Prior to this Enlightenment shift in thought, an "understanding of reality" was based on knowledge of "religious truths." What Enlightenment thinkers did was make a change in our understanding of the world, so that, as Anthony Giddens puts it, "[o]ne type of certainty (divine laws) was replaced by another (the certainty of our senses, of ... observation), and divine providence was replaced by ... progress" (48). This way of thinking about the world is associated with ideas like "reason" and "objective" knowledge rather than dogma, and for the Western world is commonly associated with modernism.

Postmodernists argue that those ideas (such as "science," "progress," and "reason") are cultural constructs, merely ways of playing with words and ideas in order to present a coherent understanding of "reality" and "history" that we can all agree makes sense. It thus rejects those very notions of "meta-narratives" and "reality" that are central to the modernist model of the world. So, in a way, the expansive storytelling structure of the *Matrix* franchise becomes exactly what postmodernism claims to reject: a grand narrative. It is the story of the enslavement and eventual freeing of humanity, with a new and better future before them as a result. There is nothing more "grand" than that! It is the very concept of "modern."

But, if we look at the American theorist John McGowan and his definition of postmodernism, we can see that it resonates almost perfectly with the *Matrix* franchise:

> Postmodernism understands contemporary capitalism as an all-inclusive order from which nothing and no one can escape ... the postmodernist insists that the social totality within which we live is a *constructed* whole that gains unity only through a process of exclusion ... Postmodernism favors internal models of transformation, relying on a return of the unsuccessfully repressed, of the outsider or marginalized who was formerly (originally) an insider. (21-22, author's emphasis)

This seems to be an almost perfect general outline of the story of the *Matrix* franchise. The matrix being the "all-inclusive order from which nothing and no one can escape" while Neo is the "unsuccessfully repressed ... outsider or marginalized" member "who was formerly an insider" who returns to effect "transformation" of the system at the end of *Revolutions*.

Another troubling aspect for postmodernists is the concept of what "real" or "reality" means because the notions that have been put forth center on the Western world with Western cultural ideas that most of the planet does not agree with. It is this idea of a "real" that Baudrillard says is not even knowable, either. How can something "reflect the truth" when we do not know what "truth" is?

Or try it this way: you go to a *Star Trek* convention, say, and buy a copy of a "phaser pistol." You are now the proud owner of a copy of a thing that does not even exist. To Baudrillard, that is a simulacrum. Much like in the matrix itself, which is a copy of a world that does not exist, Baudrillard argues that it is now possible to lose oneself in the difference between the apparent "real" or "original" and what is a "copy." So the question might be stated this way: does it matter what we decide is "real" and "unreal" if it is not possible to know the difference? It seems to matter to Morpheus, especially, but it also matters to the population of Zion. The matrix is not real, they believe, so it must be fought against. (This is a question that Russell Blackford will discuss in his essay in this volume.)

Baudrillard's *Simulacra and Simulation,* which is primarily about the ability of human industrial cultures to produce things in such detail and quantity that the copy and the original can no longer be distinguished, is pushed to the extreme in the *Matrix* franchise. This is especially so in *The Matrix.* The machine intelligences have produced the seemingly perfect simulacra, being able to recreate a copy of what agent Smith calls "the pique of human civilization."

Or have they? Baudrillard's book in the first film looks almost handmade, and appears to be leather bound. It is anything but a simulacrum, being perfectly discernable from other copies (at least, it does not look anything like our copy!) Nevertheless, some critics have hailed the *Matrix* franchise as the epitome of the "postmodern" (Felluga, Weberman).

Dino Felluga, for example, says the *Matrix* franchise is postmodern because it shows that "[t]he idea of truth or objective reality is ... meaningless" (73). Felluga's argument for the postmodernism of the *Matrix* franchise is based on his reading of Baudrillard and other postmodern theorists. He agrees with Baudrillard that the postmodern condition is not about the idea that we now inhabit an artificial world, but that "we have lost all ability to make sense of the distinction between the nature and the artifice" (Ibid.).

David Weberman agrees, since he is pleased that the *Matrix* franchise shows the "blurred or vanishing line between reality and simulation" (226). His reading of the postmodernism of the first film is also based on his agreement with Baudrillard. For Weberman, *The Matrix* is postmodern, in part, because "Neo has no way of knowing what is real and what isn't" (228). Both authors think the *Matrix* franchise is postmodern because both see within the first film that the idea of "reality" is not fully knowable.

"You're Empty!"—Agent Smith
"So Are You!"—Neo

Just because we are not sure that there is something called "reality" outside of our own experiences does not necessitate that the *Matrix* franchise, in illustrating this, must be postmodern. If the *Matrix* franchise were meant to show a postmodern future, one would expect that the characters in the films would not be spending so much time trying to uncover "the truth" and trying to show other characters "the real world." Indeed, it seems that the narrative structure's allusions to concepts from both the classical era and the modern era indicate the Wachowski brothers' desire not to move forward, but rather to return to the past, or at the very least, a place in time that is not postmodern.

We see the Wachowski brothers' opinion of postmodernism fully realized in the character of Agent Smith. Smith's ability to replicate himself in both *Reloaded* and *Revolutions* personifies Baudrillard's conception of simulacra. Smith's ability to create copies of himself that are indistinguishable from the original (especially in "The Burly Brawl" of *Reloaded*), epitomizes the idea of the simulacrum, and thus postmodernism.

When Neo tells the Architect in *Revolutions* that "the anomaly Smith is getting out of hand," viewers are finally treated to the Wachowskis' opinion of postmodernism: a set of ideas that *theorize* about, but do nothing to alleviate, social misery. Because there is no objective truth or reality in a world based on postmodernism, there is no foundation to build hope, beauty, or a better future for all of humanity. So, if we are to say that Smith is postmodernism and postmodernism is "getting out of hand" and "must be stopped," then the final destruction of the anomalous program could be interpreted as the destruction of an anomalous idea.

While some have consistently championed the *Matrix* franchise as the best examples of postmodern cinema yet produced, other critics have claimed the exact opposite. Since many of those who consider the *Matrix* franchise postmodern do so because of their reading of Jean Baudrillard, perhaps it is best to see if Baudrillard himself thinks the franchise is postmodern. In short, he does not.

In an interview with the French newspaper *Le nouvel Observateur,* Baudrillard says that the first *Matrix* film takes "the hypothesis of the virtual as a fact and carries it over to visible phantasms. But the primary characteristic of this universe lies precisely in the inability to use categories of the real to speak about it" (Lancelin). Baudrillard, whose ideas are central to the interpretation of the film as postmodern, says that the problems surrounding postmodernism stem from a much older problem:

> [T]he brand-new problem of the simulation is mistaken with the very classic problem of the illusion, already mentioned by Plato. Here lies the mistake. The world as a complete illusion is the problem that faced all great cultures and they solved it thanks to art and symbolization. What we did invent in order to put up with this pain is a simulated real, a virtual universe cleansed of everything dangerous or negative and which now overrides the real... Now, *The Matrix* is totally that! (Ibid.)

Baudrillard does not see the *Matrix* franchise as representing the issue of the simulation specifically and postmodernism in general. He sees the films as the symptom of the very issue he is trying to explain! As he puts it, "*The Matrix* is like a movie about *The Matrix* that could have produced *The Matrix*" (Ibid.). The *Matrix* franchise does not tell us what a simulacra *is,* the *Matrix* franchise itself, is a simulacrum!

For those critics who agree with Baudrillard, that the franchise is not postmodern, their arguments usually evolve around notions of reality. For example, Russell Wardlow thinks that because the franchise is about returning humans to "the real world," then they must be modernist because it accepts the notion of a "knowable reality." Thus, for Wardlow at least, the franchise is very much anti-postmodern.

We have explored whether the *Matrix* franchise is modern or postmodern, and we have seen that some scholars think it is modernist, while others see it as postmodern. The question of modernism versus postmodernism is an interesting one, to be sure. But it is a question that suggests that the *Matrix* franchise must be either one or the other and that there is a knowable difference between the two.

Earlier in the essay, we presented definitions of historical periods which allowed us to reflect on the nature of modernism and postmodernism and how the *Matrix* phenomena might be one or the other. But, if you look closely at the list delineating "classical," "modern," and "postmodern," then you have noticed already that both we and Tarnas set up the system in our favor. Each "era" on that list is defined not by itself, but *only by* its relationship to "modernism." What we and others have termed "classical" is only defined in that it came prior to the "modern," while "postmodern" is the period that followed. Indeed, we do not really find such a striking difference between classical, the modern, and the postmodern. Postmodernism places an emphasis on the ever-changing aspects of knowledge, but these trends were already inherent in the early modern thinkers like Locke and Descartes.

Thus, critics and scholars who have argued that the films are indeed postmodern do so on the strength of their opinions about what modernism means. We would suggest that the two ideas, modernism and postmodernism, are best lumped together as ways of seeing the world, and that the *Matrix* franchise embraces concepts from not only both of them, but from the classical era as well.

Jean-François Lyotard, a postmodern French philosopher, has already noted that postmodernism cannot be seen as an attack on modernism, and that it is the ideas from the classical era that are much better at voicing the attack:

> Rather than the postmodern, what would be properly opposed to modernity here would be the classical age … [which] involves a state of time (let's call it a status of temporality) in which advent and passing, future and past, are treated as though, taken together, they embraced the totality of life in one and the same unity of meaning. For example, this would be the way that myth organizes and distributes time, creating a rhythm of the beginning and end of the story it recounts. (*The Inhuman* 25)

We see then that the dispute between modernism and postmodernism assumes that their differences are interminable and cannot be rectified. However, if Lyotard, a noted postmodern scholar, concedes that modernism and postmodernism share more commonalties than either share with the mythico-classical period, then we too must consider that the previous contentions made by scholars on whether the franchise is modern or postmodern ignores its complexity. These obscure academic arguments over theory do not explicate meaning for the franchise, but rather turn it in to cannon fodder for modernists and postmodernists hell-bent on proving the emptiness of each others' positions.

The arguments between modern and postmodern scholars are exemplified best in the franchise when Neo and Agent Smith battle for the first time in the subway station near the end of *The Matrix*. Standing some distance apart, and filmed to evoke Hollywood Westerns, they rush toward each other, firing their guns at one another. Grappling and falling to the floor, each with a gun to the head of the other, Agent Smith sneers, "You're empty." Neo replies, "So are you." Like many modernist and postmodernist scholars have seemingly wished for, it appears the two schools of thought have finally come to blows.

As pragmatists, we contend that the classical, modernist, and postmodernist views each offer useful insights into the way we envision our world and our place within it. Rather than an empty and continual struggle between schools of thought, which seems to be the modus operandi of most analysts of the franchise, we agree with Neo at the end of *Revolutions* in his desire for "peace."

The *Matrix* Franchise as a Story of Hope, Renewal, and "Prophetic Pragmatism"

For us the key to understanding the philosophical underpinnings of the *Matrix* franchise is pragmatism.[2] This is a philosophy based on choice, freedom, and hope. This perspective does not disavow or do battle with the positive aspects of previous worldviews, as say postmodernism does with modernism. Cornel West calls the specific type of pragmatism we employ "prophetic pragmatism," which he explains, saying it "keeps track of social misery, solicits and channels moral outrage to alleviate it, and projects a future in which the potentialities of ordinary people flourish and flower" (*Keeping Faith* 141).

By using this pragmatic perspective, many of the difficult-to-answer questions about the *Matrix* franchise suddenly seem more understandable. Instead of questioning the meaning of "truth" or "reality," we see these issues evaporate, and what is left are issues of social hope, increased freedom, and choice. Calling the films either "classical," "postmodern," or "modern" merely limit and de-limit the amount of hope for a better future for all humanity.

This hope for a better future is first envisioned at the end of *The Matrix*. It is a very peculiar ending for an American science-fiction action film. The "good guys" are alive, but the battle goes on. Of the "bad guys," only Cypher is dead, and Smith seems destroyed while the matrix is still in place. As Neo stands at a public phone speaking to the machine intelligences of the matrix, a hint is given as to what the true outcome of this battle between human and machine is going to be:

> I know you're out there, I can feel you now. I know that you're afraid of us. You're afraid of change. I don't know the future. I didn't come here to tell you how this is going to end. I came here to tell you how it's going to begin. I'm going to hang up this phone and then I'm going to show these people what you don't want them to see. I'm going to show them a world without you. A world without rules and controls, without borders or boundaries. A world where anything is possible.

What Neo means by this soliloquy becomes somewhat clearer in *Reloaded,* and is explicitly stated in *Revolutions:* a future that is not set, but one where as many intelligent creatures as possible have "choice."

Earlier in the essay we adapted Richard Tarnas's blurry divisions of Western history into three main eras: classical, modern, and postmodern. Tarnas has hopes for the emergence of a new era. That era, he says, is one of:

> Synthesis of the long evolution from the primordial undifferentiated consciousness through the dualistic alienation. It incorporates the postmodern understanding of knowledge and yet goes beyond it. (434-5)

For us this is an apt description of the pragmatism we use to interpret the *Matrix* franchise. To dwell on its modernist conceits too much, or on its postmodernism, would be to suggest that the franchise was created and exists solely in an intellectual vacuum.

A pragmatic reading of the *Matrix* franchise aids in discarding the argument over whether the franchise is modern or postmodern in theory and design, an argument that hinges on whether there is a "reality" that is "knowable." Richard Rorty, an American pragmatic philosopher, argues that pragmatists:

Do not believe that there is a way things really are. So they want to replace the appearance-reality distinction by that between descriptions of the world and of ourselves which are less useful and those which are more useful. When the question of "useful for what?" is pressed, they have nothing to say except "useful to create a better future." When they are asked "Better by what criterion?," they have no detailed answer.... Pragmatists can only say something as vague as: Better in the sense of containing more of what we consider good and less of what we consider bad. (*Philosophy and Social Hope* 28)

This is very much the future hope at the end of *The Matrix* and it is suggested at the end of *Revolutions* as well. It is not a postmodern future, nor a modern one. To be a postmodern future it would need to be wholly removed from grand narratives of the past, Lyotard's "metanarratives." To be a modernist future it would need to be one built wholly around reason and science. As so much of the *Matrix* franchise depends on mythic elements and tells a grand story, it is neither modern nor postmodern. We contend that the future set before all of humanity at the end of *Revolutions* is one that has learned from the errors of the past, but does not reject that which is good of religion, myth, and tradition.

This prophetic pragmatism represented in the *Matrix* franchise "never [gives] up on the new possibilities of human agency" (*Evasion* 228). For West, "human agency" is the ability to see new "choices and actions" (Ibid.). As Neo notes in his conversation with the Architect in *Reloaded,* "the problem is choice"! West sees that "human struggle sits at the center of prophetic pragmatism, a struggle guided by a democratic and libertarian vision, sustained by moral courage" (229). By the end of *Revolutions,* humanity and the machine intelligences have a host of choices before them. They have a new sense of many "alternative ways of life and of struggle based on the best of the past ... [that] required memory of those who prefigured such life and struggle in the past" (229-30).

The essential component to this pragmatic reading of the *Matrix,* which disavows strict modernist or postmodernist interpretations of the franchise, does so simply because of the portrayal of willingness by both the humans and the machines to learn from the past. This acceptance includes the traditions or myths of that past and a grand narrative of progress, but progress "measured by the extent to which we have made ourselves better than we were in the past" (Rorty, *Achieving Our Country,* 28). It is prophetic because it hopes that the encounters between machine and human, myth and science, the past and present, will all make for a better hope-filled future. As Eliade notes, "This is the profound meaning of any genuine encounter; it might well constitute the point of departure for a new humanism, upon a world scale" (*Dreams* 245).

Notes

A small part of this essay was first presented at the 2001 Popular Culture Association and American Culture Association annual meeting in Philadelphia by Kapell. He thanks the many conference participants for their insightful comments at that meeting and after. A number of students at the University of Michigan–Dearborn read and critiqued drafts of this essay and we thank them all for their insights. These include Kristen Chapman, Gabriel Mahoney, and Elspeth Hetrick. Two colleagues also supplied critical comments including, at Loyola University in Chicago, Mary Fran Lebemoff and John Shelton Lawrence. We thank them both. William G. Doty, co-editor on this project, read multiple drafts and supplied the most excellent close reading on those drafts we've ever seen. Peter Wilhelm also supplied critical comments on drafts of this essay and engaged us in many fruitful conversations on the franchise: he has our thanks. Of course, after all the insights of the above people, it must be said that any errors remain wholly our own.

1. For the purpose of saving space we refer to "The Enlightenment" as the general period in Europe corresponding with the origins of Modernism. We realize this use of the term largely ignores the distinctions between German Idealistic philosophy optimized by Kant, the French Enlightenment or "Age of Reason," characterized by the work of Baron d'Holbach, and similar philosophical schools in England.

2. To save space, we will not present here much of a differentiation between pragmatism and what has come to be called "neo-pragmatism." As both the early and more recent forms of pragmatism each suggest a rejection of the "reality" question in one way or another, and both develop along lines hoping for a better future, delineating their profound differences is a topic not possible in the space we have here.

Works Cited

Baudrillard, Jean. *Simulacra and Simulation*. Trans. Sheila Faria Glaser. Ann Arbor: University of Michigan Press, 1994 (orig. 1981).

Doty, William G. *Mythography: The Study of Myth and Rituals*. 2nd. edition. Tuscaloosa: University of Alabama Press, 2000.

Eliade, Mircea. *The Myth of the Eternal Return: Or, Cosmos and History*. Trans. Willard R. Trask. Princeton: Princeton University Press, 1974 (orig. 1954).

———. *Myths, Dreams and Mysteries*. Trans. Philip Mairet. New York: Harper and Row, 1975 (orig. 1957).

Felluga, Dino. "The Matrix: Paradigm of Postmodernism or Intellectual Poseur?" *Taking the Red Pill: Science, Philosophy, and Religion in The Matrix.* Ed. Glenn Yeffeth. Dallas: Benbella, 2003.

Frankfort, Henri, and H. A Frankfort. "Myth and Reality." In Henri Frankfort, H. A. Frankfort, John A. Wilson, Thorkild Jacobsen, and William A Irwin. *The Intellectual Adventure of Ancient Man: An Essay on Speculative Thought in the Ancient Near East.* Chicago: University of Chicago Press, 1946: 3-30.

Giddens, Anthony. *The Consequences of Modernity.* Stanford: Stanford University Press, 1990.

James, William. "What Pragmatism Means." Ed. Louis Menand. *Pragmatism: A Reader.* New York: Vintage, 1997: 93-111.

Jameson, Fredric. *Postmodernism, Or, The Cultural Logic of Late Capitalism.* Durham: Duke University Press, 1991.

Kapell, Matthew. "Modernism and Postmodernism Finally Come to Blows: A Theoretical Take on *The Matrix.*" Paper presented at the annual Popular Culture Association / American Culture Association meeting, Philadelphia, 2001.

Lancelin, Aude. *Le nouvelle Observateur.* "Baudrillard Decodes Matrix: Interview." <http://www.teaser.fr/~lcolombet/empyree/divers/Matrix-Baudrillard_english.html>. Accessed 14 August 2003.

Lyotard, Jean-Francois. *The Postmodern Condition: A Report on Knowledge.* Trans. Geoff Bennington and Brian Massumi. Minneapolis: University of Minnesota Press, 1984 (orig. 1979).

———. *The Inhuman: Reflections on Time.* Trans. Geoffrey Bennington and Rachel Bowlby. Stanford: Stanford University Press, 1991 (orig. 1988).

McGowan, John. *Postmodernism and Its Critics.* Ithaca: Cornell University Press, 1991.

Rorty, Richard. *Achieving Our Country.* Cambridge: Harvard University Press, 1998.

———. *Philosophy and Social Hope.* New York: Penguin, 1999.

Tarnas, Richard. *The Passion of the Western Mind: Understanding the Ideas That Have Shaped Our World View.* New York: Ballantine, 1991.

Wardlow, Russell. "The Matrix: Postmodern or Anti-Postmodern?" <http://www.meanmrmustard.net/archives/000887.html>. Accessed 12 May 2003.

Weberman, David. "*The Matrix* Simulation and the Postmodern Age." The Matrix *and Philosophy.* Ed. William Irwin. Chicago: Open Court, 2002.

West, Cornel. *The American Evasion of Philosophy: A Genealogy of Pragmatism.* Madison: University of Wisconsin Press, 1989.

———. *Keeping Faith: Philosophy and Race in America.* New York: Routledge, 1993.

Films

The Animatrix. Various Directors. Warner Brothers, 2003.

The Matrix. Dir. Andy Wachowski and Larry Wachowski. Perf. Keanu Reeves, Carrie-Anne Moss, Laurence Fishburne. Warner Brothers, 1999.

The Matrix Reloaded. Dir. Andy Wachowski and Larry Wachowski. Perf. Keanu Reeves, Carrie-Anne Moss, Laurence Fishburne. Warner Brothers, 2003.

The Matrix Revolutions. Dir. Andy Wachowski and Larry Wachowski. Perf. Keanu Reeves, Carrie-Anne Moss, Laurence Fishburne. Warner Brothers, 2003.

9

Biomorph: The Posthuman Thing

GRAY KOCHHAR-LINDGREN

The Posthuman

*T*he *Matrix* series is a multimedia reflection on the relationship between human beings and machines, between flesh and metal. In many ways it is yet another version of the old story of the battle between the two types of beings. Humans are depicted as organic, courageous, passionate, and able to become individuals through their freedom of choice. The machines—the Agents, the Sentinels, the matrix as a whole—are unfeeling, lack freedom, and therefore the possibility of morality, and can copy themselves at will. Humans who "see the truth" become autonomous causal agents, while the machines will always remain the effects of another's programming.

If this is all the series is, then we will once again be bored into a sleep of forgetting, for the end is pre-programmed into the genre from its beginning. Humanity will triumph over mechanism and we will have only repeated what we already believe, without learning anything new. The series will be only another example of simplistic reinforcement of ideology in which the good guys defeat the bad guys. Hip, hip, hooray.

But there is already a difference at work: a third term, software, has emerged into the liminal space of the ancient enmity between flesh and metal. If Zion represents the purely human and the Machine City the purely mechanic, then the matrix itself—the place of the final battle between Neo and Agent Smith—is the software generated design-space of the encounter that will determine the fate of both human and machine.

If the *Matrix* franchise is to help us to think about ourselves, it will have to generate a new configuration of ideas and move beyond the profit-and-propaganda machine of Hollywood (which can be located anywhere on the planet) toward a work of art that will contain elements of both innovation and critique within itself. On this question we will, at least temporarily, have to reserve judgment and ask ourselves whether what culminates in

Revolutions opens up space for a vision of renewal or only, as in so many revolutions, simply repeats the violence of the same old circle.

One of the critical terms now being used to characterize our global, cultural situation is the *posthuman*. In this essay, the word will be defined as "our historical moment in which the organic and its others are crossing over into each other's domains." The body, in other words, is becoming an organism in symbiosis with various forms of machines, including computers. And, from the other side, computers are becoming more intelligent, moving in the direction of the human. The human is becoming, or has already become, a cyborg—a cybernetic organism—that marks a radical complement of the biological evolution of natural selection. A cyborg is a hybrid thing that thinks and, therefore, must have already come to speech. We are, in the early twenty-first century, the posthuman site of the crossing between the animate and the inanimate. [1]

There are many implications of this shift, but here I want to focus on only one: what happens when the "human" moves toward the "thing," and vice versa? To accomplish this, we will take a short detour and reiterate, very briefly, what the Western tradition has taught us about "person" and "thing." Immanuel Kant gives a representative version of the classical account: "Beings whose existence rests not on our will but on nature, if they are beings without reason, still have only a relative worth, as means, and are therefore called *things,* whereas rational beings are called *persons* because their nature already marks them out as an end in itself" (Kant 37). Things are natural entities without reason and therefore means with merely relative worth; people are rational entities and are therefore ends to be treated with dignity. Things are replaceable and humans are not.

The *Matrix* series, however, raises the questions of what happens when a thing comes toward language and a person comes toward thing. Once person and thing are set into motion by the turbulence of technology, where will this motion come to a stop?

Jack yourself in, then, and enjoy the ride.

Person

We all know, we think, what a person is.

Without a complete recapitulation of the development of the Western concept of the self, which includes a multitude of different streams of thought, let me briefly list some of the major characteristics of human beings that have long been central to this concept:

- Human beings are rational beings. Thinking, rational activity in and of itself, is of the essence of the person. Neither animals nor plants nor computers, it is said, think in the same manner that we do. We can do mathematics, create games and appliances, paint sunflowers, and play rockabilly music. And such things *matter* to us.
- We are in some way or another linked to the divine life. In the Judeo-Christian tradition, this will have something to do with being created in the "image" of God, and thus participating in both rationality and ethics. For the Greeks, at least for the philosophers, this will have something to do, again, with contemplative thinking. God, for Aristotle, is the Unmoved Mover who lovingly thinks thinking. Thus, the "life of the gods is completely happy, the life of men only so far as it has some resemblance to the gods' activity" (Aristotle, *Ethics* X.372).
- We are gifted, somehow or another, with "natural and universal rights," the exact content of which will vary depending upon whom we consult. "Life, liberty, and the pursuit of happiness" will serve our purposes for the time being. This is basically a legacy of the Enlightenment—Locke, Kant, Jefferson—that has become embedded into the law, both nationally and internationally, as a continuing project of modernity.
- Each of us has a personal identity (which is linked to all of the above). We are one. This is linked to the fact that we have a body. Therefore, we can love and we will die.

The person, in general outline, is rational, spiritual, political, and individual. We are called to love and commanded to encounter our own death ahead of time. In sum, we are not *things*. We are the non-thing in the world.

For all those who think human beings have a fundamentally separate status in the universe, there will be some form or another of what Pope John Paul II in his speech to the Pontifical Academy of Sciences in 1996 called an "ontological discontinuity"—a distinct separation between types of beings—between things and humans, as well as between ancestral apes and modern human beings (whatever "modern" might mean).[2] From this perspective, the human and the thing are established by God as two separate essences and are therefore destined never to cross paths, never to cross into the domain of the other. From this point of view, *the possibility of the posthuman is an impossibility.* Or, even if it is possible technically, it remains a *moral* travesty.

From a slightly different perspective, however, one that takes the history of language into account, a different image of the human is generated. Our word "person" comes from the Latin *persona,* which refers to an actor's mask or a character in a play. This, in turn, probably derives from Etruscan *phersu,* mask, which can be traced to the Greek *prosopon,* face or mask. The latter also leads to the rhetorical device known as *prosopopoeia,* a figure of speech in which an imaginary or absent person is represented as speaking or acting, or, in other words, an act of personification.

Suddenly, we see the entire philosophy of the person in a different light. The face is a mask; the mask is a face (which the Oracle, Neo, and Smith all manifest in different ways). To be a personality is to act in the ensemble cast of the very complex play called "life." Often we assume that we don a mask either to hide something or to express a character different than ourselves. We can then remove the mask to show a genuine, true self. But if we begin to understand the human being as a play in progress, a theatrical spectacle, then we begin to realize that one mask leads to another mask, not to a genuine and unchanging essence of the self. Every one of us is many. It is, indeed, perhaps the structure of the mask (which is fundamentally relational and not essential) that allows for activities such as lying, posing, taking a stand, flirting, hoping, making films, and maybe even self-consciousness itself.

This debate between essence and a relational model of subjectivity is one vector of the battle between Neo and Smith, the primary representatives of the human and the machine. Neo—the new and the one—begins *The Matrix* in an illusion, not knowing who he really is. In a journey that imitates that of other cultural heroes, he passes through a rite of initiatory vision with his guide Morpheus (the god of sleep), descends into the underworld of the fetus factory, and emerges re-born into the truth of his place in the world. *He comes to himself.* He will, therefore, be able to love Trinity, travel to Zion, and serve as the sacrificed redeemer that, through puncturing the apparent seamlessness of the software world, binds in peace the human and the machine world.

Agent Smith, on the other hand, will always remain, regardless of how many he becomes, just a smith. He is nobody, an agent of other powers until in a Promethean gesture he attempts to exceed his status as a program.

He is a self-regenerating but not rationally autonomous program, a pure mask, as is demonstrated most clearly in the Brawls with Neo in both *Reloaded* and *Revolutions*. Smith is a specific and replicable relation between ones and zeroes, while Neo is the simple oneness of the One, a unity around whom others can organize. Neo is a person; Smith is a non-person, a thing.

At this point, the *Matrix* series is simply duplicating the traditional arguments between essence and mask. Or, in other words, as Laura Bartlett and Thomas Byers have argued, "*The Matrix* places posthuman subjects at the center of its action and flirts with a theoretical postmodernism only to reject the posthumanist configuration of subjectivity in favor of resurrecting a neo-Romantic version of the liberal-humanist subject" (30). Neo is a neo-Romantic, neo-liberal, neo-humanist subject. But before making a final judgment (another archetype governing the franchise), we must briefly examine the history of the "thing."

Thing

A thing, we assume, is the simplest of all things to talk about. It is so simple, in fact, that it is not worth considering at all. In this sense, things have become invisible, part of a muted gray background of the speed of daily life. I want, in this context, to slow down and bring the thing back into visibility.

A thing is an object, an entity that stands before us as separate from ourselves. I am conscious; it is not. "Thing" has, for us, become a designator for any inert object in the world, regardless of its specific form. In front of me there is a book, a calculator, a pen, coins, a golf tee, business cards, a filing cabinet, paper and paper clips, a Zip drive, a table, a window with the blinds drawn, a mess, a pastel painting on the wall, the glimpse of a tree, a computer. These things persist in a thing we call "world" through the intermediary of the thing we call "my body."

Each thing, in turn, can be broken down into other things, other attributes. Every thing, in other words, is a field of attributes held together by something that used to be called "substance," in which all the other qualities of a thing were mysteriously bound together. Contemporary physics speaks of "fields of force" that bind things together,[3] but there remains the enigmatic separation-conjunction of things: bottle, book, fir, rock, laptop.

I prefer, following many others, to say that the field-effect of relatively stable things in a relatively stable world is produced not by substance, a kind of magical a priori adhesive, but by *language* as a general structure of signification: things cohere and can be broken apart because our language operates in the ways that it does. For human beings there is nothing recognizable apart from language as the possibility of signification, which not only mediates the world to us, but produces it. We have always already humanized the thing; the world is always ensouled with words. The object, the subject, the word, and the field of force that conjoins them come into being simultaneously and in a mutual dance. This *enwrapping* is something we have long been attempting to learn how to say.

And now the word-thing is becoming a digitized-thing, a string of bits, a data stream, and we are inventing new words and representations for this new experience. Every thing is being numbered and translated into computer code. The world, in other words, is an active and infinite combinatorial matrix. The world is, and has always been, virtual reality, not as a world copied from somewhere else—the mind of God, for example—but as an incessant reconfiguration of its own figures. It is this shift toward a new model (one that is also, in some ways, very old) that is now seeking a language. What type of reconfiguration is this? What role do human beings play in such a combinatorial world? What of freedom, meaning, ethics, and love in the time of cybernetics? These are some of the questions the series poses.

The "thing" has a long and complex history, but I want to zero in on several high points of the journey. As I have mentioned, Aristotle thought the thing to be an underlying substance (*ousia*) modified by a variety of attributes. The horse is brown, large, has a white blaze on its forehead, etc. None of these accidents is the essence of horseness, since they could all change and we could still recognize "horse." The essence of a thing, then, has a direct relationship with definition, the correct use of language and logic regarding a thing. There is also no fundamental separation between mind and body, as pattern exists as the very form of an organized thing called a human body.

But, as philosophy passed through the medieval and early modern Christian regime, this relationship shifted. René Descartes defined human beings as *res cogitans,* thinking-perceiving things, and objects in the world as *res extensa,* things extended in space (i.e., bodies). Both human beings and objects are species of *res,* an existent in the broadest sense. A thing. The person and the body, however, are regulated by different laws, the former by freedom and the latter by physical causality.

In article six of *The Passions of the Soul* (1649), Descartes writes that death never comes because of a failure of the soul, but through a disintegration of a part of the body. "Let us hold," he continues, "that the body of a living man differs from that of a dead man just as any machine that moves of itself (e.g., a watch or other automaton when it is wound up and thereby has in itself the corporeal principle of those movements for which it is designed, together with all else that is required for its action) differs from itself when it is broken and the principle of movement ceases to act" (268). Already the discourse of "machine" and "automaton" are deeply intertwined with the notion of the human, although only, as it were, with the externality of the human. The mystery, for Descartes, is how the body and the mind are connected; how the thing, in the broad sense, doubly articulates itself as *cogitans* and *extensa*.

The thing, in the nineteenth century's Industrial Revolution, moves toward an object of mass production and distribution. It becomes a kind of example of uniform and marketable serialization, which we need to keep in mind as we think about the *Matrix* series (whose final frame belongs to Time/Warner Brothers). In the *Grundrisse,* Karl Marx wrote that:

> once adopted into the production process of capital, the means of labor passes through different metamorphoses, whose culmination is the machine, or rather, an *automatic system of machinery* ... this automaton consisting of numerous mechanical and intellectual organs, so that the workers themselves are cast merely as conscious linkages.... [I]t is the machine which possesses skill and strength in place of the worker, is itself the virtuoso, with a soul of its own in the mechanical laws acting through it. (Marx 283)

Machines are already replacing the worker, leaving him or her either unemployed or working to keep the machines in running order. Machine and human are already, in this text, symbiotic and the machines necessary for capitalism are already becoming the more powerful force of production. In *The Matrix,* the machines use the plug-in of a human body (which always remains a kind of unseparated fetus) as a battery to generate energy, transforming organic energy into the inorganic energy needed to keep the matrix functioning. In order to do this, there must be a transformer working at the interface between the two domains, "translating" the one into the other.

Rainer Maria Rilke, as a twentieth-century poetic complement to Marx, mourns the loss of the thing to industrialization, equating this development— as many did—with "America." On November 13, 1925, Rilke wrote to Witold von Hulewicz:

Even for our grandparents a "house," a "well," a familiar tower, their
very clothes, their coat: were infinitely more, infinitely more inti-
mate; almost everything a vessel in which they found the human
and added to the store of the human. Now, from America, empty
indifferent things are pouring across, sham things, *dummy life....* A
house, in the American sense, an American apple or a grapevine
over there, has *nothing* in common with the house, the fruit, the
grape into which went the hopes and reflections of our forefathers....
Live things, things lived and conscient of us, are running out and
can no longer be replaced. *We are perhaps the last still to have known
such things.* (Rilke, 375)

One of the purposes of the *Matrix* franchise as a whole—along with numerous other films, novels, plays, and scholarly texts—is to raise questions
about this "dummy life," usually called "virtual reality." That will, necessarily, involve questioning the meaning of "live things" and, perhaps, coming
to different conclusions than did Rilke.

Martin Heidegger, the highly influential German philosopher with
the notoriously difficult style, lays out his understanding of things in many
texts, including "The Thing" (1950) and "The Question Concerning Technology" (1955).[4] In "The Thing," Heidegger, using an earthen jug as his primary example, moves through a discussion of the history of the thing, always
asking: "What is the thingness of the thing? What is the essence of thingness?" Heidegger wants to move away from the usual understanding of the
thing as an object separate from us, writing that:

An independent, self-supporting thing may become an object if we
place it before us, whether in immediate perception or by bringing it to mind in a recollective re-presentation. However, the thingly
character of the thing does not consist in its being a represented
object, nor can it be defined in any way in terms of the objectness,
the over-againstness, of the object. (Heidegger, "Thing" 165)

How can we translate this into (relatively) normal English? An "object,"
Gegenstand in German, is literally that which stands over against us. For this
term Heidegger wants to substitute "what stands forth," thereby attempting to think beyond the subject-object split that has determined Western
thinking and replace it with a sense of how all things come into *presence*.

A thing, for him, is what shows itself to us and can become the subject of speech. In a manner similar to our discussion about the history of "person," Heidegger notes that "thing" comes from Old High German *thing,* which was a "gathering to discuss contested matters." This, in turn, is an equivalent of the Latin *res,* the same word Descartes used for both humans and things, but which Heidegger emphasizes was also "a matter for discourse." A thing is something to talk about. Let's talk about things. How are things? I'll show you my thing if you'll show me yours. This, finally, arises from the Greek *eiro* (the root for *rhetos, rhetra, rhema*), "to deliberate on something."

A thing puts rhetoric into play. The rhetoric Heidegger brings into play is that of a re-invention of a poetics of the thing, which for him requires a language at least as rigorous as the sciences. Speaking, still, about the thingness of the jug, whose essence is the emptiness that allows pouring to occur, he writes that:

> In the gift of the outpouring, mortals and divinities each dwell in their different ways. Earth and sky dwell in the gift of the outpouring. In the gift of the outpouring earth and sky, divinities and mortals dwell *together all at once....* Preceding everything that is present, they are enfolded into a single fourfold.... The thing stays—gathers and unites—the fourfold. The thing things world. Each thing stays the fourfold into a happening of the simple one-hood of the world. (Heidegger, "Thing" 165, 179)

This is Heidegger at his finest and most enigmatic. A thing is a gift. It comes to us, for us. In every-thing (or is it only handmade and simple things like a jug?) the earth and the sky, the gods and mortals come together. That's us. Things gather and that is what we call "world." A thing, whether "natural" or "artificial," shows us the world in which we live.

A thing shows-forth the world and in our modern context, the thing—like everything else—comes under the domination of the technological worldview. The dominance of the technological transforms human beings into a type of thing like any other thing, making us into a form of stored energy—what Heidegger calls "standing reserve"—that can be inventoried for use as needed.

This is perfectly illustrated by the way the matrix uses the human body as a coppertop energy-pod. While when Neo breaks out of his pod he re-enters the "real" that is a composite of the primitive and the high-tech, for Heidegger there is no "breaking out" from the technological, since it is a dispensation of Being rather than a personal choice. It is a revealing of Being in which "everywhere everything is ordered to stand by, to be immediately at hand, indeed to stand there just so that it may be on call for a further ordering... We call it the standing-reserve" (Heidegger, *QT* 17). In the *Matrix* world, everything, including human beings, is harvestable.[5]

Finally, the last definition of thing that I want to discuss is that developed by psychoanalysis, especially by Sigmund Freud and by Slavoj Žižek, one of the pre-eminent interpreters of Jacques Lacan. For Freud, the thing is an object of libidinal cathexis. All that this means is that throughout the course of our lives we invest our erotic energy in various love-objects. Our instincts have different objects through which to attain their aim of the release of tension. "Object" here is simply a descriptive, not a derogatory, term. We bestow high importance on some objects—our mothers, fathers, and lovers, for instance—and low importance on things we could care less about. The thing of things, that thing around which identity and conflict are organized, is the penis, which Lacan prefers to call the "phallus" and is related to the "name of the father." This, patriarchal culture believes, is the Thing itself. It acts something like a sign of authority, but in fact it turns out that the phallus does not, much like the Emperor's new clothes, actually belong to anybody or to either gender. It is a fantasy of fullness that is in fact that emptiness (what psychoanalysis calls castration) around which meaning drifts.[6]

Žižek focuses his attention directly on The Matrix. As Žižek notes, the film acts as a Rorschach test, leaving itself open to all sorts of interpretations. What do you see in this cinematic inkblot? Religion, economics, questions of gender and race, a postmodern comic book, rehashed mythology, new film technologies, a love story, etc., and all of these readings are legitimate. But what Žižek is more interested in is what "leaving itself open" might mean. What are the conditions through which the series, treated as a unity, "leave open" for other readings or the very possibility of readability itself? (This is, of course, a general question for all theories of interpretation.)

The Matrix, for Žižek, shows us a paranoid fantasy that serves the function of keeping our ideology, the world we take for granted, in place. The matrix is understood to be an evil enclosure programmed by another (the Architect) to keep us under absolute control. Part of this fantasy "resides in the very belief that, outside the closure of the finite universe, there is some 'true reality' to be entered" (Žižek, *ES* 216). The "inside" is a space controlled by the "outside," but there is always a "way out" in the fantasy. If there is a Morpheus and we choose the right colored pill, we are able to get to the truth of the outside, to break out of our illusion into the freedom of the real. However, the world is in fact not so clearly divided between inside and outside: the matrix requires the influx of human bioenergy and the outside of the control surface of the program is the "desert of the real," not a utopia of freedom. The inside-outside is a Möbius strip and the realm of our everyday social life requires that we sacrifice some of our ecstatic pleasure for the sake of social coherence.

The strength of the film, for Žižek, is that it shows us our "horrible realization of this enclosure" and that if we are to be free agents this freedom *must* occur within a system of power in which we are all immersed and which, as the real, resists our attempts at escape.

> The "totalitarian" notion of the "administered world" in which the very experience of subjective freedom is the form of appearance of subjection to disciplinary mechanism, is ultimately the obscene fantasmatic underside of the "official" public ideology (and practice) of individual autonomy and freedom…. (Žižek, *WDR* 96)

In other words, in our actual daily lives all of us act like we are free agents who have individuality, choices, etc, but this fantasy *depends upon* the "fantasmatic underside" of the rule-bound society in which we, and all human beings, exist. There is no realm of pure freedom; the law must exist for the free to exist, but, so too, freedom must be exerted if the law is to come into being. The Real, which for Lacanians is that which resists the power of symbolization—the emptiness around which meaning is organized—is a "specter whose presence guarantees the consistency of our symbolic edifice" (Žižek, *WDR* 32). Everything, it seems, depends upon a ghost.

For Žižek, while the Marxist concept of the thing and of production is always near by, it is emphatically supplemented with the thing, especially the "perverse" thing, of psychoanalysis. Perversion, which again is a descriptive and not a judgmental term, stages the denial of symbolic castration, which for psychoanalysis means the denial of finitude, meaning, sexuality, and death. The humanization of the machine occurs when "it" moves toward any of these characteristics.[7]

It seems as if the Machines impose an absolute law, that as a machinic thing it imposes a machinic law on all things, including the human object. But, as the Architect says to Neo in *Reloaded:*

> Your life is the sum of a remainder of an unbalanced equation inherent to the programming of the matrix. You are the eventuality of an anomaly, which, despite my sincerest efforts I have been unable to eliminate from what is otherwise a harmony of mathematical precision.

The "anomaly," which is always generated, is what allows for the successive "Neos"—the many who have thought themselves the One—the subjective experience of freedom, which the Architect is always trying to engineer out of the total systematicity of the program, with the wish that the same will produce the same, ad infinitum. ("Beyond," in the *Animatrix,* is another example of the attempt to close the errors in a program, to suture the tears in the programmed world that allow children to do the miraculous and play.)

Programming itself, however, creates the anomaly that will try to undo the program; order creates chaos along its edges, and eventually at its center, that will un- and re-do the order of things. The same produces difference. A thing, in the posthuman era, cannot remain a thing. So, too, the person is being swept along in the digital storm into a new form of being.

The Evolutionary Space of Conversion

What, then, have we learned from this abbreviated history of the person and the thing? That *there is no such thing as a thing and there is no such thing as a person.* There is no universal definition that satisfies the requirement of different times and places. Everything changes. Philosophers and artists, responding to the sea changes of culture, provide ever-new definitions of the thing, for all things are mutable.

Secondly, and related to the openness of mutability, the thing-person depends on seriality, the capacity to be reproduced. We see this exhibited throughout the *Matrix* franchise, for the program must always be reloaded. Such seriality is shown by the development of the video game *Enter the Matrix,* the *Animatrix,* and within the plot developments of the trilogy itself. In *Reloaded,* for instance, we discover that there have been many

Ones before Neo and, of course, Smith has learned to clone himself to do battle with Neo. The writhing mass of Zion's bodies in the rave scene suggests a kind of hive-mind of the passions that must be channeled by Morpheus and Neo. This groupiness repeats itself in *Revolutions* in both the attack of the Sentinels and in the defenses staged by the Zionites, both of which serve as the condition for the emergence of the individual in what is arguably the fundamental myth of the West. (This is a reflection of the moviemaking process itself with the visibility of its stars arising out of a horde of invisible workers.) The meeting with the Architect raises the question of whether the "world" is simply an infinite series of embedded programs or whether we are to take "Zion" and the "desert of the real" as the end of a finite series of worlds.

Third, if thing and person are to become an ever more complicated symbiotic system of exchanges, then there must be multiple points of contact, overlaps, and interfaces. There, of course, are. In *The Matrix,* the metallic insert into the plug at the back of the neck hooks the humans into the electrical network that allows them to enter and exit the programmed world through telephone lines. There is the pharmacological entry through the popping of the right pill and the awakened Neo's ability to see the lines of streaming green code as they are forming the appearance of things. There is an olfactory interface, the "smell" of humans that so disgusts Smith, and, in the final battle of *Revolutions,* there is Neo's capacity to apparently become Smith, to become another encoding of the program of the excessive proliferation of unification, and then to reject that code to return to his "own" form.

The *Animatrix* also offers pertinent commentary on the interface as a space of conversion. The "Second Renaissance, Parts I and II" from the Zion Archives, for example, gives us the creation myth and fall of the human-machine relationship; the rape of a woman-machine; the million machine march; the foundation of the machine city, Zero One (the binary city of bytes), and the failed attempt by the machines to get United Nations recognition for their rights. In the long history of the oppression of machines by humans and of humans by machines, *power* and *freedom* are what are at stake for both.

And in "Matriculated," another vignette in the *Animatrix,* we see the tale of how some of the machines are "converted" to loyalty to the human side. They are offered their own freedom and begin to develop their own conscious conscience, and, thereby, a compassion for human beings. This raises the difficult question about when the non-conscious becomes conscious, of what sort of complexity of parts must exist before self-reflection and concern for the other, ethics, begins to be possible. The thing-world and the person-world are bound together irrevocably. If one is enslaved, so, too is the other; if one if free, the other is free as well.

These instances of shared code, overlapping binaries, and interfaces indicate that we are in the world of myth (as described, for instance, by Claude Lévi-Strauss), and they form a series of points of contact between the traditional world of thing, person, and story and the posthuman world of the cyborg, which is also showing itself to be generative of a wealth of mythologizing narratives. Now, however, just as we have new technologies that are rapidly extending genetic and electronic research, so, too, we also have developed new methodologies—myth-studies, psychoanalysis, semiotics, feminist analyses, cultural studies, narratology, media studies, performance studies, and deconstruction—that can help us understand the ways in which our fundamental collective and individual stories operate. The posthuman forms itself as a symbiosis between scientific rationality, technical interfaces between the organic and the inorganic, and the continuing power of the mythic imagination. In what will become more and more clearly a community of cyborgs, we will all have to decide how to shape the fundamental stories of who we are and what we are about in this world of mutability.

To an ever greater extent, then, the space of the evolution of the thing-human is becoming a form of design space. In *Chaosmosis,* Félix Guattari has asserted that "technological machines operate at the heart of subjectivity, not only within its memory and intelligence, but within its sensibility, affects, and unconscious fantasms" (cited in Bell and Kennedy 15). Always, from the earliest chipped stone axe to the latest in biomedical imaging, human beings have been technologized, supplementing the given world of nature with the design-world of artifice. The phenomenon of the *Matrix* series marks a certain intensification of this process in the posthuman era when technology is catching up to our most ancient dreams.

At the end of the day, however, the series fails to become a work of art, for though the films produce a host of technical innovations that are visually impressive, they also accede to the temptation of the technical as an end in itself, offering only the predictable excesses of one more action movie, one more metaphysical burly brawl. More importantly, however, through its concluding recapitulation of a triumphalist Christianity, *Revolutions* closes off the lush (if confused) mythological and critical opportunities opened up by the first film. Commenting only on the first film—and thereby underlining the traditional conservative logic projected through the entire franchise—Bartlett and Byers summarize the series' critical trajectory: "The story of The Matrix, like the Christian story of Earth after the fall, is basically the story of an interregnum coming to a predestined end with the (re)appearance of the messiah, the real central figure of history" (39). This move from the first through the final film, from the possibility of a critique of the ideology to a repetition of the iconography of redemption, marks a failure of vision for a posthuman future. But if the series fails to reach its own promise, it nonetheless lays out a rough schema that helps us, in a critical counterpoint to the films, to think about the travails of the biomorphing now underway.

The matrix of The Matrix, the world as the play of code with non-code and of information with noise, is being-changed, reconfiguring person and thing in the space of evolutionary conversion. The emptiness at the heart of things, the condition for all programming, is the mysterious opening of space-time necessary for the crossing over between the human and its multiple others. We all live in the planetary whirl of the human, machine, and software worlds (with the animal and the divine always close by). We are all the site of this crisscrossing; we are, all of us, mutating.

Notes

1. The posthuman is quickly becoming a common discourse of the dominant culture. For example, the Transhumanism Association's first conference was held at Yale University in June 2003. The important thing is not that there is such a group, but that they are now in enough of the mainstream to be affiliated with a major university. What used to be the fringes of sci-fi or cyberpunk is now steadily moving into the center of cultural discourse.

2. This passage is cited in Ridley's Genome. He continues: "Perhaps the ontological leap came at the moment when two ape chromosomes were fused, and the genes for the soul lie near the middle of chromosome 2" (24).

3. After a discussion of the etymology of "thing" and "reality," which David Bohm (much like Heidegger) traces back from "res" to "thinking," he concludes that: "If the thing and the thought about it have their ground in the one undefinable and unknown totality of flux, then that attempt to explain their relationship by supposing that the thought is in reflective correspondence with the thing has no meaning, for both thought and thing are forms abstracted from the total process. The reason why these forms are related could only be in the ground from which they arise, but there can be no way of discussing reflective correspondence in

this ground, because reflective correspondence implies knowledge, while the ground is beyond what can be assimilated in the content in the content of knowledge" (55). Although there is much to comment upon about this statement, it must for the moment suffice to say that his final chapter is about the "enfolding-unfolding universe," which is not a universe—how could it be for a physicist?—of isolated things and minds.

4. For a much more thorough introduction to Heidegger's texts on the "thing," see Inwood, *A Heidegger Dictionary*.

5. For one of the directions toward which such an attitude tends, see Padmanabhan's "Harvest," a play about the harvesting of human organs and their movement from the poor to the rich.

6. For a discussion of Freud's different uses of "object," see LaPlanche and Pontalis.

7. Bruce Fink has a useful chapter on perversion, in which "disavowal implies a certain staging or making believe regarding the paternal function" (170). This idea could be examined much more thoroughly in relation to the voice of the father, Deus Ex Machina, at the conclusion of *Revolutions*. The voice, echoing the New Testament, utters "It is done."

Works Cited

Aristotle, "Ethics," in *The Philosophy of Aristotle*. Trans. J. L. Creed and A. E. Wardman. New York: New American Library, 1963.

Bartlett, Laura, and Thomas B. Byers. "Back to the Future: The Humanist *Matrix*." *Cultural Critique* (Winter 2003): 28-46.

Bell, David, and Barbara Kennedy, ed. *The Cybercultures Reader*. New York: Routledge, 2000.

Bohm, David. *Wholeness and the Implicate Order*. New York: Ark, 1983.

Descartes, René. *Philosophical Writings*. Trans. Norman Kemp Smith. New York: Modern Library, 1958.

Fink, Bruce. *A Clinical Introduction to Lacanian Psychoanalysis: Theory and Technique*. Cambridge: Harvard University Press, 1997.

Heidegger, Martin. "The Thing." *Poetry, Language, Thought*. Trans. Albert Hofstadter. New York: Harper and Row, 1971.

———. *The Question Concerning Technology and Other Essays*. Trans. William Lovitt. New York: Harper and Row, 1977.

Inwood, Michael. *A Heidegger Dictionary*. London: Blackwell, 1999.

Kant, Immanuel. *Groundwork of the Metaphysics of Morals*. Trans. Mary Gregor. Cambridge: Cambridge University Press, 1997.

Laplanche, J., and J. B. Pontalis. *The Language of Psychoanalysis*. Trans. Donald Nicholson-Smith. New York: Norton, 1973.

Marx, Karl. "Grundrisse." *The Marx-Engels Reader*. Ed. Robert C. Tucker. New York: Norton, 1978.

Merriam-Webster's Collegiate Dictionary: The Voice of Authority. Springfield: Merriam-Webster, 1993.

Padmanabhan, Manjula. "Harvest." *Postcolonial Plays*. Ed. Helen Gilbert. New York: Routledge, 2001.

Ridley, Matt. *Genome: The Autobiography of a Species in 23 Chapters*. New York: Perennial, 2000.

Rilke, R. M. *Letters: 1910-1926*. Trans. Jane Bannard Greene and M. D. Herter Norton. New York: Norton, 1969.

Žižek, Slavoj. *Enjoy Your Symptom! Jacques Lacan In Hollywood and Out*. New York: Routledge, 2001.

———. *Welcome to the Desert of the Real! Five Essays on September 11 and Related Dates*. New York: Verso, 2002.

Films

Animatrix. Warner Films, 2003.

The Matrix. Dir. Larry and Andy Wachowski. Perf. Keanu Reeves, Carrie-Anne Moss, Laurence Fishburn. Warner Films, 1999.

Matrix Reloaded. Dir. Larry and Andy Wachowski. Perf. Keanu Reeves, Carrie-Anne Moss, Laurence Fishburn. Warner Films, 2003.

The Matrix Revolutions. Dir. Larry and Andy Wachowski. Perf. Keanu Reeves, Carrie-Anne Moss, Laurence Fishburn. Warner Films, 2003.

10

Strange Volutions:
The *Matrix* Franchise as a
Post-Human Memento Mori

TIMOTHY MIZELLE AND
ELIZABETH BAKER

> You had poked your head or what you thought was your
> head out of dreams or clouds unable to sustain such a
> steadfast belief in a mirror of mercy and were witness to
> the implacable spectacle of the diaspora of entire nations,
> thousands upon thousands of blind, muzzled creatures,
> fleeing from stony, blackened lands, past ashen woods
> and trickling rivers.
>
> —Juan Goytisolo, *Quarantine*

A Signpost in the Wilderness

We humans have reached a point of no return in the wilderness that is our earthly existence. Such a point does not necessarily mark the end of a good thing and the beginning of a bad. Perhaps it is best to think of such turning points as demarked by a comma and not a period. When you see them on the page, a comma and a period, you see the two dimensional representations of a sphere, the period, and a sphere with a tail, the comma. If you stare at the comma long enough, it becomes not unlike a hurricane or a tornado. There is motion in that tail, implied and captured on the page.

When we see such tails on the central sphere of our universe, the sun, we must rely on a camera to demonstrate it for us, because our eyes cannot look directly at the sun and see it. In this same way, we rely on cameras, codes, and frequencies *to see* deep space pictures provided by the Hubble Space Telescope: the images of vibrant color that we see are merely representations based on color frequencies. Right before our eyes are simulated color images of our past, in the space-time continuum, the origins of the solar system, the evidence of the big bang. We accept that the images are the right color, for, really, what would the wrong colors be? And who could answer this question?

We have become a highly visual people, creating, daily, a visual culture, a culture dependent upon our eyes, dependent upon what we can see, either as the event happens, or as evidenced by some remainder of the event, or written about the event in words, numbers, or symbols. We are also equally dependent on images of the event; more importantly, we tend to trust these images as having recorded the *true* event. We are on the move into a new millennium with dazzling new technological options for capturing truth. We are, in short, where humanity always seems to find itself when it reflects seriously.

The beauty of art, and certainly of cinematic art, is its ability to be a cultural signpost. We have reached *a wilderness moment,* where and when we are searching for order, evidence of truth, the lessons of history, searching, then, through the seemingly infinite barrage of still images and those in motion on our televisions or movie screens for the visual clues to right our course, to give meaning to events, words, symbols, to the cosmos or merely to our own individual daily lives. This is not far from the purpose, message, and intent of the *Matrix* franchise. Its component parts are woven together by many colored threads, some of which this chapter seeks to graph.

One of these threads has to do with free will and choice, a thread of fate, one could say. Another thread, or theme, has to do with appearances versus the real, whatever that may be. Another has to do with the quest to find the God, the highest one, the most high, the ghost in the machine, the ghost in the atom, Father Time, the Creator, the beyond-the-Architect, or the ultimate Source, as The Oracle indicates in *Revolutions* to explain to Neo that he gained his special powers when battling the Sentinels because he had touched the Source directly. Another has to do with relationships between the human races, different ethical codes, different codes of law, power, and control, master and slave, masculine or feminine, free or imprisoned, will and power (or will *to* power). Another deals with love, hope, faith, and pragmatism. Perhaps the most important is that thread of human spirit that unites us all, at least as we are concerned with our future as modeled—or not!—by the speculations of the *Matrix* phenomenon.

These threads run throughout each of the components of the *Matrix* franchise, giving us insight in sight and sound, giving us, too, a full cultural fingerprint or footprint for where we are now in time or history. The sign-post is not a stop sign, not a period; perhaps it is a yield sign, a yellow light-flashing comma, telling us to pause and reflect, to take note of what we have been overlooking or taking for granted. Perhaps the most important warning of the *Matrix* franchise is not to trust the eyes and act impulsively since a pause is necessary—for careful thought before taking action.

The entire set of *Matrix* components, *The Matrix, The Animatrix, Enter the Matrix, Reloaded, Revolutions,* and even the soundtracks that have been released for the movies and *Animatrix* all together, as the sum, give us a postmodern, or more accurately, perhaps, a post-human memento mori. A memento mori, a form of image from the Middle Ages, reminded its viewer or receiver (of the message in the image) to "remember thy death." One readily recognizable memento mori is the depiction of "the Grim Reaper gathering his harvest." The purpose, the message of the memento mori, is to remind the viewer that death is an unavoidable part of life, something to be prepared for at all times, not unlike The Oracle telling Neo, when they fist meet, via the writing on the wall, to "know thyself," reflecting the ancient Greek admonition to recognize one's own abilities, but also the limitations upon mere mortals.

The memento mori provided by the *Matrix* franchise is not unlike the memento mori of the Middle Ages, but it is slightly different; it has been reloaded to fit our current time, a time that thanks to Einstein's clocks is relative, a *time* and *space* fusion that leaves us devoid of any true *place*. "Reloaded" is an operative word: if we think of the word reloaded the way we think of reloading a piece of software, or a level in a game from some previously saved point, having already moved past that point—reloaded having already made choices and mistakes along the way. But we have learned from these choices and mistakes, and are given the chance to correct some of those mistakes on a second pass through the game. If we think in this way, then the second and third installment of the movies make sense: they are the first movie literally reloaded. They are merely a retelling of the first movie that has learned from its mistakes, having been made more complex, more humorous, upgraded, as you might say, in the same way that Agent Smith has been upgraded by the *Reloaded* installment of the movies.

The *Matrix* franchise is a medicine, a prophylactic, protecting us from overlooking the hard choices that we must make upon reflecting. It is best taken red pill by red pill, or component by component (the taking of the red pill starts in motion a process of rebirth; the choice to take the red pill leads one down a path to recognition that even the dialectic of free will versus pre-destination or fate is hollow, for regardless of why we make the choices we make, we must actively make them). Just as Neo is told by The Oracle in *Reloaded* that it is *why* we make the choices we do that is important, we are being told by the *Matrix* franchise to consider the why behind our choices, to consider whether we are acting with free will or whether our choices are scripted for us. We call the search for the answer to why we make choices a search for the *truth,* or for *meaning.* This search is a quest, and the *Matrix* franchise is an artistic representation of this quest as it unfolds for Neo, Morpheus, and Trinity: all three have been before The Oracle and have been told their fates; but all three must live, making choices while on the way to the fates foretold for them, learning from these choices, learning from one another, from each situation, and from *why* they make the choices they do.

There is a price to pay while searching for answers: as we receive them, we make choices that lead to changes, much the way changes are made in the matrix. Some of these changes, via choice, have what can be perceived as negative outcomes, some positive; we have no way of knowing the end result of a choice and the changes that accompany it until we have made a particular choice. Part of the message of *The Matrix* is that we make changes in the name of our own comfort, and that these changes always lead to the comfort of some but the discomfort of others. Perhaps that is why we so often resist change and invite it at the same time. We call change that which we deem acceptable progress. We long for the good old days; we long for a better future. Either way we neglect the present. When we ask the biggest of questions, the *Why are we here? Why did a Creator make us?* we often come up seemingly empty-handed. Perhaps if we keep asking, if we keep questing and questioning, we will one day be *free.*

Duty of the One, Duty of All:
Red Pill, Blue Pill; Neither Pill; Both Pills

> For he who proceeds on his own path ... encounters no
> one: that is inherent in "proceeding on one's own path."
> No one comes along to help him: all the perils, accidents,
> malice, and bad weather which assail him he has to tackle
> by himself. For his path is *his alone.*
>
> —Friedrich Nietzsche, *Preface to Daybreak*

> This was, then, the end of his walk. Or does he, only
> now, observe that he has gone in the wrong direction?
> After a few hesitant glances around, he turns back to the
> east through the woods, again walking silently, following
> the path that he had taken to reach this spot.
>
> —Alain Robbe-Grillet, *Three Reflected Visions*

In the first movie of the *Matrix* trilogy, we meet Mr. Anderson, a.k.a. Neo, a hacker, code-breaker, insomniac, potential covert operative for Zion; that is the last bastion of humanity, potentially the One, a messianic savior who is searching for Morpheus, the aptly named dreamer. Morpheus is equally searching for Neo, the potential messiah, the One, whose existence has been foretold, prophesied to Morpheus by The Oracle. At this point, in the first movie, we do not know that The Oracle is written into the *Matrix* code; we trust her, as Morpheus trusts her, for we are experiencing the movie through a combination of two points of view: that of Neo and that of Morpheus. Part of the sophistication of the Wachowski brothers is that we initially assume that these points of view overlap.

As we encounter it in the first movie, the *Matrix* story features one of two men, each on a quest to find the other. The story unfolds for us, as all components of the *Matrix* franchise do, by apparently writing the rules as we go along and then reinforcing them from franchise component to component across the many levels of information and performance. Morpheus and Neo find one another through Trinity, the eventual lover of Neo, who saves him with a kiss, as the first movie of the *Matrix* trilogy is coming to a close (our first glimpse within the franchise of salvation through love; *Revolutions* will repeat the leitmotif, though less clearly). Trinity is the third major character, and remains the third, aptly named in that she bridges between the two males.

Morpheus frees Neo from the matrix in the first film—or does he? He presents Neo with a red pill and a blue pill. Should Neo choose the blue pill, he is told he will wake from a dream, believing it was merely a dream. Should he take the red pill, Neo will be freed from the matrix, as Morpheus tells him with an allusion to *Alice in Wonderland,* to see just how "deep the rabbit hole goes."

It is important to realize that the choices are presented by Morpheus as though there is merely the choice between red and blue. It is equally important to recognize that because of the prophecies he believes in, Morpheus is sure that Neo will take the red pill (so that the choice is no choice at all but is pre-destined by fate). But actually Neo has four choices, not merely two: he can take the red pill or the blue pill, or he can choose to take neither pill or both pills. This model of more choices than meet the eye holds throughout the *Matrix* franchise; and the related model of fated choice holds with respect to every action Morpheus makes.

There are at least two very important lessons in these two models, especially with respect to our present argument that the *Matrix* franchise is a memento mori. There is, first, one true dialectic that is within our control at all times, one choice between one option and a second, perhaps in life itself, but certainly in the *Matrix* franchise: *the choice to live or to take one's own life.* Although suicide is never mentioned or demonstrated directly within the franchise, choices are made by characters who are willing to risk death in the name of some duty they consider higher or more important than their own lives. The characters, especially Neo, make choices that involve the risk of lost life because of a sense of duty.

This call of duty or drive is present for all of the major characters throughout all the components of the *Matrix* franchise, yet that they are choosing between life and death is never explicitly stated. Such a choice is implied in the option of taking the red or blue pill. It is expressed as choosing the red pill as freedom, but once the red pill is taken, one is only then truly alive and free from the black umbilical cords sustaining him or her with a sac of life-sustaining fluid—that life is sustained by the sac, however, is an illusion. It is not until *Revolutions* and *The Matrix Comics* that we see that there is no true *freedom* within the *Matrix* universe, there is only war or peace. In fact, as in some forms of contemporary philosophy, the very idea of *truth* has been reduced to being the outcome of a choice made, and the outcome of a string of choices made. Truth is always learned after the fact.

With the choice of the red pill, one is *born again,* or born, perhaps, for the first time, for one uses his or her eyes for the first time (as Morpheus tells Neo). All other seeming dialectics have hidden third, fourth, or more options or choices. The choice to keep living, to go on, is the hardest choice for the *Matrix* characters; and they all need a quest, a duty, to do so, just like all of us, and indeed like the antithesis of Neo, Agent Smith.

In the first installment of the *Matrix* trilogy, Agent Smith tells Morpheus, as he is trying to break into Morpheus's mind, that humans are not like other mammals: they are, to Agent Smith, more like a virus. Regardless of the lie in what Agent Smith says, for he tells Morpheus that no other mammals destroy their environment, that other mammals reach a symbiosis with their environment (for any mammal only reaches symbiosis by migrating before it destroys an environment—humans in cities versus nomadic humans seem to fit his description), Agent Smith does aptly reflect what he knows about humans.

As we learn from the history lessons in *The Animatrix,* choices made by humanity have blackened the sky, so that the light and the life cycle provided by the sun, the sky, and the weather have been forsaken and humanity has moved underground to live as troglodytes in a subterranean metropolis. There they plan the destruction of the very machines that they have given life (the greatest accomplishment, the source of celebration at the dawn of the age of Artificial Intelligence). To protect themselves from death, not heeding, perhaps, the memento mori always present as signposts in the wilderness, they have chosen a path that will lead to their destruction.

Unlike the movies or even *Enter,* humanity cannot reload. It cannot face catastrophic end and then regenerate. If there is any hope left, by the time we reach *Revolutions,* it is that the sixth One has broken the mold of accepting that he has to choose between the options presented to him in sight and sound, and pauses to think before acting. We learn from *Revolutions* that this does not mean that he will not be fooled again; making the right choice at each turn is not human: mistakes are made; because of free will humans lack propensity to make the right choice at every crossroads, every time we are faced with choice.

Bending the Spoon by Seeking the Truth

> But among the forces cultivated by morality was *truthfulness:* this eventually turned against morality, discovered its teleology, its partial perspective—and now the recognition of this inveterate mendaciousness that one despairs of shedding becomes a stimulant.
>
> —Friedrich Nietzsche, *The Will to Power,* 5

The emphasis on codes throughout the components of the *Matrix* franchise, on ciphering, coding, decoding, searching for meaning, for answers, coupled with choice is no accident: *it is how a quest is completed.* Choice, or more precisely, the moment at which we pause to weigh our options, to survey the landscape before us, to read the signs, to ascertain the choices we face, is a moment we often overlook and take for granted.

We place great emphasis on the choices, themselves. We weigh them out in terms of such dialectics as good vs. evil choices, right vs. wrong, intelligent vs. unintelligent, reasoned vs. unreasoned, and as we frame our choices within dialectical oppositions, we tend to be tricked into thinking we have but two choices or even that our choices have already been scripted for us. We place great emphasis on choice being something we control because of our free will, while at the same time we fear the possibility that all choices have been made for us, pre-destined, fated, and that we are hopelessly, powerlessly, being drawn forward in time, through event after event until our death.

The components of the *Matrix* franchise return repeatedly to the pause before action, the difference between *actuality* (when an action takes place) and *potentiality* (when the potential for an action exists). They constantly hold a tension between what could happen and what does happen, what could be the case, what seems to be the case, and what *is*. It does not provide viewers, receivers of the content of the franchise, with simple answers. It forces questions and demands that questions be asked.

The *ideal viewer,* the viewer who watches all the movies, plays through the game, views the comics, watches the movies again, and perhaps even reads the screenplays, will come away from the *Matrix* franchise with a great many questions and clues as to how to go about answering the ultimate questions for himself or herself. The questions will concern the threads mentioned in the opening of this essay. The more casual *mainstream viewer,* too, will come away with many questions, as the *Matrix* authors presumably have intended from the outset. This is the beauty of cinematic art, sustained throughout an extremely complex and involuted communicative vision.

As memento mori, the *Matrix* franchise has few artistic equals. It is a new kind of cinema, a *dynamic cinema,* a huge beast, the likes of which we do not yet have indexed in our cinematic bestiaries (see Doty's Introduction, on the possibly Wagnerian context of the total work of art). The *Matrix* trilogy, alone, could have stood as one of great groundbreaking cinematic epics of our time. But with the addition of *Enter, The Animatrix,* and *The Matrix Comics,* the *Matrix* franchise is one step away from what will be a full fusion of these components in future cinema.

Dynamic cinema adds the interactivity of *Enter* to the movies; it adds the fusion of animation, comics, and computer animation to the grand special effects of the movies. Will fully dynamic cinema crop up in theaters first? Most likely not, because of the expense of fusing computer interactivity with the group experience of the modern movie theater. Most likely it will come first, in the wake of the *Matrix* franchise, to our computers, via DVD or high-speed internet broadcasts.

There will still be movie theaters and eventually they will catch up to what is available to us at home, an amazing reversal of how technology has been made available in the past. This first taste of a franchise that branches out to multiple mediums, using all of the technologies available to tell the age old tale of good vs. evil, machine vs. human, maker vs. creation is telling: change is coming to cinematic art. It is not *the dangerous game* that the Architect refers to at the close of *Revolutions,* but it is a change nonetheless. It is perhaps fitting that the cinematic harbinger of such change should put so much emphasis on choice and change.

The Hidden Source: The Third Choice

You get such a strange feeling when you try to imagine what is meant by "70,000 years ago." You try to imagine it, but can't. How short is a historical period of 5,000 years, from the oldest Egyptian pyramids until today, compared with that time span! A dark night lasting perhaps twenty times longer than that entire historical period separates us from the human spirit ... Yes, it is a strange phenomenon that human spirit, that unextinguished spark, that seed that remained alive, the thread we hold in our hands that connects us, across the soundless and pitch-black night.

—M. C. Escher, *The Craft*

In *Reloaded,* we never see the Source, because Neo chooses to save Trinity, whom he loves, instead of pursuing the futile quest to save Zion by facing the Source. He learns throughout the *Reloaded* installment that he has to believe that he is the One. In *Revolutions* he is certain of his quest for truth, facing seeming dialectics, aware that other options are always available to him, that the one true dialectic is Life/Death. Death is inevitable, as he learns from Trinity's death while she was helping him reach the goal of his quest near the end of *Revolutions*.

By the end of *Reloaded*, Neo has paid attention to the Architect, noting that the two choices given him by the Architect are both hopeless. He chooses, then, a third choice: *to save Trinity and to continue to fight for Zion with Morpheus and the crew of the Nebuchadnezzar*. There is one survivor on the ship, Bane, a character inhabited by Agent Smith; both this character and Neo are in a coma-like state as *Reloaded* ends. At this point we confront a story quite familiar in Western mythology: the Christ and the Anti-Christ, the messiah vs. the ... wait a minute!

Who, from our point of view, if we are not biased by the beliefs of the characters in the movie, is the messiah if we must choose between Neo and Agent Smith? This is a hard question to answer, objectively. We know that Neo chose to save his love, himself, and allow Zion to be annihilated. We know that Agent Smith is out to kill Neo.

Agent Smith has a duty that, as we learn in *Revolutions*, is of his own volition. He is beyond the control of the machines, bent on wiping out humanity at any cost. And as an Agent, who has now become self-replicating, he is the very virus within the matrix system that he accuses humanity of being. In *Revolutions*, we are not getting a battle between merely a Christ and an Antichrist on a day of judgment to avert an apocalypse. What we get is a battle between a hero, Neo, who wishes to save life (his and that of Trinity—a potential Adam and Eve, mother and father of a new line of humanity, at the least, for he may also save the others aboard the *Nebuchadnezzar*), and Agent Smith, who wishes to end humanity (for we must keep in mind that he is not human).

Wishing, as we referred to it in the previous paragraph, is not *willing*; wishing is contingent upon that one little flaw in humanity that the Architect points out at the end of *Reloaded*, which is *hope*. Neo made his choice to save Trinity instead of going through the door to confront the Source, *hoping* that he could also save the lives of however few people would be left at Zion by the time he got there to help defend them. Agent Smith, now his direct antithesis, wishes only to replicate while snuffing out life, and he is not human, and does not have that same life. It seems almost too simple that faith, hope, and love would be what define us as humans who will survive and keep going, but in the *Matrix* universe, these three, and the knowledge that there are always many choices available, are enough to provide hope that humanity will be saved.

Strange Volutions: Riding the Spiral

If the *Matrix* franchise leaves us with one image, one memento mori, perhaps it is that our desire to control everything is what might, in the end, annihilate us. The continual spiral of war between the machines and the humans, eternally coming to a head and then ebbing again as the matrix is reloaded, Nietzsche's eternal return of the same, is a strange volution, a spiral that does not close. It cannot be represented by a circle drawn in two dimensions; it cannot be drawn as the symbol we associate with vertigo in two dimensions: it is a spiral that spins forward, out into time's future. In the *Matrix* franchise, it does not come to a close, as a circle does, for even when Neo and Smith destroy one another at the close of *Revolutions,* there is a period of peace dawning, yes, but there is already hope for Neo's eventual return.

Following the story of Christ, paralleling the story of Oedipus, with a nice twist on the morality play (Neo's interaction with the Deus Ex Machina, the odd, swirling face/voice speaking for the Machines) it is made clear to us, the viewers, that one man's journey is not his alone. Nietzsche, from our earlier epigraph, is wrong, or he is in the *Matrix* franchise; one man's journey, when he is the One, is one of choices made that have ramifications for all of those who are going along the journey with him (and even for those who are merely connected to his journey peripherally). There is hope in the memento mori that is the *Matrix* franchise. When the smoke clears, there is the hope of the return of the One and the hope for peace. But the cycle that we have witnessed through the *Matrix* franchise has already begun again: we are back where we began!

Works Cited

Escher, M. C. *Escher on Escher: Exploring the Infinite.* Trans. Karin Ford. Ed. Janet Wilson. New York: Abrams, 1989.

Goytisolo, Jaun. *Quarantine.* Trans. Peter Bush. Normal: Dalkey Archive, 1994.

Nietzsche, Friedrich. *The Will to Power.* Trans. Walter Kaufmann and R. J. Hollingdale. Ed. Walter Kaufmann. New York: Vintage, 1968.

———. *Daybreak: Thoughts on the Prejudices of Morality.* Trans. R. J. Hollingdale. Ed. Maudemarie Clark and Brian Leiter. Cambridge: Cambridge University Press, 1997.

Robbe-Grillet, Alain. *Snapshots: Stories.* Trans. Bruce Morrissette. New York: Grove, 1968.

11

Try the *Blue* Pill:
What's Wrong with Life in a Simulation?

RUSSELL BLACKFORD

In the *Matrix* trilogy, Neo learns that the urban landscape where he has lived, grown, and worked is a simulation of reality, not the real world. It does not exist in physical space but within the parameters of an infernally complex computer program. What, though, is wrong with that? If you have the choice, why not live in a reasonably comfortable world, a computer simulation of life in 1999, rather than in a desolate future where human beings are enslaved by artificially intelligent machines? If you were fully informed would you *really* take the red pill, opting for the real world?

In this essay I argue that the case for taking the red pill, preferring physical reality to a digital simulation, is far from clear-cut. Even if Neo makes the correct choice, given the set-up of the *Matrix* movies, a few changes to that set-up might make all the difference. There is nothing straightforwardly wrong with life in a simulation; it all depends on the detail. Some simulations might be better than reality.

Early in the action of *The Matrix*, Morpheus presents Neo with the choice that will determine the future course of his life: Neo must, of course, take the red pill, or the blue. "You take the blue pill," Morpheus says, "and the story ends. You wake up in your bed and you believe whatever you want to believe." The red pill is something else entirely: taking it will lead Neo out of the world he has always known, into one stranger—and far worse—than he could have imagined in his most paranoid moments. "I show you how deep the rabbit hole goes," Morpheus tells him. Then he adds: "All I am offering is the truth. Nothing more" (Wachowski and Wachowski, 301).

As we watch, Neo chooses the red pill, but is that the right decision? Cypher also chose the red pill, but, years later, he regrets doing so. As he tells Neo, "Why, oh why, didn't I take that blue pill?" (Wachowski and Wachowski, 329). The issue is debated once more (though only as the test of another character's loyalty) in the "Program" sequence of *The Animatrix*. So, is contact with reality what matters most, or can you live a perfectly good life one step removed from the real world? For his part, Cypher attempts to justify his betrayal of Morpheus and his team of human rebels. If Morpheus had properly informed the others what they were in for, so Cypher insists, they would have "told him to shove that red pill up his ass" (Wachowski and Wachowski, 357).

Those who take the red pill discover that everything they have ever experienced, every sensory datum, has been an illusion. In *The Matrix,* Neo wakes up to a hellish world—a world that is shown in more detail in the *Animatrix* sequence "Matriculated," in *The Matrix Reloaded,* and especially in *The Matrix Revolutions,* in which Neo must confront the ruling intelligence of the machines in order to save both the real world and the matrix itself.

We first see the world of the machines in *The Matrix,* when Neo is shown floating in a gelatinous substance within a womb-like capsule, his body penetrated by hoses and cables, and fed with a disgusting nutrient. His brain is directly invaded by computational machinery that feeds him a mere simulation of sense data. On the surface of this ruined, dark, and scorched future Earth, vast numbers of similar capsules, each containing a helpless human body, are banked in giant towers, soaring upward, and plunging down as far as the eye can see, and the scale of it defies our senses. Billions of human bodies are exploited as mere things, components in the machines' monstrous power plant.

The *Matrix* trilogy invites us to believe that Neo's choice, his decision to take the red pill and see how deep the rabbit hole goes, was worthwhile. His heroic actions save the two worlds—real and simulated—and restore peace between humans and machines, but we never doubt that his choice would have been a worthwhile, even if he'd failed. Better to live and die authentically, in touch with reality, than maintain an illusory existence within the simulation of a world. Or so the *Matrix* trilogy suggests. In the cut and thrust of debate with Cypher, Trinity defends Morpheus's actions in bringing others to the real world, horrific as it is: "He set us free," she says (Wachowski and Wachowski, 357).

But did he?

As science-fiction writer James Patrick Kelly observes, *The Matrix* "stacks the deck" against the actions of the machines and their creation of a simulated reality for their human enemies/slaves. For example, we are shown machines pumping a black liquid into the support capsule for a tiny human baby, and Morpheus tells Neo that the machines are feeding the humans with the liquefied tissues of the dead. Also, the machines have simulated for the living, dreaming humans, not a virtual heaven—they rejected that opportunity—but "some discount 1999" (Kelly 232). The greenish cinematography even makes this world look rather sickly, though it is lit up by brilliant virtual sunshine in the final moments of *Revolutions,* suggesting it has been redeemed.

Kelly asks what happens if we reshuffle the deck. What if the machines had fed their human batteries "a nice organically grown algae broth" or what if, instead of rejecting the virtual paradise that the machines originally provided them, "the humans had accepted it and flourished?" What if they had consciously agreed to live their lives in the simulated reality of the matrix? "Morpheus's moral crusade to wake everyone up would be at least slightly compromised, no?" (Kelly 233)

To these examples, we can add the exploitative scenario in which the towers of human bodies are used by the machines as a power source, to provide energy to initiate nuclear fusion. (This is not scientifically credible, but forget that distraction.) What more contemptible use could our violated bodies be put to? Again, the technological process by which humans are contained, kept sleeping and dreaming, and provided with a simulated reality, is repulsive and sinister partly because ... well, it *looks* so repulsive.

In *The Matrix,* Neo's body is seen shaved, pale, physically atrophied from lack of exercise (though it still looks pretty good by most standards), totally vulnerable to the tubes and cables entering it. However, any high-tech process involving living human bodies—for example any surgical operation—can be made to seem repulsive and sinister. When bodily organs, fluids, and tissues are juxtaposed against artificiality, machines, and inorganic substances, it is all too easy to produce Frankensteinian connotations. So, isn't the *Matrix* trilogy just appealing to a prejudice here? The appearance of the process surely has little to do with what is fundamentally wrong with it.

Leaving aside the precise set-up of these movies, in which the machines need all those human bodies as a power source, what if there *were* no physical bodies, merely software beings running in a computer simulation that provided as much sensory richness as the matrix? Wouldn't that get around any esthetic problem with living in a simulation?

All of this suggests that the scenario of the *Matrix* movies could be modified—the actions of the intelligent machines given some moral tidying and some prettification—and the wrongness of trying the blue pill would be less clear-cut. Even without such modifications, there are some good arguments available for trying the blue pill, or at least for regretting the loss of that option once you have committed yourself to the real world, and grasped all the implications.

David Weberman has put the arguments in substantial detail (Weberman 234-39). For a start, as Cypher is keenly aware, the simulated reality offers much in the way of sensual pleasures. We see some of these in the scene in *The Matrix* where he discusses his wishes with Agent Smith, while enjoying a superbly tender steak and fine wine in the ambiance of an elegant restaurant. More sensuality is laid on in *Reloaded* and *Revolutions* in the long sequences involving the Merovingian and his decadent followers. But the simulated reality of the matrix offers far more than that.

As Weberman suggests, the simulated reality presumably "gives us the opportunity to visit museums and concerts, read Shakespeare and Stephen King, fall in love, make love, raise children, form deep friendships, and so on" (234-35).

The gratifications available in such a world certainly include the undeniable joys of food, wine, sex, music, and every other delight experienced by the senses. Fantasies of such a richly simulated environment do not reject the pleasures of the body, though they might reject its limitations. More importantly, the matrix is not a bad world to find yourself in, even judged by loftier standards. To test this, consider how science fiction commonly depicts dystopian societies in which danger, passion, creativity, and the life of the mind have been suppressed to create a compliant, tranquil populace. A classic example is the emotionally flattened society of Aldous Huxley's *Brave New World*. Whatever its faults, the society shown within the matrix is not like that.

In *Brave New World,* the characters are seemingly happy, but they have suffered the loss of important dimensions in human life, such as anything remotely like real love or friendship. There is no scope for unique individual achievements except of the most banal kind in the service of the world government, nor for any serious artistic or intellectual pleasures. Some of Huxley's characters understand this, at least in part. One misfit in the brave new world is Bernard Marx, who complains: "I'd rather be myself [...] Myself and nasty. Not somebody else, however jolly." His temporary girlfriend, Lenina Crowne, says that everyone is "Free to have the most wonderful time" in this world. "Everybody's happy nowadays." To which Bernard replies: "But wouldn't you like to be free to be happy in some other way, Lenina? In your own way, for example; not in everybody else's way?" (Huxley 80-82).

Again, there is a famous debate between Mustapha Mond, one of the ten World Controllers of the brave new world, and the Savage, who wishes to bring back everything that causes unhappiness (Huxley 199-209). The calm, urbane World Controller deflects the Savage's criticisms, but we are clearly meant to identify with the Savage, as he grasps for the experiences that he believes are required for deep emotion and a sense of tragedy.

These exchanges highlight what has been lost in the brave new world. The trouble is not so much with the radical biotechnology that has been developed to control reproduction, nor with the promiscuous sexual relationships. It is with the way that all available forms of technology and social organization are used for an insidious, pervasive kind of control. The sexual relationships, if they can even be called "relationships," are not merely a rejection of marriage and monogamy (no longer such a frightening idea, four decades on from the 1960s sexual revolution). They are devoid of any deep or passionate feelings; any strong emotional involvement between those concerned is socially frowned upon.

By contrast, there is no reason to believe that life in the simulated reality of the matrix lacks anything in the way of rich, deep experiences. We are shown little of the relationships of ordinary people, but those who have taken the red pill and crossed over into the desolate reality of the machines' world are quite familiar with such concepts as falling in love—presumably from their original lives in the simulation. Even some of the non-human characters, the programs that serve the matrix, are capable of showing care and feeling warm emotions. Throughout the three movies, The Oracle gives long-term help and advice to Neo and other humans. Sati and her parents in *Revolutions* display a touching kind of familial love.

Nor is the simulation restricted to an urban landscape or to human beings as the only animals. In his diatribe against virus-like human beings, in *The Matrix,* Smith discusses non-human animals and their habitats in a way that suggests that they continue to exist in the simulated reality. There are pets, such as cats, and we see other animals, such as birds. In *Reloaded,* we are shown a mountainous landscape said to be five hundred (virtual) miles to the north of Neo's city. It is established that the city exists within a larger and more interesting (simulated) reality with seemingly natural elements. Indeed, the Architect (Helmut Bakaitis) shows Neo multiple images of the simulated world, making it appear just as diverse as our own.

Neo, it is true, works in what is evidently a soul-destroying job with a large computer firm, but there is no reason to believe that more people lead lives of quiet desperation in the matrix, or have to endure social control in their work and private lives, than in our own world. In short, a simulated reality such as the matrix might be well stocked with pleasures of every kind, sensual and otherwise. It might be as rich, challenging, and good as a "real" reality—or even better. At the same time, reality might turn out to be extremely harsh: not a place you want to find yourself.

In *The Matrix,* we see little of the lives of the rebel humans in the desolate, machine-governed future. We are shown none of their living spaces except the interior of Morpheus's submarine-like hovership, the *Nebuchadnezzar.* The *Nebuchadnezzar's* interior is all steel plates, rivets, wires, pipes, overhead walkways, sheets of metal grating, and flashing computer screens. Sleeping quarters are cramped and small. The only food aboard is insipid stuff that one commentator, Jennifer L. McMahon, neatly describes as "viscous gag-eliciting goop" (McMahon 170).

More is revealed in *Animatrix,* and in *Reloaded* and *Revolutions.* "Final Flight of the Osiris" (the first *Animatrix* sequence) and *Revolutions* place great emphasis on the interiors of the humans' hoverships. "Osiris" uses animation to offer a startling depiction of the weight and chunkiness of the metallic devices that are crammed into such a ships. *Reloaded* shows us more of life in Zion, and things seem rather better than we might have expected from the first movie. In particular, it shows us what Zion looks like. It is a vertical city, built far below the planet's surface, with many levels plunging down, joined by an astonishing array of crisscrossing bridges.

The total effect of the cityscape is not unlike that of the future city shown in Fritz Lang's early science-fiction masterpiece, *Metropolis* (1926). In fact, the influence of *Metropolis* pervades much of the *Matrix* phenomenon. It seems especially strong in some scenes from "The Second Renaissance Part 1" in which the machine slaves, who eventually rebel against their mistreatment and drudgery, are depicted as resembling the downtrodden menial workers shown in Lang's great movie.

Zion has adequate living quarters, and the citizens have established a wise symbiosis with their own machines. Its gigantic metal dock for hoverships such as the *Nebuchadnezzar,* and its vast, cathedral-like public spaces, are impressive. Not only that, Zion rocks with loud, rhythmic music and near-orgiastic dancing in affirmation of life and defiance of the machines. Having seen life there, we might feel that Cypher was exaggerating the privations of the real world.

Yet, no one would choose to take the red pill simply for Zion's mix of cheap pleasures and spartan living. In many ways, the matrix seems like a better place to live than Zion. As we've seen, it is far from being a science-fiction dystopia. If we took the red pill, it would not be to find a superior lifestyle, nor to discover higher and better pleasures. The problems with the simulated reality surely must relate to other values that are lost there: values to do with freedom, authenticity, and connection to objective reality.

The Wachowski brothers may have been aware of one of the most famous philosophical thought experiments of recent decades, that devised by the late Robert Nozick to refute the claim of utilitarian philosophers that subjective pleasure (or pain) is all that matters in ethics. Utilitarians do not necessarily require maximization of sensual or non-intellectual pleasures, as shown by John Stuart Mill's theory that there are "lower" and "higher" pleasures. But they do maintain that our experiences of pleasures and pains (both defined broadly) are all that have moral importance in our lives.

Nozick's *Anarchy, State and Utopia* (1974) is one of the twentieth century's magisterial works of political philosophy, still enormously influential within that field. Nozick challenges the overriding importance of subjective experience, and suggests, very persuasively, that we would not plug into a machine that could provide us with the mere simulation of experience in a pleasant pseudo-reality. Instead, we want to do certain things, be certain ways, and have contact with the objective reality; these are more important to us than any amount of pleasure or satisfaction that might be provided by machines that could do our living for us (Nozick 42-45). "Perhaps," he writes, "what we desire is to live (an active verb) ourselves, in contact with reality" (45).

Whether or not the Wachowski brothers had Nozick's thought experiment in mind, the same issues arise with the simulated reality shown in the *Matrix* trilogy, as they do with other science-fiction books, stories, and movies that depict nested realities. *The Thirteenth Floor* (1999) is another recent cinematic example. It contains no less than three levels of reality, with interactions among characters from all three levels.

It is not surprising that several philosophical commentators have discussed Nozick's "experience machine" in their consideration of *The Matrix*. Usually the point made is that Nozick's thought experiment reveals what is wrong with life in the matrix. I want to suggest that things are not so simple and to put some pressure on the assumptions made by these philosophers.

Gerald J. Erion and Barry Smith are among those who recount Nozick's argument that we want to *do* certain things, *be* a certain way, and connect in a substantial way with reality (Erion and Smith 25-26). They conclude that Cypher acts immorally because he turns his back on a life that has these characteristics. They suggest that reason compels us to face the external world "to build for ourselves meaningful lives within it, and to engage, as adults, in the serious business of living" (27). Theodore Schick, Jr. makes a similar point, then discusses whether those outside the matrix are better off than those inside it, if their fates are predetermined (Schick 90-98), an issue that I don't need to pursue here.

Lyle Zynda invokes Nozick's experience machine in order to deal with the question of whether it matters what is real (Zynda 41). However, he takes this no further than suggesting that the question of what is real does seem to matter to most people, in so far as most of his philosophy students, when questioned, say they would not plug into the experience machine (42-43).

Like Schick, Peter J. Boettke raises an issue that I don't need to pursue. He compares *The Matrix* with Nozick's thought experiment, then argues that we should build the values of freedom and responsibility into our political institutions (Boettke 151-56). While this is an attractive idea, he develops it as an argument for an unhampered market economy. Well, perhaps, but any connection between *The Matrix* and the virtues (or vices) of capitalism actually seems quite tenuous.

All of these commentators draw upon Nozick, and see *The Matrix* in terms of the moral demand that we live in contact with reality. To try to get that issue clearer, we can consider some related points made by Charles L. Griswold, Jr. (from an ethical viewpoint similar to Aristotle's) and Jennifer L. McMahon (from an existentialist viewpoint; she compares *The Matrix* with the work of Jean-Paul Sartre).

Griswold gives some examples of circumstances in which it might be said that you are not truly happy, even though you might feel content or subjectively "happy." For example, you might (unknowingly) be drip-fed a drug that makes you feel good, though your life is a mix of passivity and senseless violence. Or you might feel subjectively "happy" because of some deception, or because you are fantasizing that you are rich; or you might feel that way only when you are drunk, though you feel miserable in the morning. All of this suggests that your life must be worth living for you to be truly happy (Griswold 132-33). Griswold's conception of happiness is that you would affirm your own life as one that is worth living if you stood back and reflected upon it, considering the kind of person that you are (134). On this understanding of true happiness, so Griswold argues, you need to have a correct understanding of reality—about yourself "and about what is truly the case in the world" (135).

McMahon discusses the burdens and benefits of living "authentically," in the sense in which that word is used in existentialist philosophy, i.e., living with an acceptance of the truth about reality. As she points out, the truth may be tough: it may be that life is meaningless, as in Sartre's novels, or that we are all being exploited by sentient machines, as in the *Matrix* trilogy. Still, so the argument goes, an authentic life is better than its opposite. It is the only kind of life worthy of respect. Living inauthentically fails to eradicate anxiety about the world we live in, while it limits our freedom; conversely, living authentically enables us to live freely and honestly (McMahon 175-76). She concludes: "Though the truth may be sobering, it is all we have and all we are" (177).

Accepting the force of all this, how much are the people in the matrix really missing out on active lives and making something of themselves? To what extent do they lack freedom, truth, and personal authenticity? Weberman points out that they have as much freedom, in ordinary ways, as their opposite numbers in our own world. In the matrix, you might get stuck with a boring corporate job, just as you might in our own world, but you can also have complex relationships, exercise whatever talents you have, and shape your own identity. Presumably, you can support or oppose the government (Weberman 235). You certainly have access to complex philosophical books such as those by Jean Baudrillard.

You can even decide that everything is objectively meaningless, and commit yourself to living with that insight; the matrix probably has its due number of existentialists who swear by the literary works of Sartre and Camus. Indeed, Smith and Neo both seem to be existentialists of a kind, judging by their proclamations at the climax of *Revolutions*, when they do battle one last time. While the increasingly nihilistic Smith insists on the meaninglessness of all existence, both real and virtual, Neo makes what seems an effort of existentialist heroism, *choosing* to act in defiance of meaninglessness and seemingly unavoidable defeat.

In any event, Weberman makes the critical point: the only things you can't do in the simulation—the only things that incur the wrath of the machines and their Agents—are unplug or assist others to do so. And the only important truth you cannot know is that your whole world is unreal—

if that matters: "it feels real as real can get. And there's no reason to suspect that it's unreal unless Morpheus or one of his team visits you. So should you care? Does it matter? Is it in the end really unreal? What makes it unreal?" (235)

This takes us to the root of the problem. Is a simulated reality less real than an unsimulated reality? The actions and experiences that Neo has had in the matrix, such as visits to restaurants, all stand in a coherent relationship to each other, and even to those of other people (Weberman 236-37). They correspond to something that actually happened, and in principle one could even "find traces of it in the brains of other human beings lying in pods plugged in to the matrix" (237). For those in the matrix, their world is as real as ours is to us. Although objects in the matrix do not exist in physical space, Weberman rejects the idea that something must exist in space in order to be real (238).

Up to a point, this analysis seems right. Try another thought experiment. What if our entire experienced world (including we, ourselves) somehow emerged from computations within an underlying substrate that was not actually part of this world? In a sense, only that substrate would be physical reality, but it might be nothing like the physical objects, particles, fields, forces, and so on perceivable via our senses or detectable by scientific instruments. Imagine that it is impossible in principle for us ever to discover this deepest level of reality, that we are totally insulated from it. (This is something like the "dust" theory in Greg Egan's novel *Permutation City*. I'm not sure that we are any better off if avant-garde theories in contemporary physics, such as string theory, turn out to be true.)

If that were the situation in the *Matrix* trilogy, I would agree with Weberman. Being able to live a meaningful life does not seem to depend on access to knowledge about the deepest levels of explanation for our universe. For all we know, we are in a situation where our ability to discover truth has fundamental boundaries. It seems we must bracket off some possibilities and get on with our lives. It is pointless complaining that we are not living in contact with reality if it is only in *that* sense.

The possibility of fundamental boundaries to our knowledge does not prevent us having lives that can be full of activity, self-creation, and authenticity. In every meaningful sense, we can be free. At an ultimate level, the world might not be as it seems, but does it matter? And, really, at what previous period in history have human beings had even the knowledge of reality available now, through the advance of science? Yet, we do not dismiss all people who ever lived before, say, the discoveries of Darwin and Einstein, as living inauthentic lives. Judgments about whether or not people are living authentic, or inauthentic, lives must be relative to the knowledge of reality that is reasonably available to them if they are clear-eyed and honest.

That, however, does not justify taking the blue pill. The point here is that the matrix is not totally insulated from the machines' world. Instead, we have a set-up where sentient programs (the Agents) are in touch with both worlds; such characters as Morpheus, Trinity, and Niobe (Jada Pinkett Smith) move freely between one and the other; and various of them—Neo, Cypher, and Trinity, among many others—are given a clear choice whether or not to experience the underlying reality. A decision to take the blue pill would be a deliberate rejection of available knowledge, not the result of some fundamental boundary to what human beings can know.

On the other hand, those who are not given the choice cannot be accused of living inauthentic lives. It is not clear that there is anything wrong with living in the simulation, until they are actually faced with the conscious choice (that they may have unconsciously accepted the matrix, in the sense of finding the illusion compelling, does not seem relevant). On reflection, their situation is surprisingly *different* from those who use Nozick's experience machine, and have the machine live their lives for them.

This might suggest that it is wrong to take the blue pill, but that it is also wrong of Morpheus to offer the red pill! By what right does he impose such a terrible choice on people whose lives were satisfactory, until he interfered—satisfactory even by criteria such as those specified by Nozick and Griswold? Against this, British science-fiction writer Stephen Baxter sums up one reason why we might be angered and outraged upon discovering how we have been used by the machines: "If we are being contained and deceived, whatever the motive, we are in a relationship of unequals, and are thereby diminished. We have a moral responsibility to ourselves to try to break down the walls and challenge our captors" (45).

Perhaps so. Once we become aware of it, we are outraged by our exploitation. Perhaps, too, this is a justification for the choice that Morpheus offers, and for his struggle. It might be better if he could inform individuals such as Neo more fully before they made their choice ... but how could he? No one would believe it. This is a powerful argument for offering and taking the red pill, but it is based on the precise scenario of the *Matrix* trilogy, not on an argument that any life in a simulation must be lacking in authenticity. It cannot be used successfully as a general argument against living in a simulated reality, and I do not believe that any such general argument is available.

In what circumstances, then, might it be okay to live in a simulation?

Earlier, I asked whether a few changes might make all the difference. We have imagined some of them already. Consider, now, a more drastic scenario than that in the *Matrix* trilogy. Some science-fiction writers, such as Greg Egan, have imagined worlds populated by characters of complex software in simulated environments. In his novel *Diaspora,* for example, Egan's characters include "polis citizens" who are beings of pure software running within simulated-reality communities maintained by well-protected supercomputers. The word "polis" refers to both a community of citizens (the original Greek use) and to the physically secure hardware that sustains the software infrastructure for its shared reality.

Diaspora is set in the distant future. Egan reveals that the original polis citizens were human beings who converted into software form and entered their simulated environments in the late twenty-first century. This mass exodus into simulated reality is recalled, appropriately, as "the Introdus." That word, in turn, gives a name to "Introdus nanoware," still available for uploading the neural properties of "fleshers," i.e., flesh-and-blood humans (or genetically altered transhuman beings), onto radically advanced computer hardware.

One of the issues with which *Diaspora* grapples is what kind of significance can be given to maintaining a connection with physical reality, if posthuman technologies and richly simulated environments are available. For most of Egan's characters, and seemingly for the author himself, there is still value in using scientific instruments and other devices to investigate the physical world and exert some control over it.

This leads me back to Nozick's experience machine, and to one last commentator on the subject, the Extropian philosopher Max More, who embraces the development of radical technologies to transform the human condition. Like other thinkers about life in simulations, More uses Nozick's thought experiment as a starting point. He contrasts the experience machine with a possible simulated reality in which you really do interact with others, in which you might retain some contact with the physical world and ability to change it, and in which you can create things, "even if these things are information and datastructures" (8).

He sets out the case against living in Nozick's experience machine as six points (see More 9-10), but these can be repackaged cogently as follows. First, we want to achieve certain things, not just have the subjective sensation of achieving them. We want the world we are in to give us the opportunity to exercise our capacities and talents. Second, we each want to be a certain sort of person, not just have the subjective sensation of being like that. Third, we want to live in a world that is deep and rich, not one that is limited by preprogramming. We want to have the richness of experience that comes from really interacting with other people, and the interplay of many minds. We also "want endless worlds to explore for new knowledge, more profound understanding, fresh ideas and perspectives" (10). Fourth, we do not want to be helpless, trapped in a virtual substrate that may be threatened from outside, unknown to us, and we want to be able to exercise some control if our immediate reality is sustained by machines in the external physical world.

Judged by these criteria, some imaginable simulated realities are superior to the experience machine in every way. The polises described in Egan's *Diaspora,* at least those that have chosen to retain contact with the physical world, do not suffer from any of its disadvantages. In the end, nothing seems to be intrinsically, inevitably, wrong with living in a simulation of reality. Perhaps the trilogy eventually accepts this in the last redemptive moments of *Revolutions.*

It seems that there is nothing intrinsically wrong with living in a simulation, despite the heavy propagandizing in favor of the "real" that dominates most of the *Matrix* trilogy. It all depends. It is not simply a matter of the inferiority of a virtual existence.

When Neo meets Morpheus in *The Matrix,* Morpheus informs him that the world he has known is an illusion: "It is the world that has been pulled over your eyes to blind you from the truth." Neo responds with just two words, "What truth?" (Wachowski and Wachowski 300), and similar terse dialogue continues throughout the *Matrix* trilogy. Do we wish to live in the real world, or can it be okay to live in a simulation? The answers are not clear-cut, despite the interpretations of commentators who have gone back to Nozick's thought experiment. We need to see the detail, to check the fine print.

What is wrong with life in a simulation of reality? We can only reply: "What life? What simulation? What reality?"

Works Cited

Baxter, Stephen. "The Real Matrix." Haber 31-46.

Boettke, Peter J. "Human Freedom and the Red Pill." Yeffeth 145-57.

Egan, Greg. *Permutation City.* London: Orion-Millennium, 1994.

——. *Diaspora.* London: Orion-Millennium, 1997.

Erion, Gerald J., and Barry Smith. "Skepticism, Morality, and *The Matrix.*" Irwin 16-27.

Griswold, Charles L., Jr. "Happiness and Cypher's Choice: Is Ignorance Bliss?" Irwin 126-37.

Haber, Karen, ed. *Exploring the Matrix: Visions of the Cyberpresent.* New York: St. Martin's, 2003.

Huxley, Aldous. *Brave New World.* First published 1932. Repr. London: Flamingo-Harper-Collins, 1994.

Irwin, William, ed. *The Matrix and Philosophy: Welcome to the Desert of the Real.* La Salle: Open Court, 2002.

Kelly, James Patrick. "Meditations on the Singular Matrix." Haber 223-35.

McMahon, Jennifer L. "Popping a Bitter Pill: Existential Authenticity in *The Matrix* and *Nausea.*" Irwin 166-77.

More, Max. "Virtue and Virtuality: From Enhanced Senses to Experience Machines." Based on a talk to The Future of the Senses conference, Bonn, January 1997. <http://www.maxmore.com/virtue.htm>. Accessed November 8, 2003

Nozick, Robert. *Anarchy, State and Utopia.* New York: Basic Books, 1974.

Schick, Theodore, Jr. "Fate, Freedom, and Foreknowledge." Irwin 87-98.

Wachowski, Larry, and Andy Wachowski. *The Matrix* (screenplay). *The Art of the Matrix.* Ed. Spencer Lamm. New York: Newmarket Press, 2000. 271-394.

Weberman, David. "*The Matrix:* Simulation and the Postmodern Age." Irwin 225-39.

Yeffeth, Glenn, ed. *Taking the Red Pill: Science, Philosophy and Religion in The Matrix.* Dallas: Benbella, 2003.

Zynda, Lyle. "Was Cypher Right? Part II: The Nature of Reality and Why it Matters." Yeffeth 33-43.

Conclusion

At the Edge of the World, Again.

MATTHEW KAPELL

O n a Saturday morning in 1999, I sat with my then nine-year-old stepdaughter Kristen, and viewed the science-fiction movie *Deep Impact* (1998). The film depicts the effects of a comet striking the earth; the heroes who save the world from a second, larger comet; and the lives of people who live through the events. As the movie ended, the nine-year-old turned to her stepfather and asked a pointed question. "When did that happen?" When told that the story was made up and, that, it never happened she replied, "That's too bad. It would have been really cool to have an African American president." Stunned, I told her that one day there would be an African American president, and she would be a woman too.

What followed was a long discussion of the ways in which (a) race, (b) gender, and (c) class function in society. It was decided that before there would be a person of color in the White House then we would need cultural models such as motion pictures in which, at the end, all the "white" characters were dead while the people of color and women mostly survived. It was Kristen's hope that such films would also feature a lot of women who don't "just scream and yell until the man comes and saves her."

With the *Matrix* franchise, it may be that we finally have a work that comes pretty close to what Kristen hoped for. Well, *maybe!* Certainly King and Leonard, Lipp, and Lawrence would disagree by their contributions to this book. Yet, as Sexson notes in his essay, whatever the *Matrix* franchise is, it is something to learn from.

The *Matrix* Phenomena and the New Multi-Media Panoramic Franchise in Popular Culture

When the first of the *Star Wars* films was released in 1977, it quickly received immense cultural popularity. What then happened helped change popular culture forever. But this change, ushered in by *Star Wars* and similar films, was only one of quantity, in that there were more products to purchase, but they did nothing to help tell the story of the films. Already in the 1950s, children could and did buy toy rifles emulating those favored by of the most popular Saturday movie cowboy heroes. Long before that they could read their A. A. Milne "Pooh" stories while holding their own Pooh Bears. But in the late 1970s, the cross-marketing phenomenon exploded.

Suddenly there was a plethora of merchandise that one could buy with respect to *Star Wars* alone. Trading cards with screen shots, lunch boxes, models of the ships, the list could go on and on. But the *Matrix* phenomenon has done its extra-filmic franchising in a far different manner. Now, rather than just producing products that let the buyer re-live the filmed experience, *the products themselves* have become part of the story.

The game, *Enter*, fills in how Niobe and Ghost move through their volunteer mission to where they actually save Morpheus in *Reloaded*. The *Animatrix* sequence not only fills in the back-story for a number of characters (most notably Kid), it fills in the entire history of how the matrix itself came into being ("Second Renaissance, Parts I and II").

Unlike the case with *Star Wars* or any other similar franchise, the Wachowskis have shown us that it is now possible to add needed details to the entire franchise through the use of different media. We believe this makes the *Matrix* franchise a new form of entertainment, and one likely we will be seeing more of in the future. It did not take long for the Wachowski brothers to get from toying "with the idea of continuing the story in comic book form when the movies are finished" (Wachowski brothers interview, 1999) to publication of "volume one, Fall 2003" of *The Matrix Comics*.

From a Multi-Media Story to an Interdisciplinary Book on the Franchise

We began this volume by discussing how many different ways there are "to read" the *Matrix* franchise. The prisms of "race" and gender are certainly important, and what we hope for the next generation of this planet is that the inequalities that have existed for so long will vanish. But what Lipp, and King and Leonard, note in this book remains true: our culture still exhibits thousands of examples of racism and sexism. If Gray Kochhar-Lindgren is correct in his contribution, it seems as though the entire definition of what it means to be "human" is changing, and with it many other important ideas in our world. Perhaps the old definitions of "race" and gender will cease to be important factors. But this is not the first time that such definitional changes have occurred within Western culture, nor in all likelihood will it be the last.

Beyond the sort of non-involved scholarship of rationalism (see Doty's Introduction), postmodernist voices (a) recognize *the embedded ideological quality* of any institutionally produced research. It is now a difficult task to track just how extremely post-World-War-II research was driven largely by what either government or commerce indicated as "most productive"—and screw those earlier transcendental ideals worshipped yea these many generations in Western idealism.

At the same time, (b) the last decade or so of postmodernist discussions have engaged *ethical* issues that earlier postmodernist theorists considered out of bounds. The collection of essays by Jacques Derrida, *Acts of Religion,* is representative, as is O'Leary's *Foucault and the Art of Ethics,* and *Philosophy and the Turn to Religion* (de Vries).

We hope that this volume will stimulate reflections beyond those proposed in the secondary literature to date. Can our contributions seed important new ways of accessing the *Matrix* data?—we hope so.

At the Edge of the World, Again. Now Where to?

Nearing the year 1000 C.E. was difficult for those living in the Western world. The so-called "Dark Ages" covered the continent like a thick fog. Many thought that perhaps the world would end on New Year's Day 1000, others hoped that Christ would return to begin his millennial reign. The American historian William Manchester calls the period leading up to the year 1000 C.E. one of "incessant warfare, corruption, lawlessness, obsession with strange myths, and an almost impenetrable mindlessness" (3). Thankfully, the world did not end!

A millennium later, approaching the year 2000 C.E. in the Western world was like déjà vu all over again. People worried about the Y2K bug destroying the entire electronic infrastructure of the planet, about planes dropping from the sky like locusts. They stocked up on bottled water and non-perishable foods "just in case." Certainly, at the time, taking the blue pill seemed like a fine alternative, as Blackford suggests in his essay here.

And as 1999 arrived, few suspected that an inconsequential film, written and directed by two virtually unknown brothers and co-writers/directors, would become a worldwide phenomenon. But somehow *The Matrix* did exactly that.

Four and a half years later, it is hard to remember the "millennial fears" that gripped many. But the first *Matrix* film seemed to be made at the perfect time to exploit those fears. And with those fears (like those at the end of the first millennium) a Christ figure of renewal appeared in Neo, of *The Matrix,* as John Shelton Lawrence notes in his essay in this volume.

Yet as many of our contributors in this book have noted in one way or another, the *Matrix* franchise has utilized more than just Christian symbolism. Flannery-Dailey and Wagner relate the *Matrix* materials to both "Eastern" and "Western" religions, while Isaacs and Trost, and Jones, identify in the franchise searches for a mythic underpinning in our postmodern times. We did not find the fact that the franchise was replete with religious allegory all that surprising. To us, what was surprising was how quickly and easily much of the moviegoing public recognized the various types of symbolism. Maybe the Western world was ready for images of a huge and dramatic change—primed to expect them as the year 2000 hullabaloo had shaped them. Maybe it was simply that we were all ready for a change. Maybe we had, in fact, primed ourselves for it.

The Canadian cultural theorist Richard Dellamora notes in the introduction to his edited volume, *Postmodern Apocalypse,* that "in cultural history, there are a number of moments that provide an allegorical figure of a particular movement" (1). He recounts the suicide of the wonderful English novelist Virginia Woolf, who died in early 1941, trying to escape a violent death at the hands of the Nazis for herself and her Jewish husband. For Dellamora, Woolf's suicide marked the immediate end of a certain way of writing, a certain artistic aesthetic, and the beginning of something new.

We believe that the release of *The Matrix* is a similar (though obviously not as dramatic) allegorical moment. The older movement (likely the one initiated in late 1960s through the early 1980s during the height of popularity for *Star Wars, Star Trek,* and similarly styled fictions) found the beginnings of its own end as new stylistic forms began to emerge.

The end of that previous style can be found in the very first scenes of the first film. It is in the moment when Trinity leaps into the air, arms extended, black vinyl shining like the carapace of a deadly spider. As the camera rips around her before she lands her first kick on a police officer, puny light-saber battles and "going where no one has gone before," could no longer create mass public excitement.

But, millennial fever and changes of the guard aside, as The Oracle notes in *Revolutions,* "everything that has a beginning has an end." We have a new aesthetic, but eventually there will be another allegorical shift and the world created by the Wachowski brothers will seem as dated to many as the earliest episodes of *Star Trek* appear to the generation that first embraced the *Matrix* franchise. Like Neo in the first film, we don't know how the aesthetic introduced by the franchise will end, for as Mizelle and Baker note, the *Matrix* franchise is not about closed loops with ends easily seen. But like The Oracle in the closing scenes of the final film, we have hope that whatever new style replaces this current one, it will be as rich, dizzying, and open to multiple readings as is the entire *Matrix* phenomenon.

Works Cited

Dellamora, Richard, ed. *Postmodern Apocalypse: Theory and Cultural Practice at the End.* Philadelphia: University of Pennsylvania Press, 1995.

de Vries, Hent. *Philosophy and the Turn to Religion.* Baltimore: Johns Hopkins University Press, 1999.

Derrida, Jacques. *Acts of Religion.* Ed., intro. Gil Anidjar. New York: Routledge–Taylor and Francis, 2002.

Manchester, William. *A World Lit Only By Fire: The Medieval Mind and The Renaissance.* New York: Little, Brown, 1992.

O'Leary, Timothy. *Foucault and the Art of Ethics.* New York: Continuum, 2002.

Wachowski brothers interview on Matrix Virtual Theatre. 6 November 1999. <http://www.warnervideo.com/matrixevents/Wachowski.html>. Accessed 1 January 2004.

Films

Deep Impact. Dir. Mimi Leder. Perf. Robert Duval, Tea Leoni, Elijah Woods. Paramount Pictures, 1998.

Star Wars. Dir. George Lucas. Perf. Mark Hamill, Harrison Ford, Carrie Fisher. Twentieth Century Fox, 1977.

Getting With the Program/s of the Franchise: User's Information

1. List of items in the franchise, with abbreviations used in this book:

Full Titles:	Shorthand use:
The Matrix (1st film)	*The Matrix*
Matrix Reloaded	*Reloaded*
The Matrix Revolutions	*Revolutions*
the three films	the *Matrix* trilogy
the franchise	the *Matrix* franchise
ref. to the matrix within the films	the matrix [e.g., "they live in a matrix constructed by externals"—this is already Wiliam Gibson's use]
general ref. to the Matrix phenomenon	the Matrix phenomenon (a bit broader than the franchise)
Enter The Matrix (p.c./video game)	*Enter*
The Animatrix (9 short animé films)	*Animatrix*
"Final Flight of the Osiris"	"Osiris"
"The Second Renaissance Part I"	"Second Renaissance Part I"
"The Second Renaissance Part II"	"Second Renaissance Part II"
"Kid's Story"	"Kid's Story"
"Program"	"Program"
"World Record"	"World Record"
"Beyond"	"Beyond"
"A Detective Story"	"Detective Story"
"Matriculated"	"Matriculated"
The Matrix Comics so far: vol. 1, Fall 2003, has been issued	*Comics*
The Matrix Online (Massively Multiplayer Online Role-Playing Game, or MxO)	*Online*

2. Glossary of Names and terms in the franchise:

Some of the terms of symbolic resonance in the *Matrix* franchise are briefly discussed in this section. The names of the actors who perform some of the most important roles are discussed here in terms of possible referents intended by the directors. Note that actor's names are not always indicated in individual chapters, only in this segment. Excellent resources for determining the full casts and crews of the films will be found on sites listed below in part 3. We point to "The Matrix Glossary" in *Taking the Red Pill: Science, Philosophy, and Religion in* The Matrix, edited by Glenn Yeffeth (Dallas: Benbella, 2003: 243-55) as a useful resource for symbolic meanings of numbers in *The Matrix,* many technical terms, and such items as particular colors and phrases, and the many Chicago street names.

Anderson, Thomas A. (= Neo; Keanu Reeves): Thomas Anderson must refer to the doubting Thomas of the New Testament. "Anderson" means, literally, "Son of Man." Thomas in Greek is a traditional twin name; the Gnostic Gospel of Thomas, for instance, is said to be written by Judas Thomas, acclaimed by Syrian Christians as the twin brother of Jesus and the apostle to the Syrians. Neo also acts as Osiris in the Isis/Osiris myths, where the god is killed, but resurrected by his sister-wife, Isis (represented here by Trinity). Another reference may be to the Inanna/Tammuz myth in Mesopotamia, or to that of Persephone in Greece. (See Persephone).

APUs: Armored Personnel Units. (See Cyborg.)

Architect, The (Helmut Bakaitis): The "father" of the matrix. In Egyptian myth Imhotep is the god of architecture and writing. A historical Imhotep was the designer of the first step pyramid, which initially reflected the Egyptian primeval mound that represents order over chaos. Several commentators refer to The Architect's "Freudian" appearance and mien.

B1-66ER: The first robot that rose up against its master and crushed his head in order to prevent its own death; the incident led to a pivotal court case that is argued on the basis of rulings in the (historical) Dredd Scot case ("The Second Renaissance" and "Bits and Pieces"). The MATRIX 101 observes: "It's been suggested the robot's name came from 'Bigger Thomas,' the main character of *Native Son,* a novel [by Richard A. Wright] about a black man in 1930s Chicago who commits a murder he believes he has no choice but to commit" (http:www.thematrix101.com/revolutions/synopsis.php, accessed 1 January 2004).

Bane (Ian Bliss): Fatal injury or ruin; a cause of death (from Old English for "slayer"), destruction, or ruin; a deadly poison. A rebel onboard the ship *Caduceus,* his body is taken over by Smith and he attempts to kill Neo, but is foiled by the Kid. He causes further mayhem, killing a medical officer with a scalpel. Later he and Neo fight and Bane burns Neo's eyes with the power from broken electrical cables—but Neo can still psychically "see" enough to bash his head in with a metal pole.

Birth: Neo's re-birth from the nurturing machines pretty clearly signals his steps toward eventual messianic status, although we have to wait until the apotheosis scenes in *Revolutions* to be absolutely sure of that status.

Brothers, The: See Wachowski, Andy; Wachowski, Larry.

Cyberpunk: A term used to identify William Gibson's influential sci-fi novel *Neuromancer* (1984—here already is the "jacking in" of our title), and later writers such as Bruce Sterling, John Shirly, and others. "Cyber" derives from control and comm systems, "punk" from the relationship of the authors to popular culture. Authors already influencing cyberpunk writers are no less part of the literary and filmic atmosphere in which the Brothers work: William Burroughs, Thomas Pynchon, Raymond Chandler, J. G. Ballard, Philip K. Dick, and Samuel Delaney.

Cyborg: Literally a "cybernetic organism" (coined by Manfred Clynes in 1960 in the context of the space program, the concept suggests a life form that is part organic and part technological, or in the words of the American theorist Donna J. Haraway, "a hybrid of machine and organism"—think of the anti-hero of the *Terminator* movies. In the *Matrix* franchise the use of Armored Personnel Units (APUs) is the most striking visual example, in which humans interface with defensive armored machines. However, the very process of "jacking in" also represents a hybrid of the organic and mechanistic in which the human element is enhanced through the use of technology. (See also APU, Cyborg, Simulation, and Kochhar-Lindren essay, in this volume.)

Cypher (Joe Pantoliano): Perhaps short for "Lucifer," as well as "to cipher," to calculate (mathematics) or to put into secret writing or code. The classic betrayer, Cypher weighs the odds between the free humans and the matrix, and makes a bet on the matrix as the winning side. People who see *The Matrix* primarily as a Christian allegory equate Cypher with Judas. (See Blackford essay in this volume.)

APPENDIX

Deus Ex Machina: See God.

Dozer (Anthony Ray): The major reference is to the earth-moving bull-dozer (which may be from obsolete *bulldose,* a severe beating). However, a secondary reference may be to Djoser, the Egyptian vizier for whom Imhotep designed the first step pyramid (see Architect, The). In *The Matrix,* Dozer is a natural-born-human from Zion who piloted the *Nebuchadnezzar.* He was killed by Cypher, using a plasma rifle.

Franchise, The *Matrix:* An inclusive term for all the components of the materials developed by the Wachowski brothers in tandem with the original movie, *The Matrix.* See the "List of items in the franchise" that precedes this glossary, and discussion of the "Total Work of Art" concept in the first part of Doty's introductory chapter.

Ghost (Anthony Wong): He and Niobe are the alternative personalities for the game-player in *Enter.* Otherwise, as a rebel aboard the *Logos,* his major skill has to do with firearms—helpful when he strafes enemies to cover Captain Niobe as she carries out missions.

Gnosis: "Knowledge," but of a special sort—a sort of mystical kit of symbols thought to bring experience of the ultimate spirit beyond all physical incarnations of it. In fact the physical is often treated as merely a hindrance. In forms of Christian Gnosticism, Jesus is either a transcendent being from elsewhere or just a human teacher, who in either case brings highly coded sayings that will enable the believer to rejoin the All (*plêroma*) which was fragmented by evil powers. A Hovercraft name mentioned by an old woman to Neo in *Reloaded.*

God: While the Latin *deus ex machina* is applied to mechanical devices in Greek drama that bring an actor representing a deity onto or above the stage, often to resolve a insolvable dramatic conflict, the Brothers' Deus Ex Machina, the apparent face in the shimmering golden bowl at the end of *Revolutions,* merely provides one indirect suggestion of "salvation": the trilogy is never so obvious as to suggest any single "answer." Perhaps the deus ex machina here could be thought of as "the machine intelligence par excellence." It sees the danger of the takeover of everything (and subsequent annihilation) by Smith, and understands that Neo's acquiescence and attempt at peace making at the end of *Revolutions,* represents more of a possibility for the future than the martial fighting to the end between Neo and Smith.

Hamann, Councilor (Anthony Zerbe): The reference here is doubtless to the philosopher Johann Georg Hamann (1730-88), a contemporary of

Immanuel Kant. Hamann underwent a sort of conversion that involved giving up his early commitment to the secular Enlightenment in favor of a more orthodox view of Protestant Christianity. As a consequence, he embarked on a career of trenchant and often scathing criticism of Enlightenment thought, stressing the need for intuition in understanding nature, the use of genius, and a faith in God—none of which were understandable through reason alone. Hamann's work greatly influenced Søren Kierkegaard, who is quoted by Ghost in *Enter*.

Key Maker, The (Randall Duk Kim): In certain versions of the Isis/Osiris myth of Egypt, the *Ankh* hieroglyph symbolizing the life force includes the significance of representing "The Key to the Nile." This key was needed to allow Isis and Osiris to stay together, and for Isis to aid in the resurrection of Osiris. In the trilogy, the Key Maker is a program designed to make keys for everything and he deals Hermes-like with a variety of exits and entrances. The Oracle sends Neo to him for assistance on getting to the machine source. (See The Architect, Neo, Trinity, Persephone).

Kid, The (= Michael Karl Popper; Clayton Watson): In *Animatrix*, "Kid's Story," teenager Neo has communicated with him in computer chatrooms, and who believes in Neo deeply. Agents come for him at school, but thanks to a call from Neo he escapes, using his skateboard to get to the roof. He jumps and wakes up in the real world, believing that Neo had saved him—we overhear Trinity saying "I didn't think self-substantiation was possible." On Zion in *Revolutions*, he manages to open the gates for the triumphal scene of the end of the war.

Link (Harold Perrineau): Most obvious reference for Link is that as an "operator" on the *Nebuchadnezzar*, he is the "link" between the real world and the virtual world of the matrix. A Zion-born human, he is married to Zee (whose siblings were Tank and Dozer).

Lock, Commander (Harry J. Linnix): The obvious reference is to safety ("situation locked down"), since he is in charge of the defense of Zion. Lock does not believe in Neo, and believes that devoting resources to his quest will ensure Zion's destruction. Since there are references throughout the franchise to philosophers familiar to the Brothers, this may be a reference to John Locke. Locke is famous for his conception of *tabula rasa*, namely that humans are born with no innate ideas ("a blank slate"). For Locke (and both Hume and Berkeley), knowledge was derived from experience. Locke's two treatises on government had a profound impact on the late eighteenth-century revolutions in France, Haiti and, especially, the British Colonies (United States). Locke's distinction between primary and secondary qualities and his distinction between intuition and demonstration may also have been in the mind of the Wachowskis.

Logos: Greek for "word," but eventually specified in Greek thought as representing the rational rather than mythical statement (as witnessed in "logical"). In some early Christian contexts, the Christ figure was entitled The Logos or Word (Gospel of John 1.14, "The Word became flesh"), probably derived from Stoic teachings about a world pattern or spirit behind and in people and the world order, as well as Hellenistic Jewish concepts of the active "Word" (Hebrew *dabhar*) of the deity in creation. The primary use of the term is for Niobe's hovercraft that Neo and Trinity use to travel to the machine city.

Matrix: Derived from Greek *mêtêr and* Latin *mater,* mother or breeding animal, the term refers to the surrounding substance within which something else originates, develops, or is contained, the womb, a mold or die, an array of quantities subject to mathematical operations. We capitalize the "m" in references to the *Matrix* films and other parts of the franchise, and use the word matrix in lower-case, for the implied machine construct of the fictional world being referred to.

MetaCorTechs: The company for which Thomas Anderson worked (it echoes a real company, CorTechs). There may be some play upon the cerebral cortex, the outer gray matter of the brain responsible for sensation, thought, and memory. An online game set in the matrix universe has appeared called *Metacortex*. The idea is to follow clues to uncover secrets and, inevitably, more clues. If there is a "prize" of any kind or insights into the future of the *Matrix* franchise is anybody's guess, all we can do is search and see.

Merovingian, The (Lambert Wilson): Merovingians were Frankish kings who ruled what is now mostly France, from the time of Clovis I (481-511 CE) until 751 CE. Myths have been built around this family, including magical powers; for instance, Clovis I was buried with the severed head of a horse, and that has led to some modern myths among the American Mafia. A Merovingian Gnostic Church, supposedly founded by Joseph of Arimathea in 54 CE, was charged with protecting the Holy Grail. There is a strong hint in the franchise that the Merovingian and Persephone might be earlier incarnations of The One and Trinity. Note Persephone's statement, "a long time ago he used to be like you."

Mifune, Capt. (Nathaniel Lees): Head of the defensive APU squadron protecting the home Zion. Possibly a reference to Toshiro Mifune, a Japanese actor in many Akira Kurosawa films, especially samurai films. (See APUs.)

Morpheus (Laurence Fishburne): Greek and Roman God of Sleep, who could take on many forms while sending images into the dreaming mind. He is not known for attempts to find a messianic leader or as a prophet leading revolutionary teams, as in the franchise. Indeed the name, from Latin into French, leads to the name of the drug *morphine,* which causes morbidity and sluggishness. Part of the dream-world, perhaps, the Wachowskis use him as a further heightening of the repeated/implied question: "Is this real or not—reality or a dream?"

Mouse (Matt Doran): The youngest member of the crew of the *Nebuchadnezzar* who does programming for the training systems.

Nebuchadnezzar: The hovercraft ship that flies through the abandoned subway and sewer lines beneath the destroyed surface of the earth. The name is that of the King of Babylonia (605-562 BCE) who captured (597) and destroyed (586) Jerusalem, and carried the Israelites into captivity in Babylonia. He was the most powerful and longest reigning king of the Neo-Babylonian period, who brought the state to a pinnacle of power, and sponsored several impressive building projects that beautified his capital, Babylon.

Neo (Keanu Reeves): Neo means "new" (cf. *neonate,* a newborn child), but it is also an anagram of "One," and rhymes importantly with "hero." In many ways, the entire franchise can be seen as comprising the Epic of Neo, whose presence looms even when he is not personally present. (See Thomas Anderson, Trinity, Persephone.)

Niobe (Jada Pinkett Smith): The tragic tale of Niobe is one of the most memorable in Greek mythology. It features a striking example of the consequences of hubris (arrogance or excessive pride): she offends the goddess Leto by boasting that while she herself had given birth to twelve children, the goddess only bore two (the god Apollo and the goddess Artemis). Leto sends her two children to punish the foolish woman, as treated in Homer's *Iliad* and Ovid's *Metamorphoses.* Immediate applications to the chief butt-kicker of *Enter,* Niobe, are not self-evident. She is the only hovercraft pilot who can pilot *The Hammer* through belowground tunnels never meant for hovercraft travel.

Oracle, The (Gloria Foster and Mary Alice): The Oracle at Delphi was famous for giving good, but difficult to comprehend, advice. However, it was always true, and this motif seems to be prevalent in the trilogy, although characters seldom know just "how" true or when. As the "mother" of the matrix, she discovered the need for choice in order for the virtual projection to work, and as the one who consistently throughout the film trilogy keeps prodding the action along, she perhaps foresees what will happen when the opposition between Neo and Smith is broken when Neo lets go. Taken over by Agent Smith, and speaks to Neo through him; but after the final defeat of Smith by Neo, she returns to her normal appearance, and attends the cosmic-golden-sky scene with Sati, at the end of *Revolutions*.

Osiris, **The:** Like four others of the ten rebel ships, the *Osiris*—made, we are told in the USA in 2079—it carried a reference to a verse of the Gospel of Mark, in this case it is to Mark 6.16, "But when Herod heard of it, he said, 'John, whom I beheaded, has been raised.'" This curious reference to the death of John the Baptist leads to as few associations as the obvious reference to the Isis/Osiris story of ancient Egypt does. The ship provides the transition between its battle with the evil Sentinels, and the beginning mission of *Reloaded*. (See Neo.)

Persephone (Monica Bellucci): The beautiful daughter of Demeter and Zeus, Persephone is the goddess of the underworld in Greek myth (contrasts with Neo as Osiris) and is the focus of the story resulting in the division of the seasons, giving us the sweetness of Spring and the bitterness of Winter. Persephone is a parallel myth to the Isis/Osiris and Inanna/Tammuz myths of the ancient near-East. These myths are obviously referred to in the story line of Trinity and Neo—thus, it is not surprising that Persephone would be seen as a threat to both, but especially to Trinity. The powerful goddess quality of Persephone is only hinted at in the few spoken lines that Bellucci is given in the films. (See Neo, Trinity.)

Posthuman: That which comes "after" the human. Intimately related to the concept of the cyborg, the idea of the posthuman suggests that humanity is in the process of making itself over, through the use and development of technology, into a new kind of creature. A merging of the organic and the mechanistic, it is the hope that through the use of technology humanity will be able to overcome previous inequities based on class, gender and "race," since those divisions will no longer remain important. (See also Cyborg, Virtual.)

Rama-Kandra (Bernard White): Parent with Kamala (Tharini Mudaliar) of Sati, who teaches Neo a lesson about the ability of the machine's ability to love—not as human love would be understood, but as something of a connection to someone or something else. (See Sati.)

Roland (David Roberts): Captain of the *Mjolner/Hammer,* his name is likely both a reference to Roland Barthes, French myth and literature critic and analyst, and to *The Song of Roland,* an epic that concerns bravery and sacrifice, and is often treated along with *Beowulf* as representative of the main medieval European literary "hero" texts.

Sati (Tanveer Atwal): "Daughter" of the programs Rama-Kandra and Kamala, the little girl was to be deleted from the machine world because she had no purpose, but she is saved when Rama delivers to the Merovingian the deletion codes to the outer shell of The Oracle. The sunrise she orchestrates at the end of *Revolutions* apparently prophesies a utopian outcome, and certainly indicates faith in youth.

Seraph (Collin Chou): From seraphim, the highest order of angels in Christian myth, also known as guardian angels. These are the Angels closest to God and from their number come all the archangel princes. Beings of pure light and thought, they are described as fiery flying serpents— the impression that Seraph gives in some of his spectacular wired action scenes where he operates as bodyguard for The Oracle.

Silver, Joel: The primary producer of the films. The Wachowski brothers are notably reticent to explain their work or comment upon it, whereas Silver has been quite loquacious in interviews.

Simulacra, Simulation, Virtual Reality: In the 1970s, Jean Baudrillard pulled together several lines of thought to argue that commodities or values and the signs pointing to them have become fused. Those within such a system fail to realize how signs themselves are now taken for realties that never were ("hype" would be one form of this). A simulacrum results when the mass media arrange "reality" to merchandise some company's products, or a political institution fabricates a sanitized representation of its power. Such a hyperreal representation then becomes "virtually" a reality—a construct (something fabricated) that looks real, but is false all the way down. The question posed by the *Alice in Wonderland* (that "down the rabbit hole" line) and *Wizard of Oz* aspects of the

Matrix realities can only be resolved on the basis of the perspectives on truth and reality one brings to the franchise—or the "real" world we are stalled in.

Smith, Agent (Hugo Weaving): "Agency" or the ability to act to further one's own agenda, is one of the cliquey terms of contemporary theory and analysis. And of course there are "agents" in discovery, protection, and enforcement institutions such as the Federal Bureau of Investigation. His excesses in the franchise may indicate some impatience with the hyper-efficiency of institutional government officials today. His primary associates are Agents Brown and Jones.

Soren (Stephen Bastoni): Captain of the *Vigilant* who attempts to assist in finding the source of the matrix. The ship is hit by a sentinel bomb and the ship and crew are destroyed. Probably a reference to existentialist philosopher Søren Kierkegaard. His major work, *Either/Or,* posits that there are in place of "universal truths," logical gaps—thus he accepted "leaps of faith" as necessary. If this was in mind, it explains why Soren is the first to volunteer to find the *Nebuchadnezzar*. Kierkegaard was greatly influenced by the anti-Enlightenment philosophy of Hamann. (See Councilor Haman.)

Switch (Belinda McClory): A rebel on the *Nebuchadnezzar* who at one point holds Neo at gunpoint for the safety of the crew when they remove an Agent's tracking bug in Neo. She is killed when Cypher pulls out her head jack while she is still connected to the matrix. The name perhaps emphasizes the nature of the binary logics upon which contemporary electronic communication and computation is based: zero and one *switching* back and forth in an infinity of combinations.

Tank (Marcus Chong): A Zion-born human, he is onboard the *Nebuchadnezzar* when Cypher betrays the crew, shooting Tank and his brother Dozer, and pulling out the head jacks of several others. When Cypher prepares to kill Neo in the same fashion, Tank suddenly revives enough to kill Cypher.

Tirant (Frankie Stevens): The captain of the ship *Novalis;* he and his crew were slaughtered by Sentinels ("squiddies"). Likely from *Tirant lo Blanc—The White Knight*—a famous book referred to twice in *Don Quixote,* about the life and tragic death of the Knight and his princess. White Knight Hackers is also the name of a well-known Internet security company.

Trainman (Bruce Spence): Not always clear whether he is or is not the bizarre looking bum ... or the guy who opens his trench coat to display cheap watches for sale, but he is an important "agent" in terms of actions at the train station and in the moving trains in *Revolutions* and *Animatrix*. A minion of the Merovingian, he uses the train to smuggle exiled programs into and out of the matrix; as a sort of lord of the underworld, another analogy would be with the Greek ferryman, Charon.

Trinity (Carrie-Anne Moss): The first mate on the *Nebuchadnezzar*. Perhaps the most obvious reference of her name is to the Trinity of Christian myth, but there is also the Hindu trinity, called the *trimurti,* of Brahma, Vishnu, and Shiva. The name also refers to both the Inanna and Isis myths in which the goddess helps resurrect a fallen or killed god who then becomes a god of the Underworld. Isis was portrayed as the literal throne of the Pharaoh, without which Pharaoh could not rule—he who was the reborn Osiris, god of the underworld. (See Neo, Persephone, and Lipp essay, in this volume.)

Virtual reality: See Simulation.

Wachowski, Andy; Wachowski, Larry: The directors of the whole enterprise of the *Matrix* franchise, often referred to by the crew and critics as the Brothers. One key interview in 1999 laid the basis for what has appeared in much of the mass communications coverage of the franchise (and it has been huge; see the Matrix Virtual Theatre interview, 6 November 1999: http://www.warnervideo.com/matrixevents/Wachowski.html).

West, Councilor (Cornel West): Well-known Princeton philosopher, his best book remains *The American Evasion of Philosophy.* It traces pragmatic philosophy from Emerson through Peirce, Dewey, William James, Davidson, Quine, and others. One theoretical key to the franchise is probably James's "Will to Believe" essay, which is why West appears here. (See Wilhelm and Kapell essay, in this volume.)

Zion: A name for the historic land of Israel as a symbol of the Jewish people, it may also be synonymous with Jerusalem or the City of David. It can be generalized to refer to a place or religious community regarded in rather utopian terms—which is the way it functions in the *Matrix* franchise, referring to a zone below the destroyed surface of the earth where free humans live. But it is also a machine-construct that has been restarted several times!—that is the revelation Neo receives in the terminal scene with the Architect in *Reloaded,* and that leads him to choose the door for Trinity, rather than activate yet another cloning experiment with respect to Zion.

3. Useful Internet sites

The *basic site* is Warner Brothers' well-designed and -maintained Mainframe homepage: www.whatisthematrix.com. It takes a while to learn how to negotiate the homepage (the second panel from the right, "Flash Version," identifies what the otherwise unidentified click-on boxes lead to), but there is a wealth of material here. The films of the trilogy each have sub-pages, with cast, bios, photos, sometimes interviews, etc. *Online* is accessed here. There are special sub-pages for *Enter,* and for *Animatrix*—a nine-minute preview of "The Second Renaissance," synopses of the animé films, and downloads. The Matrix Shop opens off the homepage, as does the News—the place many of us kept up with the ongoing development of all aspects of the franchise, over the last few years. The Mainframe Archive has trailers, detailed graphics of sets, audio files, screensavers, and more. *The Comics* adds to the franchise online analogue comics (not just those of the printed book, *The Matrix Comics*). The Philosophy section has been expanded twice (March and December 2003) since its November 2002 debut. It has included articles by several authors, including our contributors Rachel Wagner and Frances Flannery-Dailey ("Wake up! Gnosticism and Buddhism in *The Matrix*"; this was originally published in the *Journal of Religion and Film* 5/2 [October 2001], and is still available at that Web site, but not on the homepage). News also has active links to items it covers, including film scenes such as the Burly Brawl.

Matthew Kapell has compiled some *links* on his website for this book: www. personal.umd.umich.edu/~kapellm; follow the link to *Jacking In.*
For Hollywood *movie news* of all sorts, one can find mentions of the actors and films for about three previous years at www.hollywood.com, under "News."
Character/actor lists: Internet Movie Data Base (for *Revolutions,* for instance the URL is http://us.imdb.com/title/tt0242653/fullcredits—click on "full cast and crew" option); "The MATRIX 101": select "characters" under each of the trilogy films, "Matrix Character Database"; http:// matrix.thescarymonkeyshow.com: an impressive listing of characters from across the franchise, along with Ship Log, Machine World, Comic Section, and Sources—all handy for checking franchise data. Of course the Warner Bros. homepage for the series has cast and crew lists, bios, and often interviews.
Generally useful sites beyond the Warner Bros. sites: "Open Directory" by *dmoz:* see "top: arts: movies: titles: m: matrix series"—this has an

excellent selection of links that lead to fan sites, message boards, and other resources. "The MATRIX 101" presents a wealth of information compiled, we are told, by "fans"; it is one of the few Web presences that includes the entire franchise, and has very balanced synopses, mini-articles on "meaning and interpretation," many downloads (under "Get Stuff!"), and very rich FAQs. The search engine, Google, is always useful in providing a very wide range of hits. Other search engines, of course, including those that work like Web crawlers, are often as useful. The Yahoo! directory has a useful page of links, "The Matrix Series," in its Entertainment segment. The *dmoz open directory project* has excellent lists of fan sites and Matrix Series pages in several languages other than English. Several fan-run sites have chat rooms and bulletin boards. "Jen's Matrix" gets hundreds of hits and is well organized.

Religious discussions proliferate. A couple that are well developed include Brian Takle's "Matrix Religion" (http://wylfing.net/essays/)—he argues that in the films we have first a story about the expulsion from Eden in Genesis, The Architect being the Creator; then in "The Matrix: Reloaded Explained," the quest for the Holy Grail and Ascension of Christ, as well as transition from sixth to seventh day of creation. Mark Saunder's review-essay, "The Matrix Trilogy" (http://www.facingthechallenge.org/revolutions.htm posted by Focus Radio, David Couchman, dir.) suggests that the films do not really pull authentically from biblical messages.

4. Recommended bibliography

A number of books, mostly collections of essays, that treat some aspect of the franchise are indicated in essays and works that are cited throughout this book, and need not be collated here. Peter B. Lloyd, author of *Exegesis of the Matrix* (published in November 2003, but from what we can tell available only in the UK), has posted tables of contents, and in one case synopses of each contribution, for most of the books in philosophy mentioned, and the table of contents of his own volume—which treats both philosophical and technological aspects: http://ursasoft.com/matrix/ exegesis-book-contents.htm, accessed 13 January 2004. Background in terms of postmodernist ideas is also treated in the book—we're thinking of writings by Baudrillard and the fiction of William Gibson—again references to such materials can be found in the Works Cited portions following each chapter in this volume.

William James, "The Will to Believe" (1897), available online (Bob Corbett's outline at Webster University is handy), may well be one of the most significant influences, or at least one may say that it establishes the background in pragmatic philosophy for the sort of intellectual climate of the franchise themes. (See Wilhelm and Kapell, this volume.)

The editors compiled boxes of mass media accounts of the franchise, although it was rare to find any coverage of sophistication or depth. Persons with access to research library or online search engines (such as Ebsco Host Research Databases) can easily generate reading lists—and often actual texts—online. A few items we have found of special interest and depth:

Laura Bartlett and Thomas B. Byers, "Back to the Future: The Humanist *Matrix*" in *Cultural Critique* 53 (Winter 2003): 28-46 (available online through Project Muse). Its scope includes only the first film, but it contains some of the most "righteous" wrestling with issues raised by the franchise that we know.

Julien R. Fielding, "Reassessing *The Matrix / Reloaded*" (*Journal of Religion and Film* 7/2 (October 2003), six pages on line, is quite brief, but establishes that syncretism, rather than any particular religious-philosophical system, underlies the Wachowskis' epic.

Jake Horsley, author of *Matrix Warrior: Being the One, The Unofficial Handbook* (Gollancz, 2003), self-styled pseudo-voodoo-gonzo-guru, renegade preacher or enlightened fool, is the author of "Gnosticism Reborn: The Matrix as Shamanic Journey": www.foxfireinstitute.com/ review_matrix.htm, which treats the first film as perhaps "the outstanding American movie of the 90s," and develops a view of Neo as a sort of Gnostic-shamanic savior.

Jennifer Daryl Slack's "Everyday Matrix: Becoming Adolescence" (*Animations of Deleuze and Guattari*, ed. Slack, 2003: 9-29) is a dense and sophisticated analysis of the first movie in the light of the thought of these two French philosophers, and a Gnostic reading of current educational practices.

INDEX

INDEX